Variable Income Equivalence Scales

Contributions to Economics

www.springeronline.com/series/1262

Further volumes of this series can be found at our homepage.

Claus Brand
Money Stock Control and Inflation Targeting in Germany
2001. ISBN 3-7908-1393-1

Erik Lüth
Private Intergenerational Transfers and Population Aging
2001. ISBN 3-7908-1402-4

Nicole Pohl
Mobility in Space and Time
2001. ISBN 3-7908-1380-X

Mario A. Maggioni
Clustering Dynamics and the Locations of High-Tech-Firms
2002. ISBN 3-7908-1431-8

Ludwig Schätzl/Javier Revilla Diez (Eds.)
Technological Change and Regional Development in Europe
2002. ISBN 3-7908-1460-1

Alberto Quadrio Curzio/Marco Fortis (Eds.)
Complexity and Industrial Clusters
2002. ISBN 3-7908-1471-7

Friedel Bolle/Marco Lehmann-Waffenschmidt (Eds.)
Surveys in Experimental Economics
2002. ISBN 3-7908-1472-5

Pablo Coto-Millán
General Equilibrium and Welfare
2002. ISBN 7908-1491-1

Wojciech W. Charemza/Krystyna Strzala (Eds.)
East European Transition and EU Enlargement
2002. ISBN 3-7908-1501-1

Natalja von Westernhagen
Systemic Transformation, Trade and Economic Growth
2002. ISBN 3-7908-1521-7

Josef Falkinger
A Theory of Employment in Firms
2002. ISBN 3-7908-1520-9

Engelbert Plassmann
Econometric Modelling of European Money Demand
2003. ISBN 3-7908-1522-5

Reginald Loyen/Erik Buyst/Greta Devos (Eds.)
Struggeling for Leadership: Antwerp-Rotterdam Port Competition between 1870–2000
2003. ISBN 3-7908-1524-1

Pablo Coto-Millán
Utility and Production, 2nd Edition
2003. ISBN 3-7908-1423-7

Emilio Colombo/John Driffill (Eds.)
The Role of Financial Markets in the Transition Process
2003. ISBN 3-7908-0004-X

Guido S. Merzoni
Strategic Delegation in Firms and in the Trade Union
2003. ISBN 3-7908-1432-6

Jan B. Kuné
On Global Aging
2003. ISBN 3-7908-0030-9

Sugata Marjit, Rajat Acharyya
International Trade, Wage Inequality and the Developing Economy
2003. ISBN 3-7908-0031-7

Francesco C. Billari/Alexia Prskawetz (Eds.)
Agent-Based Computational Demography
2003. ISBN 3-7908-1550-0

Georg Bol/Gholamreza Nakhaeizadeh/
Svetlozar T. Rachev/Thomas Ridder/
Karl-Heinz Vollmer (Eds.)
Credit Risk
2003. ISBN 3-7908-0054-6

Christian Müller
Money Demand in Europe
2003. ISBN 3-7908-0064-3

Cristina Nardi Spiller
The Dynamics of the Price Structure and the Business Cycle
2003. ISBN 3-7908-0063-5

Michael Bräuninger
Public Debt and Endogenous Growth
2003. ISBN 3-7908-0056-1

Brigitte Preissl/Laura Solimene
The Dynamics of Clusters and Innovation
2003. ISBN 3-7908-0077-5

Markus Gangl
Unemployment Dynamics in the United States and West Germany
2003. ISBN 3-7908-1533-0

Pablo Coto-Millán (Ed.)
Essays on Microeconomics and Industrial Organisation, 2nd Edition
2004. ISBN 3-7908-0104-6

Wendelin Schnedler
The Value of Signals in Hidden Action Models
2004. ISBN 3-7908-0173-9

Wilhelm J. Meester
Locational Preferences of Entrepreneurs
2004. ISBN 3-7908-0178-X

Carsten Schröder

Variable Income Equivalence Scales

An Empirical Approach

With 23 Figures
and 63 Tables

Physica-Verlag
A Springer-Verlag Company

Series Editors
Werner A. Müller
Martina Bihn

Author

Dr. Carsten Schröder
University of Kiel
Department of Economics
Institute of Public Finance and Social Policy
Olshausenstraße 40
24098 Kiel
Germany
u2261@bwl.uni-kiel.de

ISSN 1431-1933
ISBN 3-7908-0183-6 Physica-Verlag Heidelberg New York

Cataloging-in-Publication Data applied for
A catalog record for this book is available from the Library of Congress.
Bibliographic information published by Die Deutsche Bibliothek
Die Deutsche Bibliothek lists this publication in the Deutsche Nationalbibliografie; detailed bibliographic data is available in the Internet at <http://dnb.ddb.de>.

Physica-Verlag is a part of Springer Science+Business Media

springeronline.com

Printed in Germany

Softcover Design: Erich Kirchner, Heidelberg

SPIN 10986783 88/3130/DK-5 4 3 2 1 0 – Printed on acid-free and non-aging paper

Acknowledgements

Many learned people have contributed to the development of this disertation. First, I like to thank everyone who has participated in the empirical surveys and the EU, without whose TMR network "Living Standards, Inequality and Taxation" the data collection would not have been possible. I am also indebted to Constantinos Constantinou, Xenios Demetriou, Stalo Krassa, Alex Michaelides, Charis Panagides, and Michalakis Petrou for their generous voluntary assistance in data collection for Cyprus, to Professor Erik Schokkaert from the Katholieke Universiteit Leuven whose invitation gave me the chance to collect the Belgian data, and to Peter Grösche who programmed the virtual internet questionnaires. I would also like to thank all my colleagues for stimulating discussions and advice, especially Professor Ulrich Schmidt, Professor Christos Koulovatianos, and PD Stefan Traub. Moreover, I have to thank Thomas Drabinski, Thilo Krienke, and Phil Faust for carefully reading through the manuscript and providing a lot of helpful comments.

In particular, I would like to thank my advisor Professor Christian Seidl who encouraged my research activities far beyond what one could expect, and his wife Christine for her heartiness and hospitality.

My final thank goes to my family and to Yvonne for being who they are.

Kiel
December 2003

Carsten Schröder

Contents

1

Introduction

1.1 A Brief Overview

An extensive body of empirical and theoretical literature deals with the measurement of social welfare. This body can be decomposed in several different but related topics, all of which have implications for empirical studies in welfare economics. One of these topics are household *equivalence scales* which help to compare welfare levels across households that differ in composition. An equivalence scale relates the income of any arbitrary household type to the income of a *reference household* such that both households are equally well–off.

Differences in household needs arise from differences in the households' *demographic composition* which is, for instance, given by the number, age, and sex of the household members. The increase of household needs is not necessarily proportional to the increase in the number of household members. Such a non–proportionality, for example, results from differences in the needs of adults and children, *economies of scale* arising from the division of *fixed costs* among the household members, welfare gains from *household production*, and from common consumption of commodities bearing a within–household *public good* component.

The measurement of differences in household needs has a long tradition going back to studies of *Ernst Engel* in the middle of the 19th century. In his empirical studies, Engel especially analysed the consumption patterns of working–class families in Belgium and introduced a relative measure for making household needs comparable. According to this measure, two households are equally well–off if their expenditure shares for food are equal. *Engel*'s approach was strongly criticised because of its lack of a utility–theoretical foundation, yet it opened a new field of theoretical and empirical research. Since *Engel*'s early studies, three approaches to determine equivalence scales established. The *economic approach* derives equivalence scales from a two step procedure. The first step comprises the specification of a functional form of household preferences and hence of a household–demand system. In a second step, equivalence scales are calculated from the estimates of the single demand functions using household budget data. The *expert approach* refers to assessments of household (minimal nutrition) needs by *experts*. Such scales underlie the definition of various socio–political determinants like the German social assistance or the OECD poverty line. A third approach refers to *survey techniques*. Different types of questionnaires have been suggested and have been applied empirically to derive information about household needs.

Each of these approaches possesses specific weaknesses and strengths. For example, the economic approach is highly recommended by many economists and econometricians since equivalence scales derived by it are built on models of household behavior. A variety of restrictive and/or controversial assumptions that underlie these models and their econometric implementation, however, question the derived empirical results. On the other hand, survey approaches directly target the original problem, the derivation of equivalence scales, yet researchers often doubt whether this approach leads to reliable and valid results. One fundamental objection to this approach is that respondents might not be able to assess correctly the needs of households that are different from their own. A similar reasoning holds for the expert approach that crucially depends on the assessments of the so–called experts.

1.2 Objective of the Thesis

This thesis presents a new survey approach for measuring equivalence scales which traces its origin back to the *contingent valuation method*. The contingent valuation method is a rather prominent tool in cost–benefit analysis, and in the assessment of public and non–market goods. The idea of this method is to ask respondents for their valuation of the item of interest, for example the preservation or renunciation of a biotope. This evaluation problem can be designed in two ways depending on whether the property right is assigned to the interviewee by asking her/him for her compensation demanded for the renunciation of the biotope (willingness to accept), or the property right is assigned to another party by asking the interviewee for her/his willingness to pay for preserving the biotope. In our surveys, we asked our respondents for their valuation of the impact of family size on monetary household needs. A typical question reads as follows:
"Which family income level can make a single adult with two children achieve the same well-being as a single adult without children and an income of 1,000 *Euro, according to your opinion?"*
Thus, respondents were asked to assess the welfare–equalising income of a well–defined hypothetical household type compared with the income of a reference household, a childless single adult in the example given above. Dividing the welfare equalising income by the given income of the reference household

gave the corresponding equivalence–scale value. With respect to *all* previous survey approaches for measuring equivalence scales suggested in the literature so far, our approach differs in one main aspect. In our questionnaires, we use *income* as the dimension for both, stimulus *and* response, as opposed to income and a verbal proxy for household welfare in all other survey approaches. This procedure eliminates two problems concerning the data quality of previous survey approaches. Firstly, the choice of income as the dimension for both, stimulus and response, evades the necessity of specifying a functional or parametric utility system in order to derive equivalence scales from our data base. Secondly, by avoiding verbal specifications of household welfare we reduce the risk of misjudgement and of biases arising from *habit formation* or *haziness* of our respondents' knowledge.

The questionnaire design was applied in a number of empirical surveys conducted from 1999 to 2002 in Germany, Cyprus, and Belgium with an overall number of about 600 participants. Each of the respondents were asked to assess the needs of a number of well–defined hypothetical household types. The available resources unfortunately did not allow for collecting a representative data set, yet we observed that respondents understood very well even household arrangements that substantially differed from their own. Thus, our methodology also allows the use of data from small samples. Besides testing the new methodology empirically, the surveys were conducted to provide insights into determinants of household needs, poorly understood up until now.

A first determinant is the aforementioned *economies of scale in consumption*. Different commodities exhibit different possibilities of joint consumption by the household members if the level of rivalry in consumption varies across commodity groups: for instance, the level of rivalry in consumption is plausibly less for household appliances than for food. Our surveys' intention was not to quantify the commodity–specific degrees of rivalry in consumption. Instead, we were interested in determining whether overall rivalry in consumption (economies of scale) systematically vary with household income. For example, if equivalence–scale estimates of our surveys were negatively related to the level of reference income, then overall rivalry in consumption would decrease with rising household income. The estimates might also be positively related to income indicating increasing rivalry with rising household income. However, according to our respondents, equivalence scales are negatively related to the income of the reference household. This finding has basic implications for the economic approach for measuring equivalence scales. In this branch of research, a large body of literature estimates equivalence scales assuming that household expenditure functions across different family types are proportional to the level of reference income. The consequence is that, by assumption, equivalence scales are independent from income. This assumption was independently suggested by *Blackorby* and *Donaldson* (1991, 1993) who called it *equivalence scale exactness* (ESE) and by *Lewbel* (1989) who introduced the notion *independence of base* (IB).

A second determinant of household needs is the level of *household production* activities. Already in 1965 *Becker* argued that households do not only consume market goods and services, but a lot of them are converted to final consumption within the household by using time and household appliances. The available time for household production is crucially dependent upon whether the household member is employed in the labour market or not. This implies that the income gain of a further household member is starting to work in the labour market is partly lost because her/his time for providing household–production activities shrinks such that the income gap between, for example, a one–earner and a two–earner couple systematically overestimates the difference between the two households' living standards (*Homan et al.* 1991). A proper comparison of the two households' situations therefore requires a measure of *compensated* income including the difference in the level of household production. From a theoretical perspective, the determination of these compensated incomes is a standard problem. The empirical determination of such compensated incomes is more complicated since available data in general do not contain the necessary information for assessing the value of household production as a function of household characteristics. We hope to help closing this gap by letting our respondents assess the needs of households that differ in the employment status of adult household members. We asked them questions such as
"Which family income level can make a household with one unemployed adult and two children achieve the same well-being as a household with one employed adult and two children and an income of 1,000 Euro, according to your opinion?"
The income gap corresponds to the monetary equivalent the respondent demands for compensating the household for the reduction of its available time for household production (or leisure).

1.3 Structure of the Thesis

The thesis is organised as follows. Chapter 2 presents the different approaches to equivalence scales, the expert approach, the survey approach, and the economic approach. For each approach, we summarise the results from the literature and draw conclusions regarding its validity.

Chapter 3 and 4 review the literature dealing with the impacts of income and of employment on equivalence scales. For two reasons the related literature to these two issues is rather limited. Firstly, the economic approach is based on an ordinal utility function which describes the household's preferences. Ordinality, however, means that there exists a broad range of possible equivalence scales for each utility or income level. To reduce this scale variety, the IB/ESE concept has been introduced which simply makes equivalence scales independent on income or utility by *assumption*. Economic approaches that make use of this assumption take a dominant position in the estimation of equivalence scales. Secondly, empirical data in general do not contain sufficiently differentiated variables which contain information on the time allocation of households. Still, such data are a prerequisite for measuring the impacts of employment on household needs and equivalence scales. For these reasons, the impacts of both variables, income and employment, have been neglected in equivalence scale measurement. Yet, it is by no means self–evident that their quantitative impacts on equivalence scales are small.

Chapter 5 presents the new survey approach for measuring equivalence scales. The chapter comprises a description of the new methodology and a comparison with previous survey methods.

Chapter 6 and Chapter 7 present the empirical results of four survey studies based on the suggested approach. Methodologically, a focal point will be to demonstrate that the use of hypothetical households in the questionnaires is valid and that the interviewees were able to assess the needs of hypothetical households even if these households differed from their own individual household type. Regarding the impacts of the two stimulus variables, income and employment, on equivalence scales, responses are very homogeneous within each sample and across the samples. According to our respondents, equivalence scales substantially *decrease* if reference income increases and *increase* the more adults become being employed in the labour market.

Chapter 8 summarises the study and draws conclusions regarding the usefulness of the collected data for empirical research on poverty measurement and on income distributions.

2

Equivalence–Scale Measurement

This chapter is devoted to a presentation and discussion of the three main approaches to measuring equivalence scales which are the *expert approach*, the *economic approach*, and the *survey approach*. Most attention will be paid to the economic and to the survey approach since both are applied in this thesis. Already here, we would like to point out that equivalence scales derived in previous studies now and then are of dubious value. Thus, the reader should not think of typing errors if she/he finds that equivalence scales for the same household type lie in a rather wide range.

2.1 Expert Approaches

The expert approach refers to evaluations of household needs by *experts*. In general, these experts are asked to define household specific *minimal* needs for goods and services. The ratios of entailed cash amounts give equivalence scales which are frequently applied in practical social policies. Germany's social assistance scale or the OECD equivalence scale are examples. The following subsections review the related literature, evaluate the methodology of the expert approach, and present a number of expert equivalence scales.

2.1.1 Literature Survey

The expert approach to equivalence scales originates in the early empirical works of *Engel* (1857, 1895). In this first ideal type of expert scales, the needs of different household members are assessed by referring to the expert–defined needs of an infant. Adjacent, the needs of older household members are extrapolated with factors called *centimeter weights*. The *centimeter weight* of an individual is the product of its individual weight in kilogramme and its size in centimeters. Though this procedure seems a bit curios, it is applied in official

Switzerland's statistics on household budgets of employees and pensioners.[1]

The second ideal type of expert scales was proposed by *Rowntree* (1901). In his analysis, *Rowntree* refers to household specific subsistence quantities for essential commodities as defined by experts. The ratios of corresponding monetary equivalents for different household types give equivalence scales for the subsistence level. Until 1990, the determination of German social assistance, for example, was based on this procedure.

Orshansky (1965) suggested a third ideal type of expert scales by extending the expert approach with expenditure analytical elements. More precisely, *Orshansky* combined household expenditure data for food with diets as suggested by experts. *Orshansky*'s suggestion became practically relevant for the definition of household specific poverty lines in the US.[2] In the UK, expenditure data on income and budget shares for necessities were used by *Bradshaw et al.* (1987) to design one of their budget standards.

Table 2.1 lists the equivalence scales for adults according to studies of *Engel* (1895), *Rowntree* (1941), and *Orshansky* (1965). The empirical data reveal that across the studies expert equivalence scales differ substantially and that among experts there is not much agreement on household needs. While, for example, *Engel* finds that each additional adult in the household is as costly as the first, *Rowntree* finds substantial economies of scale: according to his analysis, the second adult costs about 65% less than the first adult. Of course, the choice of the methodology is not necessarily the only factor to be made responsible for the quantitative differences in the equivalence scales derived. The three cited studies were conducted in a time interval of 70 years and refer to data of different countries.

Table 2.1. Expert Scales

Number of Adults	Engel[a]	Rowntree[b]	Orshansky
1	1.000	1.000	1.000
2	2.000	1.351	1.538
3	3.000	1.757	1.969
4	4.000	2.162	2.400
5	5.000	2.568	2.846
6	6.000	2.973	3.323
7	7.000	3.365	3.785
8	8.000	3.770	4.492

[a] values result from addition of individual weights.
[b] values for unemployed adults.
Sources: *Engel* 1895, p. 5; *Rowntree* 1941, p. 30; *Orshansky* 1965, p. 75.

[1]Compare *Deiss, Guillaume* and *Lüthi* 1988, p. 10.
[2]Compare *Atkinson* 1983, p. 49.

2.1.2 Evaluation

The reliance on expert judgements is often seen as a great failing of the expert approach per se since these (arbitrary) judgements directly affect the size of obtained equivalence scales. Such judgements involve, for example, the choice of "necessary" commodity categories and the respective quantities as well as the choice of which household characteristics should be considered. The definition of a price vector which is required to assess the monetary values of the commodity quantities is a further necessary judgement. Since none of these judgements is free from arbitrariness, derived equivalence scales – in the end – are arbitrary as well. Especially the pragmatic mixing of methodology suggested by *Orshansky* (1965), is questionable since "there is no real conceptual coherence in this mixture of methods" (*Bradshaw* 1991, p. 14). Another shortcoming is that expert scales, in general, are defined only for the subsistence level. As outlined above, fundamental doubts are advisable whether such subsistence scales should be applied for assessing household needs at higher income or welfare levels.

2.2 Economic Approaches

2.2.1 Demand Theory

The economic approach aims at deriving welfare–equalising incomes and equivalence scales from the consumer behavior of households. The starting point of microeconomic demand theory is that households behave *rationally.* This means that a consumption unit chooses the consumption bundle which maximises its utility. The hypothesis of rationality is embodied in the *completeness* and *transitivity* assumptions about the preference relation ($\succeq$). Completeness means that the household has a well–defined preference between any two pairs of consumption bundles. Transitivity rules out cycling preferences. If, in addition, household preferences are *continuous*, then there exists a continuous *utility function* that represents $\succeq$. This function is *increasing* and *quasiconcave* and assigns a single real number to each commodity bundle. It is, however, important to notice that if there exists at least *one* utility function that has these properties then these properties are preserved for any increasing transformation of the utility function.[3]

What is the decision problem of a household? Given a strictly positive price vector p and the household's disposable income y, the *primal problem* is to maximise the utility function $u(x, s)$ under the *budget constraint* $\sum_{i=1}^{I} p_i x_i \leq y$. The budget constraint requires that overall expenditures $\sum_{i=1}^{I} p_i x_i$ do not exceed disposable household income y. The solution of the primal problem

[3] Compare *Mas–Colell et al.* 1995, pp. 6–50.

yields the *Marshallian demand functions* $x_i = x_i^m(y, p, s)$ which specify the optimal consumption level of commodity i depending on the variables y, p, and household demography s. Analogously, *Hicksian demands* $x_i = x_i^h(u, p, s)$ result from the solution of the *dual problem*: each household minimises total expenditures $\sum_i p_i x_i$ under the condition that $u(x, s) \geq u$. The Hicksian demand function $x_i = x_i^h(u, p, s)$ gives the household's consumption level of commodity i, given household utility u, the price vector p, and household demography s.

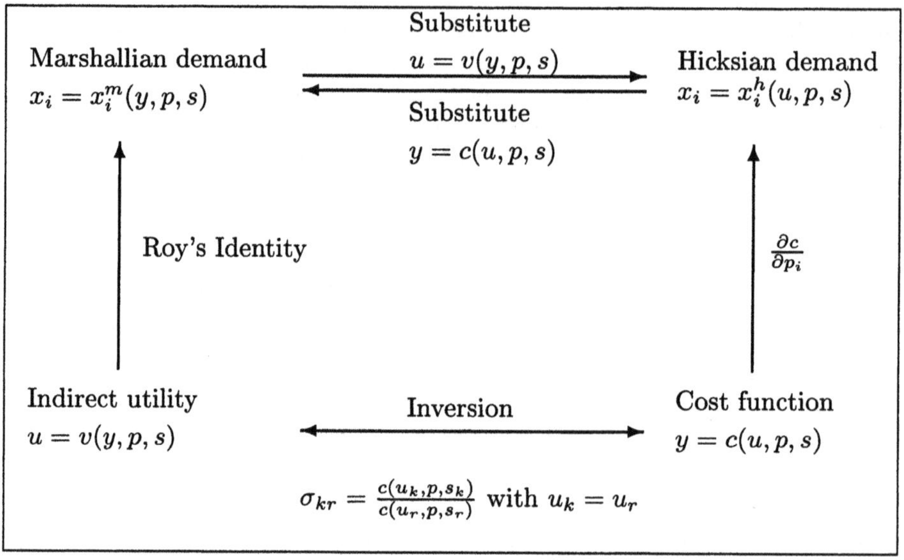

Figure 2.1. Fundamentals in Neoclassical Demand Theory
Source: *Deaton* and *Muellbauer* 1980, pp. 38–41.

Irrespective of its concrete specification, the utility function imposes several conditions on the derived demand system (*Deaton* and *Muellbauer* 1980). If household preferences are characterised by *non–satiation*, overall expenditures add up to household income. *Homogeneity* means that demands remain unaffected for a simultaneous and proportional change of all prices and of household income. The two further conditions of *non–negativity* and *symmetry* refer to the reaction of household demands on price changes.

A basic concept for the calculation of equivalence scales is the *cost*/or *expenditure function* $y = c(u, p, s)$. The cost function identifies minimal expenditures that are necessary to reach a specific utility level, given prices p and household demography s. For the utility levels of two different household types, k and r, to be identical, k's equivalence scale is is $\sigma_{kr} = \frac{c(u_k, p_k, s_k)}{c(u_r, p_r, s_r)}$.[4]

In the following, we give an overview of the most prominent economic models that are employed for the estimation of equivalence scales. The first subsection comprises a brief literature survey which is subsequently taken as a guideline for an extensive evaluation.[5]

2.2.2 Literature Survey

The utility function is the core concept for the construction of parametric demand systems since it defines the resulting demand functions. Table 2.2 summarises the most prominent demand systems and underlying specifications of household utility functions.

Table 2.2. Economic Models

Author	Model	Demand Function
Engel	$u = u\left(\frac{x_1}{\sigma(u)}, ..., \frac{x_I}{\sigma(u)}\right)$ constant prices $\sigma = \sigma(y, s)$	$\frac{x_i}{\sigma} = \theta\left(\frac{y}{\sigma}\right)$
Rothbarth	$u = min[u_1(x_A, x_B^a), u_2(x_B^c, n_C)]$ constant prices $\sigma = \sigma(y, s)$	$\frac{x_A}{\sigma} = \theta\left(\frac{y}{\sigma}\right)$
Prais and Houthak-ker	$u = min\left(\frac{x_i}{m_i \alpha_i(u)}\right)$ constant prices $\sigma = \sigma(m_1, ..., m_I, y)$	$\frac{x_i}{m_i} = \theta\left(\frac{y}{\sigma}\right)$
Barten	$u = u\left(\frac{x_1}{m_1}, ..., \frac{x_I}{m_I}\right)$	$\frac{x_i}{m_i} = \theta\left(\frac{p_1 m_1}{y}, ..., \frac{p_I m_I}{y}\right)$
Pollak and Wales	$u = u(x_1 - l_1, ..., x_2 - l_2)$	$x_i = l_i + \theta(p, y - \sum_{i=1}^{I} p_i l_i)$
Gorman	$u = u\left(\frac{x_1 - l_1}{m_1}, ..., \frac{x_I - l_I}{m_I}\right)$	$\frac{x_i - l_i}{m_i} = \theta\left(\frac{p_1 m_1}{y - \sum_{i=1}^{I} p_i l_i}, ..., \frac{p_I m_I}{y - \sum_{i=1}^{I} p_i l_i}\right)$

Notation: σ equivalence scale; i commodity group; l_i translating parameter of i; m_i equivalence scale of i; s vector of demographic characteristics; n_C number of children; x_A quantity of adult goods; x_B^a quantity of non–adult good that is also consumed by adults; x_B^c quantity of non–adult good exclusively consumed by children.
Source: *Muellbauer* 1977, p. 463, and *Pollak* and *Wales* 1992, pp. 74–79.

[4]An alternative approach is the direct estimation of equivalent incomes. For an overview compare the survey by *Jorgenson* 1990 and the papers by *King* 1983, and *Apps* and *Savage* 1989.

[5]For a more extensive literature survey compare, for example, *Lewbel* 1985, or *Faik* 1995. Our evaluation takes *Coulter et al.* 1992 as a guideline.

Rather simple yet still popular models are the *single–equation models* of *Engel* (1895) and of *Rothbarth* (1943).[6] In the *Engel* approach, two household types are assumed to be equally well–off if the expenditure share of commodity i is the same for any two household types k and r. *Engel*'s idea is illustrated in Figure 2.2.

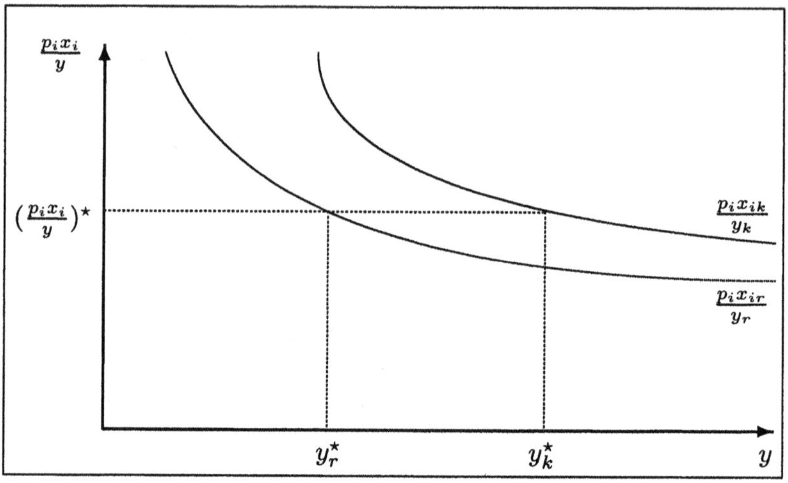

Figure 2.2. Engel Approach
Source: *Coulter et al.* 1992, p. 88.

Here, $\frac{p_i x_{ik}}{y_k}$ is the budget share of commodity i for household type k, while $\frac{p_i x_{ir}}{y_r}$ is the corresponding share for household type r. According to the *Engel* approach, k and r are equally well–off if the budget share of commodity i is the same for both household types. This condition holds for $y_r^\star$ and for $y_k^\star$. Assuming identical prices for all household types, the equivalence scale of household type k relative to r is $\sigma_{kr} = \frac{y_k^\star}{y_r^\star}$ such that $\frac{p_i x_{ik}}{y_k^\star} = \frac{p_i x_{ir}}{y_r^\star}$. Obviously, *Engel*'s approach faces several weak points. Firstly, the choice of a *relative* standard of comparison requires *identical* consumption patterns for all household types. For example, the standard is meaningless if the expenditure share for commodity i is a decreasing function of income for household type k but an increasing function for household type r. Secondly, though it is a normative and arbitrary choice which commodity is taken as the standard of comparison, this choice directly determines the derivation of equivalence scales. In general *food* is chosen since food is an essential commodity and the consumption pattern is rather similar for all household types: its expenditure share is a strictly negative function of household income, the so–called *Engel law*.[7] Thirdly, the *Engel* approach by no means guarantees the intuitively ex-

[6] For current applications compare, for example, *Betti* 1999, *Browning* 1992, and *Tsakloglou* 1991.

[7] For empirical confirmation compare *Klein* 1994, *Deaton* and *Muellbauer* 1986, and *Tsakloglou* 1991.

pected outcome that $\sigma_{kr} = \frac{y_k^\star}{y_r^\star} > 1$ whenever k is the "larger" household. On the contrary, for $\frac{\partial(p_i x_i)}{\partial y}\frac{y}{p_i x_i} < 1$ the expected outcome only arises if $p_i x_i$ increases with *in*creasing family size for a given income. For $\frac{\partial(p_i x_i)}{\partial y}\frac{y}{p_i x_i} > 1$ the expected outcome only holds if $p_i x_i$ *de*creases with increasing family size for a given income.[8] Fourthly, derived equivalence scales are conditional on the functional specification of the estimated *Engel curve*. The choice of a linear specification, for instance, might lead to different equivalence scales compared with a quadratic one.[9] A further characteristic of the Engel model is that estimated equivalence scales are invariant relating to prices, a characteristic which is fundamentally criticised by *Deaton* (1997).

While *Engel*'s equivalence scales are based on a *relative* standard of comparison, *Rothbarth* refers to an *absolute* standard by distinguishing *absolute* expenditures for two commodity bundles, x_A and x_B.[10] Commodity bundle x_A comprises *adult goods*, commodities that are exclusively consumed by adults like alcohol and adult clothes, while x_B comprises either those commodities that are consumed by adults *and* children or by children only. According to *Rothbarth*, two households are equally well–off if *total* expenditures for x_A are the same for two households k and r. Thus, the equivalence scale for household type k is $\sigma_{kr} = \frac{y_k^\star}{y_r^\star}$ such that $p_A x_{Ak} = p_A x_{Ar}$ taking r as the reference. For an illustration compare Figure 2.3.

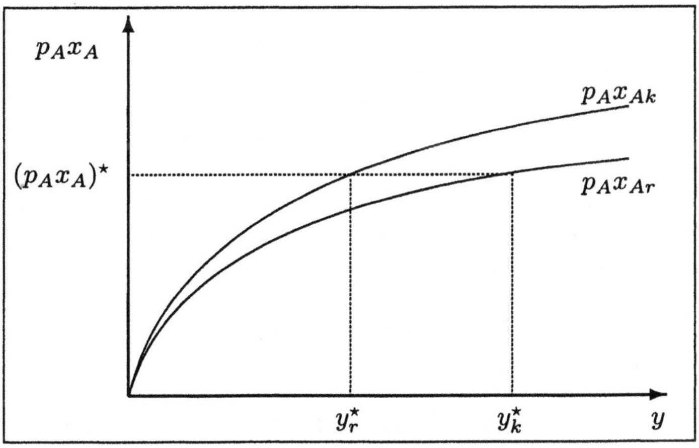

Figure 2.3. Rothbarth Approach
Source: *Coulter et al.* 1992, p. 88.

[8] Compare *Gronau* 1988.

[9] An overview of possible specifications and respective equivalence scales gives *Faik* 1995.

[10] The *Rothbarth model* is broadly presented and discussed, for example, in *Rothbarth* 1943, *Henderson* 1949, *Nicholson* 1949, *Fiegehen et al.* 1977, *Deaton* and *Case* 1988, *Bradbury* 1989, *Deaton et al.* 1989, and *Tsakloglou* 1991.

Rothbarth's criterion is meaningful only if households differ in the number of household members (children) which do not participate in the consumption of the *adult good*. *Rothbarth* scales, therefore, are used for the quantification of equivalence scales of households with different numbers of children but an identical number of adults. The cost function resulting from the *Rothbarth* model is $c(u, p_A, p_B, n_C) = c_1(u, p_B, n_C) + c_2(u, p_A, p_B)$ where p_A is the price of the adult good, p_B is the price of the non–adult good, $c_1(.)$ are *variable* costs related to children and $c_2(.)$ are *fixed* costs for the adult good. Finally, n_C gives the number of children. Taking a childless adult as the reference, the equivalence scale for household type k with one or more children is $\frac{c_1(u_r,p_B,s_{kc})+c_2(u_r,p_A,p_B)}{c_2(u_r,p_A,p_B)}$.[11] Alike the Engel model, *Rothbarth scales* are sensitive to the chosen functional specification of *Engel curves*. Moreover, derived equivalence scales are conditional on the definition of the *adult good*. Comparing the approaches of *Rothbarth* and *Engel*, *Engel*'s approach avoids the rather implausible assumption that having children affects expenditures on different commodity groups in an identical way. On the other hand, the *Rothbarth* approach might provide researchers with information on the intra–household allocation of resources.[12]

Besides these *single–equation models* there exists a variety of *multi–equation models*. In the *Barten* model (*Barten* 1964), household demography affects both, household preferences as well as household prices and the household's budget constraint. According to *Barten*, indifference maps of the household are identical only if preferences are defined over *equivalent* consumption, that is, the consumption of commodity i divided by its specific equivalence scale value, rather than over consumption per se. This procedure is called *demographic scaling*. Differences in household demography, however, also cause differences in *equivalent* prices, the products of commodity specific market prices and equivalence scales, and therefore affect the slope of the budget constraint in terms of equivalent consumption. For example, since children do not consume alcohol but milk, an additional child does not only increase household demand for milk, but it also increases the equivalent price of milk relative to that of alcohol. Such changes in relative equivalent prices might cause substitution effects.

By assumption, such substitution effects remain unconsidered in the *Prais–Houthakker model*. *Prais* and *Houthakker* (1955) define standardised consumption quantities $\frac{x_i}{m_i}$ for any commodity i where m_i is a commodity specific scale as a function of household–equivalent income $\frac{y}{\sigma}$ where σ is the general equivalence scale: $\frac{x_i}{m_i} = x_i^\star = \theta_i\left(\frac{y}{\sigma}\right)$. Since $x_i^\star$ is a function of equivalent income but not of relative prices, the model is consistent from a demand–theoretical perspective only if there is no price substitution (*Deaton* and

[11]Compare *Tsakloglou* 1991, p. 347, and *Coulter et al.* 1992, p. 89.

[12]For a more extensive discussion compare *Deaton* and *Muellbauer* 1986, p. 733.

Muellbauer 1980). Then, also *Hicksian demands* x_i^h are independent of prices such that the equivalence scale is $\sigma_{kr} = \frac{\sum_{i=1}^{I} p_{ri} m_{ki} x_{ri}(u_r)}{\sum_{i=1}^{I} p_{ri} x_{ri}(u_r)}$. Figure 2.4 sketches the procedure underlying the *Prais* and *Houthakker* model.

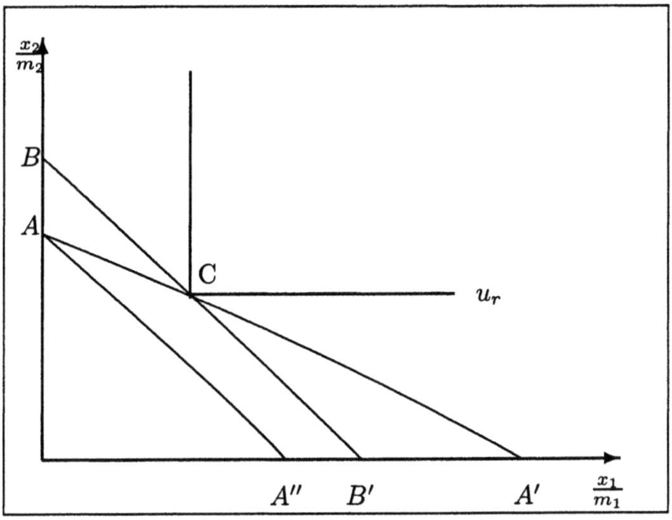

Figure 2.4. Prais and Houthakker Model
Source: *Seel* 1992, p. 136.

Under the assumption that an additional household member only increases the commodity specific scale m_1 and leaves m_2 unchanged, the household's budget line shifts from AA' to AA'' since axes measure standardised consumption quantities. By shifting AA'' through point C where AA' and BB' intersect and utility u_r remains constant, the equivalence scale in terms of commodity 2 is given by the ratio $\frac{0B}{0A}$. As opposed to the right–angled indifference curve in the *Prais–Houthakker* model, a substitutional shape of the indifference curve would lead to a new consumption point C' different from C. Such a case is depicted in Figure 2.5 and the equivalence scale is given by the ratio $\frac{0B''}{0A}$.

An alternative to considering household size by *demographic scaling* is *demographic translation* as suggested by *Pollak* and *Wales* (1981). In their model, differences in household size or structure lead to differences in equivalent consumption. These differences are no longer measured in relative but in absolute terms such that household utility is represented by $u = u[x_1 - l_1(s), ..., x_I - l_I(s)]$. l_i denotes commodity specific *translating* parameters. Then, indirect utility is given by the function $v = v[p, y - \sum_{j=1}^{I} p_j l_j(s)]$. With regard to the structure of household cost functions, demand functions (compare Table 2.2) imply a fix–cost element already found in the *Rothbarth* model.

Gorman (1976) suggested a synthesis of *demographic scaling* and *demographic translation* defining household utility as $u = u\left(\frac{x_1 - l_1(s)}{m_1(s)}, ..., \frac{x_I - l_I(s)}{m_I(s)}\right)$, such that the indirect–utility function is $v = v[p_1 m_1(s), ..., p_I m_I(s), y - \sum_{j=1}^{I} p_j l_j(s)]$ and $x_i^m = l_i(s) + m_i(s) f_i[p_1 m_1(s), ..., p_I m_I(s), y - \sum_{j=1}^{I} p_j l_j(s)]$ is the Marshallian demand function of commodity i.

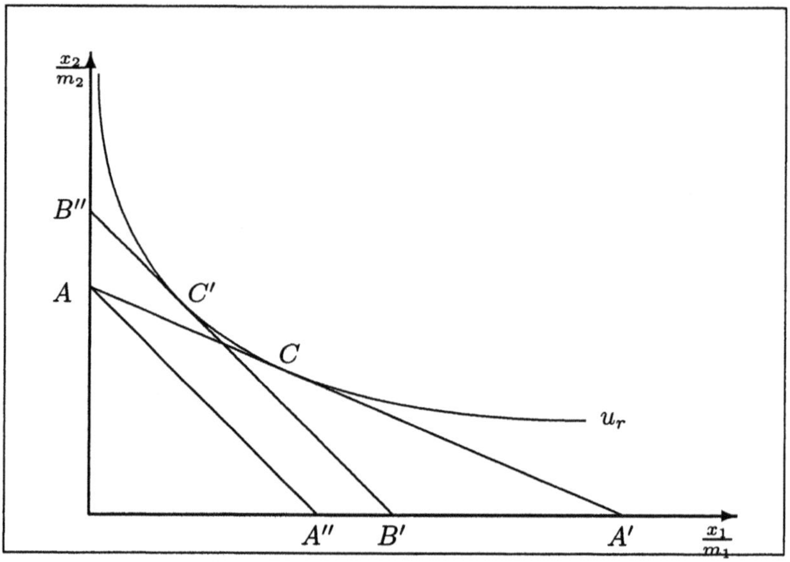

Figure 2.5. Substitutional Case
Source: *Seel* 1992, p. 136.

There exists an enormous number of empirical applications of the economic approach to equivalence scales and it is impossible to give a complete picture of derived equivalence scales. In any case, differences in quantified equivalence scales across the empirical studies are substantial. It is, however, in most cases impossible to assign these differences to different model specifications or to differences in the considered empirical data. The intention underlying Table 2.3 is to summarise equivalence scales that are *comparable* since all of them are calculated from the same data base, the 1983 income and expenditure survey for Germany (*Einkommens- und Verbrauchsstichprobe*), and since household size is always considered by the number of household members. This far differences in equivalence scales reported are solely caused by methodological differences. Table 2.3 reveals that quantitative differences across the studies are still substantial. For example, the scale value for a two–person household varies between 1.340 (*translating*) and 1.810 (*Engel*).

Table 2.3. Comparable Economic Scales

Number of Persons	Engel[a]	Barten[b]	Translating[b]	Prais/ Houthakker[b,c]
1	1.000	1.000	1.000	1.000
2	1.810	1.480	1.340	1.550
3	2.190	1.730	1.530	1.840
4	2.450	1.890	1.640	2.020
5	2.770	1.980	1.720	2.170
6	3.040	1.930	1.710	2.222

Note: equivalence scale for two–adult households with one child.

[a] equivalence scales for expenditure category food.

[b] calculations for arithmetic mean income of DM 24,906.08.

[c] commodity specific scale for food was a–priori fixed.

Source: *Faik* 1995, p. 202, p. 209, pp. 244–245, pp. 262–263.

2.2.3 Evaluation

From a theoretical viewpoint the economic approach is rather interesting since it is based on models that systematically connect household demand and utility as well as demography. Especially multi–equation models – for which rather flexible functional forms have been developed – are persuasive due to their theoretical foundation. Nevertheless, none of the economic approaches are immune to criticism.

In 1979, *Pollak* and *Wales* have already stressed the so–called *identification problem* resulting from *numerous* cost functions that can be derived from the same expenditure data such that equivalence scales are not unequivocal: suppose that preferences are correctly depicted by the utility function $F(u(x,s),s)$ and $\frac{\partial F}{\partial u} > 0$, then the resulting cost functions $c^F(.)$ are identical to cost functions $c(.)$ obtained from u(.). Equivalence scales that are based on $c^F(.)$ are sometimes called *unconditional scales* while *conditional scales* are the ones derived from $c(.)$. A *conditional scale* takes household demography as exogenous while an *unconditional scale* takes household demography as endogenous. The implications of the two concepts can be illustrated by an example of *Pollak* and *Wales* (1979). In the economic approach, the presence of children can change equivalent prices and reduces their parent's consumption possibilities. However, "the expenditure level required to make a three–child family as well off as it would be with two children and \$ 12,000 depends on how the family feels about children" and observed differences in consumption patterns do not reveal "whether the third child is regarded as a blessing or a curse" (*Pollak* and *Wales* 1979, p. 219). A family that behaves fully rationally with perfect foresight would only opt for a third child if the child was perceived as a "blessing". In the case of imperfect foresight, however, it is possible that the decision proves to be false ex post, yet it is irreversible.[13] Therefore, *Pollak* and *Wales* (1979, p. 220) argue that conditional equivalence scales "cannot be used to make welfare comparisons." Other authors remark that this conclusion is too negative since at least some useful information about relative household costs can be derived from estimates of economic models. *Blundell* and *Lewbel* (1990, p. 7) line out that given the true values of unconditional scales "in one price regime, Marshallian demands can be used to uniquely recover the true values of all equivalence scales in all other price regimes". However, there remains the question what these "true" values are. *Blackorby* and *Donaldson* (1988), *Lewbel* (1989), and *Blundell* and *Lewbel* (1990) suggest to restrict the range of possible specifications of $F(.)$ by assuming that equivalence scales are IB or *exact*.[14] IB/ESE requires homothetic household–utility and household–cost functions. Homothety means that a doubling of a household's consumption level increases its utility by the same factor. Given that prices are constant this again guarantees equivalence scales to be invariant to income. For empirical analyses IB/ESE are clearly attractive, yet the plausibility of this assumption is debatable. We will address IB and ESE in more detail in Section 3.

A number of other arguments reinforces that demand data alone are unsuitable for deriving equivalence scales. *Fisher* (1987) doubts that observed behaviour alone is sufficient to derive ethically attractive results. For example, one might think of differences between the assessment of a child's welfare by the society compared to its parents' assessment. Still household expenditure data only reflect the latter. Thus, consumer sovereignty should not be taken as the single standard for welfare judgements. Sen (1984, Chapter 15) gives an illustration of this point by the issue of "gender bias" in the parents' expenditures on children.

In his critique, *McClements* (1978) goes even further and questions that household choices as reflected by demands in fact reveal preferences since "existing behavioural pattern is unduly constrained" (*McClements* 1978, p. 117). According to *McClements* (1978, p. 117), demand patterns of pensioners are an instructive example since "incomes of pensioners are generally low and since most pensioners receive retirement pensions the estimated equivalence scales may simply reflect existing relativities." This train of thought can be applied equivalently to single mothers, for example.

Further (conceptual) problems of the economic approach arise concerning the specification of the economic models and corresponding estimation equations. One weakness is that the models (including the underlying data

---

[13]Compare *Deaton* and *Muellbauer* 1980, pp. 208–211, for a broader analysis of potential biases of conditional scales.

[14]The IB label is introduced by *Lewbel* 1989, and *Blundell* and *Lewbel* 1990, while ESE was introduced by *Blackorby* and *Donaldson* 1988.

bases) are static and consequently ignore all inter–temporal aspects. Households, however, optimise their inter–temporal consumption flow by savings. For a single period which does not incorporate the whole space of time, there may be a gap between disposable income and total expenditures. As *Muellbauer* (1978, pp. 343f.) shows, equivalence scales are sensitive with respect to whether they are defined on disposable income or on total expenditures since the expenditure share for savings varies with the income level.

A further conceptual weakness of the economic approach is the existence of various possible specifications of household utility functions, which again determine household demands and household cost functions. For reasons of convenience and of data limitations it is, for instance, assumed that only the consumption of market goods and services enter the utility function while other potential factors like leisure, household production and other non–cash items, remain unconsidered. These limitations are now and then overcome by more extensive models that include the household's time–allocation decision and household–production functions.[15] On the other side, these extensions lead to serious measurement problems. Moreover, time allocation does not necessarily reveal preferences, for example because of constraints in the labour market.

All these problems are intensified by data limitations, limitations in applicable estimation techniques, and by necessary yet arbitrary working assumptions. For example, it is a purely normative judgement whether expenditures for take–away food are assigned to the composite commodity group "food" or to "services." Moreover, there are no longitudinal data available in most countries. Thus, single period models are frequently applied. Yet, these models retain the problem of how durable commodities should be considered. Should durable commodities be excluded from the analysis, or should they be included and treated as non–durable commodities, or should only depreciations be considered? The choice of the "correct" strategy again is more or less arbitrary.

Equivalence scales depend on the specification of the relation between household characteristics and equivalence scales, too, i.e. the specification of commodity–specific equivalence scales m_i and translating parameters l_i. The researcher not only has to specify these functions but it is also up to her/him to decide about the demographic variables to be considered. Is it, for example, appropriate to include only the mere number of household members rather than to distinguish between adults and children? Furthermore, should we differentiate for gender and age? In general, severe limitations are already imposed by the set of available data. But even if a sufficiently broad data base existed, this

---

[15]Compare, for example, *Muth* 1966, *Apps* and *Savage* 1989, and *Apps* and *Rees* 1996.

would not necessarily be reliable. One might think of expenditures for alcohol where huge understatements are to be expected. Even though this problem is well–known, alcohol frequently serves as the *adult good* in empirical applications of *Rothbarth scales.*[16] Moreover, owing to under–identification not all economic models can be estimated from a single cross–section.[17] An example is the *Prais–Houthakker model.* The under–identification problem results from the mutual dependence of general equivalence scales and those that are commodity specific: commodity specific scales by definition require the existence of a general equivalence scale, yet commodity specific scales are employed to calculate the general scale.[18] There are two approaches that aim at solving the *under–identification problem.* One simply defines a single commodity–specific scale a–priori, a procedure that is rather arbitrary.[19] Another suggestion is the iterative estimation of general and commodity specific equivalence scales, a suggestion that again suffers from an arbitrary a–priori scale definition. Furthermore, scale values do not necessarily converge.[20] In any case, different assumptions and estimation techniques again lead to different equivalence–scale values.

Altogether, economic equivalence scales are rather popular among econometricians and economists but, as outlined above, suffer from a variety of necessary assumptions, data restrictions, model limitations and statistical shortfalls. In no case do they lead to a unique "correct" equivalence scale and "decades of research have failed to produce a generally accepted methodology" (*Bradbury* 1989, p. 387), a conclusion that is topically now as ever and explains the interest in alternative methodologies.

2.3 Survey Approaches

While economic approaches measure the relative welfare levels of different household types *indirectly* from demand data, *survey methods* attempt to evaluate the links between income, welfare, and demography in a *direct* way by asking a sample of respondents about the needs of different household types.

Following *van den Bosch* (1999), whose rather comprehensive representation of survey techniques is taken as the reference in the following, two branches of survey methods can be distinguished. The *consensual approach* aims at identifying equivalence scales by reference to people's views about the incomes of families in *general.* It employs survey questions about how much

[16]Compare, for example, *Lancaster* and *Ray* 1998, p. 7, or *Faik* 1995, p. 202.
[17]Compare *Deaton* and *Muellbauer* 1980, p. 202, and *Buchegger* 1986, p. 41.
[18]Compare *Klein* 1986, p. 41.
[19]Compare, for example, *Muellbauer* 1980, and *Buchegger* 1986, pp. 79–80.
[20]Compare *McClements* 1977, p. 197.

income a *hypothetical* household, which is defined by a set of demographic characteristics, needs in order to achieve a specific living standard. Relating the welfare–equalising incomes of two different household types gives the equivalence scale. Consensual approaches are to be distinguished from *subjective approaches*, where people are asked about their *own* income needs or living standard instead about the income needs or living standard of other, hypothetical households. Thus, no information is collected about how people judge the needs of a specific household in general but they are asked to assess their own individual situation. Here, two branches of surveys can be distinguished. The *income evaluation method* asks respondents what income they think, in their own situation, suits to a specific living standard. The *income satisfaction method* asks the subjects to rate their feeling of income satisfaction on a welfare scale. In the following two sections, we review the survey approaches that have been suggested so far, we present the corresponding empirical findings, and discuss their suitedness for measuring equivalence scales.

2.3.1 Consensual Approach

The consensual approach aims at identifying (minimal) living standards by reference to people's views about the incomes or the possessions and activities of different household types in the community in general. In sample surveys, interviewees are asked how much income a hypothetical household of a given type needs in order to reach a specific living standard. From these answers, an unequivocal and correct equivalence scale could easily be derived, provided there was a complete consensus among interviewees, i.e. that all respondents' answers were identical. Yet, this outcome is not very likely such that, in general, the median answer is taken as the standard.

Literature Survey

As Table 2.4 reveals, a number of different consensual approaches for measuring equivalence scales have been suggested so far which differ regarding the chosen stimulus material and response categories. The studies of *Saunders* and *Bradbury* (1991), *Saunders* and *Matheson* (1992), *Kilpatrick* (1973), *Rainwater* (1990) and *Vaughan* (1993) are mentioned only to complete the picture. Since these studies asked for the incomes of a single household type only, the data collected obviously do not allow the quantification of equivalence scales.

In the *Boston Social Standards Survey* interviewees are asked about the income amounts that are necessary to make different household types attain pre–defined living standards. Six different living standards (poor, getting along, being comfortable, prosperous, substantial, and rich) of six different household types (couple with zero to five children) are distinguished and each respondent is asked to state the income amount for a single household type at a single living standard. Given these data, *Rainwater* (1974) calculates the geometric means of incomes for each household type and welfare level and derives equivalence scales that turn out to be rather flat: for example, a family size elasticity of 0.312 implies an equivalence scale of 1.27 for a couple with two children, taking a childless single adult as reference. Further data are reported in Table 2.6. Interestingly, *Aguilar* and *Gustafsson* (1988, pp. 262f.) apply the same methodology for Sweden but get equivalence scales that are significantly steeper. Taking a single adult as reference household, they get a scale value of 1.70 for a couple, and 2.61 for a family with two children aged between 4 and 10 (compare Table 2.6).

Table 2.4. Consensual Survey Questions

Author	Question/Stimulus Material	Response
Kilpatrick (1973), Rainwater (1990), Vaughan (1993)	"What is the smallest amount of money a family of four (husband, wife, and two children) needs each week to get along in this community."[a]	Income
Rainwater (1974), Aguilar and Gustafsson (1988)	"Now I'm going to describe several different couples in their thirties and forties – and their levels of living. For each description I give you, please tell me the income that that family probably has so that they can live at that level."[b]	Income
Riffault and Rabier (1977)	Respondents were presented a set of hypothetical family types and, for these family types, they were asked for the incomes that make ends meet.[c]	Income
Dubnoff (1985)	Respondents were presented a set of hypothetical family types with incomes that were set in a range between 25% and 160% of a median family income of 21,000 Dollar.[d]	Answers on a six–point poor/prosperous scale
Saunders and Bradbury (1991), Saunders and Matheson (1992)	"In your opinion, what is the smallest amount a family of four – two parents and two children – need a week to keep in health and live decently – the smallest amount for all expenses including rent?"[e]	Income

[a] *Gallup Poll*, US. [b] *Boston Social Standards Survey*, US; Similar for Sweden. [c] name unknown, nine European countries. [d] name unknown, US. [e] *Morgan Gallup Poll*, Australia.

Dubnoff et al. (1981, 1985) switch the dimensions of stimulus and response that are used in the *Boston Social Standards Survey*. Instead of defining welfare levels and asking for welfare–equalising incomes across households, respondents are asked to rate the living standard of a household with given income and demography on a welfare scale. By regressing these ratings on income and household size, *Dubnoff et al.* (1981, 1985) calculate welfare–equalising incomes across households. The respective ratios of welfare–equalising incomes give equivalence scales for different household types. The resulting average equivalence scales over all welfare levels are reported in Table 2.5 to the base of a single adult household taking the welfare–equalising incomes from *Dubnoff et al.* (1985, Table 3, p. 294) for households without retired members.

Table 2.5. Equivalence Scales of Dubnoff et al. (1985)

	Number of household members					
Welfare Level	1	2	3	4	5	6
Poor, near poor, just getting along, reasonably, comfortably, very comfortably, prosperous	1.0	1.271	1.463	1.616	1.746	1.860

Note: own calculations based on the data in *Dubnoff et al.* 1985.

The equivalence scales derived are constant over all welfare levels. However, this does not mean that the answers of the interviewees were independent on the welfare level as well. Constancy is simply due to the estimation procedure which is applied in the underlying regression model. Compared to the findings of *Rainwater* (1974), the scales in *Dubnoff et al.* (1981, 1985) are much steeper. We will comment on these differences in an evaluation that follows in a later part of this section.

Riffault and *Rabier* (1977) estimate equivalence scales for nine European countries by the ratios of median answers to questions about minimum incomes for three different household types (single person of 30–50 years, two–person household of persons of 30–50 years, a family consisting of a man and a woman and two children between 10–15 years). The equivalence scales derived (compare Table 2.6) are rather similar across the considered countries. Compared to *Rainwater* (1974) and *Dubnoff et al.* (1981, 1985), the equivalence scales estimated by *Riffault* and *Rabier* (1977) are higher but flatter compared to the equivalence scales from *Aguilar* and *Gustafsson* (1988).

Altogether, consensual income methods differ with respect to the choice of the stimulus variables, to the type of questions, and to the dimension of pre–defined answer categories that is either welfare or income. The spectrum of consensual scales is rather extensive: taking a childless single adult as the reference, the equivalence scales for a couple with two children, for instance, lie in a range between 1.61 (*Dubnoff* 1981) and 2.61 (*Aguilar* and *Gustafsson* 1988). Of course, differences may partially be caused by country specific characteristics. But this can only be seen as one potential source. Other sources will be touched in the next section which will deal with the methodological features of the cited approaches.

Table 2.6. Consensual Equivalence Scales

Author	Country	A	AA	AAC	AACC	AACCC
Rainwater (1974, p. 105)	U.S.	—	1.00	1.12	1.27	1.30
Dubnoff et al. (1981)	U.S.	1.00	1.49	1.57	1.72	1.85
Dubnoff et al. (1985)	U.S.	1.00	1.27	1.47	1.61	1.74
Riffault and Rabier (1977)	Belgium	1.00	1.56	—	2.00	—
	Denmark	1.00	1.41	—	1.85	—
	Germany	1.00	1.47	—	2.06	—
	France	1.00	1.56	—	2.23	—
	Ireland	1.00	1.47	—	2.04	—
	Italy	1.00	1.45	—	2.07	—
	Luxemburg	1.00	1.45	—	1.93	—
	Netherlands	1.00	1.32	—	1.63	—
	U.K.	1.00	1.41	—	1.90	—
Aguilar and Gustafsson (1988)	Sweden	1.00	1.70	—	2.61	—

Notation: each A denotes an adult. Each C denotes a child.
Source. Authors cited and own calculations.

Evaluation

Consensual income surveys collect information about what the public thinks is the relation between incomes of well–defined household types and their living standards. Thus, the validity of the consensual method rests on three requirements. Firstly, interviewees were required to take a general viewpoint when answering the questions and should not refer to their own family situation. An indicator whether this demand is met would be that respondents' answers are only slightly affected or unaffected by their own personal characteristics. The results of *van den Bosch* (1999, pp. 160–166) reveal that this condition is satisfied: responses in the cited studies are either slightly correlated or uncorrelated with personal characteristics, indicating that interviewees take the required general viewpoint. Secondly, phrases that describe different living standards should evoke a concrete image of material living standards and this image should be rather similar across the sample of respondents. This prerequisite does not only mean that respondents attach an identical meaning to a phrase like "prosperous", but that the phrase is also related to a particular living standard which subjects are able to translate into a cash amount. On the respondents' side, this requires the definition of some kind of market basket which then is to be converted to a monetary equivalent. With respect to these requests, the picture is less convincing. The derivation of a "correct" equivalence scale would require that the living standards, as employed in the questionnaires either as stimulus or as response category, have an identical meaning for all respondents, and that subjects are capable to define (priced) market baskets for the respective welfare levels. Yet, the data variation is rather high. *Rainwater* (1974, p. 59) explains this finding by errors that arise when people have to transform incomes into welfare levels (or the inverse task) but there might also arise pricing errors as to the monetary assessment of the market baskets. Thirdly, differences in the answers finally might be due to imprecise descriptions of the hypothetical household types. Is it, for instance, sufficient to distinguish among adult and non–adult household members or is there a necessity to provide a more detailed description regarding the gender, employment status, or health status of the household members?

The statistical results of all consensual surveys indicate that data variation is not simply random. This means that interviewees' responses are sensitive to the values of the stimulus variables. Moreover, the equivalence scales derived are "reasonable" in the sense that they increase with increasing size of the hypothetical households and they are only slightly affected by the interviewee's personal characteristics. The latter result indicates that respondents are not too rationally bounded for answering the survey questions, but take a rather general point of view.[21] There is, however, high data variation within and across the studies. This finding is very likely driven by different ideas about the meanings of the verbal notions of welfare across the respondents. It would therefore be interesting to test whether the verbal descriptions of welfare evoke similar images in the respondents' minds. Unfortunately, such a test is not possible which means that there is good reason to doubt the data quality of consensual approaches.

2.3.2 Subjective Approach

The previous section worked out two important arguments that question the validity of consensual equivalence scales. Firstly, in the consensual approach respondents make assessments of the income needs of hypothetical households that are different from their own which are, secondly, not always well–defined. A way to overcome these weak points is to ask the interviewees about their own, personal situation instead of referring to hypothetical household types. The idea behind this strategy is that a respondent might better assess the needs of her/his own household type as compared to any other household type since she/he has clear ideas of her/his household's characteristics. This is the subjective approach.

[21]The concept of *bounded rationality* was introduced by *Simon* 1957. Compare, especially, pp. 196–204.

Two branches of subjective approaches can be distinguished differing in the stimulus variables and response categories employed. Using the *income evaluation method*, subjects are asked what income they attribute, in their own familiar circumstances, to a specific *living standard*. On the other hand, interviewees in *income satisfaction* surveys rate their income satisfaction on a particular *welfare* scale. At first glance, these differences seem to be of semantic nature only such that one would expect rather similar empirical results across the studies. It will become obvious, however, that the empirical findings are crucially dependent upon which branch is followed. The following two sections review the literature that is related to the two branches of subjective approaches, comprising a presentation of equivalence scale estimates and a discussion about the usefulness of each of both subjective approaches to equivalence–scale measurement.

Income Evaluation Approach

Income evaluation methods employ the so–called *minimum income question* (MIQ) or the *income evaluation question* (IEQ). The minimum income question typically reads as:

"We would like to know which net family income would, in your circumstances, be the absolute minimum for you. That is to say, that you would not be able to make ends meet if you earned less."

The most prominent income evaluation question as suggested by *van Praag* (1971a) is:

"Please try to indicate what you consider to be an appropriate amount for each of the following cases. Under my (our) conditions I would call a net household income per week/month/year of:
about .... very bad
about .... bad
about .... insufficient
about .... sufficient
about .... good
about .... very good."

There exists a number of different versions of MIQ and IEQ, and differences especially showing in the verbal description of the household welfare levels. We refrain from summarising all of them here. A common feature of these questions is that they do *not* ask for public–regarding evaluations (consensual approach), but that they ask for self–regarding evaluations given the individual demographic situation of the interviewee. The major difference between *IEQ* and *MIQ* is that *IEQ* does not only refer to the subsistence level (MIQ) but that it collects income data for a range of different welfare levels. A common feature of both questions is that they deal with the personal evaluation of one's own income rather than directly providing "general" conclusions about household needs. Thus, income evaluation surveys measure respondents' subjective welfare such that the equivalence scales derived represent income ratios that equalise income evaluations across different household types.

Literature Survey

Although income evaluation surveys are conducted with various interests, like the definition of poverty lines or the derivation of welfare functions of income, the following remarks confine themselves only to those studies that are related to our topic. Still, the number of studies remains impressive. Table 2.7 lists the main empirical results with a focus on the impacts of household income and household size on equivalence scales. Moreover, empirical results of different statistical approaches are summarised to show the sensitivity of the findings to the choice of the underlying model. The parameters α_{FS} and α_y denote the regression estimates of the logarithms of family size (FS) and of household income (y). HSE is the equivalence scale's elasticity with respect to household size and is defined as $\frac{\alpha_{FS}}{1-\alpha_y}$. The equivalence scale of a couple with three children (2A3C) is given by the ratio $\frac{F_A}{F_{2A3C}}$. F_{1A} denotes the equivalence factor of a single adult and F_{2A3C} is the equivalence factor of a couple with three children.

The elasticity α_y is worth some further explanation since it captures in how far responses are influenced by the respondent's real income situation, the so–called *preference drift*. *Preference drift* means that people get used to their actual income: if income increases, people adapt to their new living standard and judge their past situation worse than they realised it at the time they were actually living in that income situation. Thus, subjects with a "high" actual income are expected to state higher incomes for pre–specified welfare levels than subjects with a "low" actual income.[22] Across the studies, the variation of α_y is rather high with a minimum of 0.19 in the study of *van Praag* (1971b) and a maximum of 0.80 in *Hagenaars et al.* (1984). A value of 0.80, for example, means that an increase in personal income by 1% increases the average answer to the imposed questions by 0.80%.

While high variation appears for α_y across the studies, variation is less extensive for $log(FS)$, the logarithm of household size. Except for some outliers, about 60% of the estimates stated range between 0.10 and 0.20. Higher coefficients in some studies are not due to differences in the empirical data, but result from different specifications of the regression model: in some surveys, children are replaced by equivalent adults causing relatively high coefficients.[23]

[22] Compare, for example, *van Praag*, 1971b, p. 362.

[23] In Table 2.7, the respective coefficients are marked by a ^{g}.

Table 2.7. Income Evaluation Equivalence Scales

Author	Ctr.	Year	Inc. Ev.	α_{FS}	α_y	HSE	F_{1A}	F_{2A3C}	σ_{2A3C}	R^2
v. Praag (1971b)	Be	1969	$\mu(y)$	0.30	0.19	0.37	77	140	1.82	0.20
Kapteyn, v. Praag (1976)	Ne	1971a	$\mu(y)$	[a]	0.64	0.30	nr	132	nr	0.65
Goedhart et al. (1977)	Ne	1975	$\mu(y)$	0.13	0.53	0.28	83	129	1.56	0.60
	Ne	1975	$log(y_{min})$	0.12	0.60	0.30	81	132	1.62	0.57
v. Herwaarden et al. (1977)	Be	1969	$\mu(y)$	0.14	0.68	0.44	74	149	2.02	0.61
	Be	1970	$\mu(y)$	0.13	0.66	0.38	77	142	1.85	0.59
	Be	1973	$\mu(y)$	0.14	0.61	0.36	78	139	1.78	0.51
	Ne	1971	$\mu(y)$	0.14	0.60	0.35	78	138	1.76	0.63
	Ne	1974	$\mu(y)$	0.11	0.66	0.32	80	135	1.68	0.66
v. Praag et al. (1980)	Be	1979	$log(y_{min})$	0.13	0.53	0.28	83	129	1.56	0.58
	De	1979	$log(y_{min})$	0.10	0.74	0.38	77	142	1.86	0.78
	Fr	1979	$log(y_{min})$	0.08	0.68	0.25	84	126	1.50	0.71
	WG	1979	$log(y_{min})$	0.14	0.63	0.38	77	141	1.84	0.65
	UK	1979	$log(y_{min})$	0.14	0.54	0.30	81	132	1.63	0.57
	Ir	1979	$log(y_{min})$	0.18	0.53	0.38	77	142	1.85	0.57
	It	1979	$log(y_{min})$	0.16	0.56	0.36	78	140	1.80	0.54
	Ne	1979	$log(y_{min})$	0.15	0.54	0.33	80	135	1.69	0.58
v. Praag et al. (1982)	Be	1979	$\mu(y)$	0.10	0.43	0.18	89	117	1.33	0.70
	De	1979	$\mu(y)$	0.08	0.63	0.22	86	122	1.42	0.83
	Fr	1979	$\mu(y)$	0.06	0.51	0.12	92	112	1.22	0.68
	WG	1979	$\mu(y)$	0.11	0.58	0.26	83	127	1.52	0.69
	UK	1979	$\mu(y)$	0.12	0.36	0.19	88	119	1.35	0.58
	Ir	1979	$\mu(y)$	0.17	0.46	0.31	80	133	1.66	0.64
	It	1979	$\mu(y)$	0.16	0.38	0.26	84	127	1.51	0.51
	Ne	1979	$\mu(y)$	0.10	0.54	0.22	86	122	1.42	0.66
Danziger et al. (1984)	US	1979	$log(y_{min})$	0.21	0.33	0.31	80	133	1.66	0.48
Colasanto et al. (1984)	US	1981	$log(y_{min})$	0.26	0.45	0.47	72	154	2.14	0.45
	US	1981	$\mu(y)$	0.20	0.45	0.36	78	140	1.80	0.42
Hagenaars et al. (1984)	Ne	1983	$\mu(y)$	0.003	0.80	0.02	99	101	1.02	0.66
Hagenaars et al. (1985)	Be	1979	$\mu(y)$	nr	0.46	0.21	86	106	1.23	0.59
	De	1979	$\mu(y)$	nr	0.64	0.27	75	108	1.44	0.82
	Fr	1979	$\mu(y)$	nr	0.48	0.22	83	103	1.24	0.64
	WG	1979	$\mu(y)$	nr	0.57	0.28	93	128	1.38	0.65
	Ir	1979	$\mu(y)$	nr	0.47	0.24	87	129	1.48	0.63
	It	1979	$\mu(y)$	nr	0.41	0.25	81	117	1.44	0.53
	Ne	1979	$\mu(y)$	nr	0.47	0.17	79	113	1.43	0.64
	UK	1979	$\mu(y)$	nr	0.42	0.16	75	114	1.52	0.51

Table continues

Continuation of Table 2.7

Author	Ctr.	Year	Inc. Ev.	α_{FS}	α_y	HSE	F_{1A}	F_{2A3C}	σ_{2A3C}	R^2
Janssens et al.	Be	1976	$log(y_{min})$	0.18	0.44	0.32	80	134	1.68	0.55
(1985)	Be	1982	$log(y_{min})$	0.23	0.31	0.33	79	136	1.71	0.35
Kapteyn et al.	Ne	80/82	$\mu(y)$	0.10	0.42	0.17	89	117	1.32	nr
(1985)	Ne	80/82	$log(y_{min})$	0.12	0.45	0.22	86	122	1.42	nr
Homan et al. (1986)	Ne	1983	[b]	0.12	[b]	0.42	nr	147	nr	nr
de Vos et al.	Ne	1983	$log(y_{suf})$	nr	[c]	0.46	78	153	1.96	0.72
(1987)	Ne	1983	$log(y_{min})$	nr	0.56	0.34	84	138	1.64	0.33
Kapteyn et al.	Ne	1982	$\mu(y)$	0.76[g]	0.55	0.33	78	126	1.62	0.59
(1988)	Ne	1982	$log(y_{min})$	0.22[g]	0.43	0.39	76	134	1.76	0.56
Poulin (1988)	Ca	1983	$log(y_{min})$	0.10	0.36	0.16	90	115	1.29	0.36
v. Praag et al.	Be	1979	$log(y_{ins})$	0.25	0.31	0.36	78	139	1.79	0.40
(1988)	De	1979	$log(y_{ins})$	0.20	0.58	0.48	72	155	2.15	0.65
	Fr	1979	$log(y_{ins})$	0.15	0.41	0.25	84	126	1.51	0.42
	WG	1979	$log(y_{ins})$	0.28	0.25	0.37	77	141	1.82	0.32
	Ir	1979	$log(y_{ins})$	0.13	0.41	0.22	86	122	1.43	0.38
	It	1979	$log(y_{ins})$	0.20	0.30	0.29	82	130	1.58	0.31
	Ne	1979	$log(y_{ins})$	0.15	0.48	0.29	82	130	1.59	0.54
	UK	1979	$log(y_{ins})$	0.21	0.29	0.30	81	131	1.61	0.26
	US	1983	$log(y_{ins})$	0.14	0.65	0.40	76	144	1.90	0.76
Callan et al. (1989)	Ir	1987	$log(y_{min})$	0.32	0.27	0.44	74	149	2.02	0.49
Moriani	It	1987	$\mu(y)$	0.23	0.32	0.34	79	136	1.72	0.66
(1990)	It	1987	$log(y_{min})$	0.29	0.31	0.42	75	147	1.97	0.66
Muffels et	Ne	1985	$log(y_{min})$	0.06	0.44	0.11	93	110	1.38	nr
al. (1990)	Ne	1985	$log(y_{min})$	0.23*	0.35	0.36	78	114	1.46	nr
	Ne	1985	$\mu(y)$	0.05	0.45	0.09	94	109	1.16	nr
	Ne	1985	$\mu(y)$	0.17*	0.35	0.29	82	111	1.35	nr
	Ne	1985	$log(y_{min})$	0.16	0.40	0.27	83	128	1.54	nr
	Ne	1985	$log(y_{min})$	0.59*	0.40	0.29	80	126	1.58	nr
	Ne	1985	$\mu(y)$	0.16	0.39	0.26	83	127	1.53	nr
	Ne	1985	$\mu(y)$	0.55*	0.37	0.29	81	123	1.52	nr
	Ne	85/86	$log(y_{min})$	0.20*	0.35	0.31	81	121	1.49	nr
	Ne	85/86	$\mu(y)$	0.17*	0.38	0.27	83	116	1.40	nr
	Ne	85/86	$log(y_{min})$	0.15*	0.20	0.15	90	111	1.23	nr
	Ne	85/86	$\mu(y)$	0.20*	0.23	0.20	87	115	1.32	nr
de Vos, Gar–	Ne	1983	$log(y_{min})$	nr	0.55	0.35	78	132	1.69	0.34
ner (1991)	US	1982	$log(y_{min})$	nr	0.43	0.38	72	145	2.01	0.49
Flik, v.	Ne	1983	$\mu(y)$	0.08	0.71	0.28	83	129	1.56	0.63

Table continues

Continuation of Table 2.7

Author	Ctr.	Year	Inc. Ev.	α_{FS}	α_y	HSE	F_{1A}	F_{2A3C}	σ_{2A3C}	R^2
Praag (1991)	Ne	1983	$log(y_{min})$	0.11	0.59	0.27	83	128	1.54	0.31
Stanovnik	Sl	1983	$log(y_{min})$	[d]	0.71	0.52	nr	nr	nr	0.71
(1992)	Sl	1988	$log(y_{min})$	[d]	0.52	0.59	nr	nr	nr	0.62
v. Praag,	It	1987	$\mu(y)$	0.25	0.32	0.37	78	140	1.81	0.51
Flik (1992)	It	1987	$\mu(y)$	–	0.32	0.33	85	139	1.64	0.51
	It	1987	$\mu(y)$	0.27	0.27	0.37	77	140	1.81	0.54
	Fr	1989	$\mu(y)$	0.16	0.45	0.29	82	131	1.60	0.62
	Fr	1989	$\mu(y)$	nr	0.46	0.23	88	127	1.44	0.62
	Fr	1989	$\mu(y)$	0.12	0.42	0.21	87	121	1.40	0.64
	Be	87/88	$\mu(y)$	0.18	0.42	0.31	81	133	1.65	0.57
	Be	87/88	$\mu(y)$	nr	0.43	0.36	82	130	1.59	0.57
	Be	87/88	$\mu(y)$	0.17	0.37	0.27	83	128	1.54	0.60
Saunders et al. (1993)	Au	1988	$log(y_{min})$	[e]	0.26	0.17	85	112	1.32	0.32
Saunders	Au	1988	$log(y_{min})$	[e]	0.3	0.19	88	119	1.35	0.25
et al. (1994)	Sw	1992	$log(y_{min})$	[e]	0.32	0.44	80	155	1.94	0.39
Halleröd (1995)	Sw	1992	$log(y_{min})$	[f]	0.25	nr	77	149	1.94	0.43

Note: data of authors cited, calculations in *van den Bosch* 1999, and own calculations.

Notation: nr: not reported; country: Sw: Sweden; Au: Australia; Be: Belgium; Ca: Canada; De: Denmark; Fr: France; Ir: Ireland; It: Italy; Ne: Netherlands; Sl: Slovenia; Sw: Sweden; UK: United Kingdom; US: United States; WG: West Germany. Inc. Ev.: income evaluation variable used: $\mu(y)$: average income; log: logarithm; y_{min}: minimal income; y_{ins}: insufficient income; y_{suf}: sufficient income.

[a] Authors use more complex specifications that are not outlined here. [b] Results for single–earner couples. Authors use specifications with $log(y)$ and $log(y)^2$. [c] Authors use specifications with $log(y)$ and $log(y)^2$. [d] Instead of log(FS), log(equivalent household size) entered the equations. [e] Number of adults and number of children entered the equations. [f] Equivalence scales are calculated from regression results reported by the author in Table 2, Equation 9i. [g] Children entered the regression as equivalent adults.

Comparing the values of α_y and $log(FS)$, both are inversely related across the studies: $log(FS)$ is always large whenever α_y is low. An explanation for this finding is a strong correlation of household size and household income in most countries such that their estimates "in the μ and logYmin equations will be inversely correlated" (*van den Bosch* 1999, p. 233).[24]

[24] $exp(\mu)$ is the level of income that is evaluated by 0.5 which is the middle of the welfare scale. logYmin is the logarithm of minimum income which is interpreted as poverty line (*Hagenaars* 1985, p. 49).

Estimates of household size elasticity (HSE) substantially vary across the studies with a minimum of 0.09 for 1985 in the Netherlands (*Muffels et al.* 1990) and a maximum of 0.48 for Denmark (*van Praag* and *van der Sar* 1988). Consequently, there also is high volatility among the equivalence–scale estimates. For example, equivalence scales of a five–person household range from 1.02 (*Hagenaars et al.* 1984) to 2.15 (value for Denmark, *van Praag et al.* 1988) taking a single adult as reference. As more detailed results of *Hagenaars* (1985, pp. 241–246) reveal, the weights for each household member follow rather peculiar patterns in some countries. For example, children cause almost no additional costs in the Netherlands and the UK. One possible reason for this astonishing finding is that the impacts of children on household needs are smoothed away by applying the log(FS) specification in the regressions. On the other hand, taking the logarithm of a variable is a rather comfortable way to increase the explanatory power of the regressions. Yet, the explanatory power highly differs across the studies: the coefficient of determination (R^2) varies between 0.20 (*van Praag* 1971b) and 0.83 (value for Denmark, *van Praag et al.* 1982). The inclusion of further explanatory variables (like sex, level of education, profession, etc.) only slightly increase regressions' explanatory power.[25]

Evaluation

Compared to equivalence scales from the consensual approach and the economic approach, income evaluation equivalence scales in general are rather flat, i.e. the income needs of households do not increase much if family size rises. Which potential sources can be made responsible for this observation? In the following, we will give an answer to this question. Moreover, we summarise the technical problems related to the estimation procedures and conclude with a comment on the merits of the income evaluation method for the measurement of equivalence scales.

A first potential source that might explain the flatness of the equivalence scales derived are preference and life–style changes that arise whenever the family structure varies. *Goedhart et al.* (1977, p. 516) argue that low equivalence scales reflect

"the fact that the preferences within the family shift in such a way that material needs do not increase very much. For example, a two–person family (husband and wife) may be accustomed to a life–style which includes relatively high holiday expenditures. When the first child is born, the parents decide to spend their holidays at home, thus saving money which may be used to compensate for the additional expenditures caused by the increase in family size."

[25] Compare, for example, *Saunders* and *Matheson* 1993 and *Saunders et al.* 1994 where different sets of explanatory variables are included in the regressions.

If this interpretation is correct, then it would support the validity of equivalence scales that are based on the income evaluation method. But there is at least one possible other interpretation, namely that childcare simply reduces the parents' time from opportunities to spend money and that equivalence scales derived are not the right indicator for welfare equivalence among household types. Furthermore, *Goedhart et al.*'s argument may have some appeal for parents that are financially well endowed, but the suggested kind of behavioural adjustment seems to be rather difficult for low–income recipients.

A second source of distortion are *reference–group effects*. *Bradbury* (1989, p. 400) argues that equivalence scales derived are valid only "if reference group effects are independent of family composition" and continues:

"The overall lack of responsiveness of the attitudinal scales to family size may reflect some tendency for families to judge their standard of living relative to other families of the same composition. If this were entirely the case, the equivalence scale would be equal to unity for all groups."

Given the available empirical data, a test of this hypothesis seems to be not viable at present.

A third potential source of distortions is quite similar to the aforementioned reference–group effects: equivalence scales could be affected by what respondents regard as a "reasonable" income given a pre–specified welfare level. Irrespective of their own household size, respondents may have an idea of what constitutes such a "reasonable" income. If this were the case, respondents' answers would be distorted indicators of household needs since they would adapt their actual ideas about household needs towards these "reasonable" values. The following example demonstrates the impacts of such behaviour on equivalence scales. Assume that a respondent with a partner and three children perceives the German social assistance of about Euro 800 for a couple as a "merely sufficient" income. Asked about a "merely sufficient" income given her/his own actual demographic situation she/he might have Euro 1,800 in mind. However, owing to the huge difference of Euro 1,000 between both incomes, she/he might judge Euro 1,800 as unreasonably high and state Euro 1,400. Inversely, a person in a one–person household might regard Euro 600 as "merely sufficient" and therefore she/he might state Euro 700 such that the resulting equivalence scale of $\frac{1{,}400}{700} = 2.0$ is substantially flatter than the "correct" one of $\frac{1{,}800}{600} = 3.0$.

The respondents' consideration of family allowances might be a fourth reason for flat scales when answering MIQ or IEQ (compare *O'Higgins* 1980). If respondents do not consider such income sources when answering the questions, the "correct" income corresponding to a specific level of household welfare on average is higher than the actually stated one. This idea is in line with *O'Higgins* (1980, p. 19) observation that "countries with the most generous levels of child support (Belgium, France and the UK) have the lowest equivalence scales." Results of later studies, however, no longer confirm this observation (compare *Bradshaw et al.* 1993, p. 265).

Also, there is a number of technical problems that raise doubts on the validity of income evaluation equivalence scales. Firstly, there exists no consensus about how to control biases in equivalence scales which are caused by *preference drift*. As was outlined above, it is a well-observed phenomenon that stated incomes for any given welfare level are positively related to the actual income level of the respondent. If, for example, an interviewee who lives in a "large" household has a lower income than an interviewee who lives in a "small" household, preference drift may lead to the outcome that the former states a lower income for a given welfare level compared to the latter. In such a case, preference drift would lead to an equivalence-scale value below 1.0 for the larger household. Of course, such a result is inappropriate for any socio-economic analysis. *Deleeck* (1989) suggests a rather comfortable way to control preference-drift effects. He argues that if the "true" response to MIQ or IEQ is the same as the current income of the interviewee, preference drift plays no role since the interviewee's answer is the same as the current income. Thus, considering only the group of interviewees that give answers near to their own actual income generates unbiased equivalence scales. This procedure, however, causes the loss of a large share of collected data.

Secondly, the *Leyden School* assumes that utility functions of income $u(y)$ are s-shaped which implies a low marginal utility of income for very poor subjects which contradicts *Gossen's first law*. *Van Praag* (1968) argues that low marginal utility results from critical consumption quantities such that quantities which are below this critical level are practically worthless. On the opposite, *Seidl* (1994, p. 1646) argues that

"when an agent may freely switch among a large set of different commodities, it is absurd to assume that he will spend his money on goods representing low welfare. Rather he will buy units of goods which [...] provide the highest marginal welfare in successive order. Such consumption patterns obviously provide for a positive, but uniformly decreasing marginal welfare of living."

Moreover, low marginal utility of income at low income levels "might cause nonconvexity of the social welfare function, violating thereby desirable axioms of poverty indices, especially the transfer axiom [...]" (*Seidl* (1987), p. 95). *Seidl* continues upon the subject of indivisible commodities. He states indivisibility does not provide a justification since it is implausible to assume that subjects purchase goods, knowing that the available quantities do not contribute significantly to their welfare. Furthermore, the s-shape implies that utility is bounded from above and from below. Consequently, $u(y)$ can be normalised such that $0 \leq u(y) \leq 1$ for all income amounts y. Boundedness, however, generally causes a further problem for cardinal utility functions. If, for instance, a subject states a utility level of $u(y) = 0.7$ for an income of Euro 3.000, and then this subject is asked for the additional income that would double her/his utility, she/he should answer (Seidl 1994, p. 1641): "Sorry, no amount of money can double my present welfare, since my utility function is bounded." On the contrary, psychological experiments reveal that the utility function of money is concave and limited from below, but the function is unlimited from above.[26] The difficulties of the upper bound become even more relevant if one considers that according to empirical studies in the Netherlands, "couples with one individual working have average welfare of 0.72."[27] Although these incomes were not unimaginably high, only (excessively) large additional incomes would lead to significantly higher utility levels. Substituting cardinality by ordinality would solve the problems caused by the proposed s–shaped form.[28] The *Leyden School*, however, always emphasized cardinality as an important advantage of their approach.

Thirdly, categories of the IEQ are assumed to be equally spaced on the welfare continuum, the so–called *equal quantile assumption*, though this assumption was repeatedly rejected in empirical tests.[29] Moreover, *Seidl* (1987, p. 95) argues that the equal quantile assumption is sensitive to the number of welfare categories employed in the questionnaires. The claim that the income evaluation method is a cardinal measure, however, rests on both, s–shaped utility functions and an equally spaced welfare continuum.

Further problems are related to the identification of individual welfare functions of income. Following *van Praag* (1968), these functions follow a lognormal distribution functions with a location parameter and a parameter that measures welfare sensitivity. However, "a power welfare function combined with a lognormal-distribution welfare evaluation function and a lognormal welfare function are all *observationally equivalent*" (*Seidl* 1994, p. 95). Moreover,

"when a logarithmic function or a power function rather than the lognormal distribution function happen to be the true individual welfare functions, it makes no sense whatsoever to superimpose a normal or a lognormal distribution function which serves only the evaluation purpose [...]. As superimpositions of such evaluation functions are not linear transformations, they change the properties of the welfare function" (Seidl 1994, p. 1655f.).

Altogether, there arise strong doubts on *van Praag*'s view that the results of the income evaluation method are valid almost by definition and, consequently, build the standard for assessing the validity of all other approaches to measuring economic welfare. On the contrary, respondents' answers towards IEQ and MIQ provide biased estimates of their "true" income needs. This finding also questions the validity of equivalence scales derived. That equivalence–

[26] *Seidl* 1994 provides an overview of this literature.
[27] *Hartog* 1988, p. 260.
[28] Compare *van Praag* and *van der Sar* 1988.
[29] *Seidl* 1994 provides an overview of this literature.

scale estimates tend to be flatter than in other approaches emphasises the relevance of aforementioned concerns. These concerns will be reinforced by the analysis in the following section which will show that equivalence scales of the closely–related *income–satisfaction approach* are significantly steeper compared to the income–evaluation approach.

Income–Satisfaction Approach

When using the income–satisfaction method respondents are asked to rate their own living standard or income on a scale of ordered categories. A typical question (*Bradbury* 1989) reads "How satisfied are you with the financial situation of your household?", and answers are to be given on a pre–specified welfare scale with a number of response categories. The income–satisfaction method is used for numerous purposes,[30] yet the following discussion is confined to those studies and results that are related to the topic of equivalence scales. In income satisfaction surveys, equivalence scales are derived in a two–step procedure. At first, the level of household k's income satisfaction (S_k) is regressed on the explanatory variables household log–income, $log(y_k)$, and other household characteristics, Z_{kj}, with $j = 2, ..., J$, and $V_0, ..., V_J$ are the parameters to be estimated. Then, the equivalence scale for household type k relative to reference type r can be calculated as the income ratio $log\left(\frac{y_k}{y_r}\right) = \frac{1}{V_1}[-\sum_2^J V_j(Z_{kj} - Z_{rj})]$ that for k and r creates the same feeling about their own income, respectively. If we are interested in deriving equivalence scales for different numbers of household members (FS) only and avoid the logarithm, the equivalence scale is $\frac{y_k}{y_r} = \left(\frac{FS_k}{FS_r}\right)^{-\frac{V_2}{V_1}}$ where the exponent is the equivalence–scale elasticity with respect to household size. In this case the equivalence scale only depends on the parameters V_1 and V_2 and household size, but not on the income or on the welfare level.[31]

Literature Survey

As to our knowledge, seven different types of *income satisfaction* surveys have been conducted. Differences in the methodology are of semantic nature and also refer to the definition of the pre–defined welfare scale. A summary is given in Table 2.8. Table 2.9 summarises the equivalence scales of these seven surveys. *Dubnoff et al.* (1981) and *Melenberg et al.* (1995) get rather flat scales that are quantitatively rather similar to the equivalence scales of the income evaluation approach. On the opposite, *Douthitt et al.* (1992) and *Bradbury* (1989) estimate equivalence scales that are partly beyond any rational level. For instance, *Bradbury* (1989) derives an equivalence–scale value of 181.39 for

---

[30]For an overview, compare *Andrews* and *Withey* 1976.

[31]Compare *van den Bosch* 1999, pp. 454–455.

a single with two children. It is also hard to imagine that a couple with three children needs about twice the income of a couple with two children such that the income satisfaction is the same for both (*Douthitt et al.* 1992).

Though quantitative differences in equivalence scales are substantial across different household types (consider, for example, an equivalence scale of 3.91 for a single adult with one child and 181.39 with two children), *Bradbury* (1989) finds that some of these differences are insignificant. According to *Bradbury*, this is due to large standard errors in the regression coefficients. In any case, there is no evident reason that explains the substantial differences in equivalence scales across the seven studies: the underlying questionnaires are rather similar and, except for Slovenia, all data are exclusively collected in industrialised and highly developed countries.

Table 2.8. Income Satisfaction Methods

Stimulus Question	Response Category
"How do you feel about the income you (and your family) have?"[a]	Answers on a seven–point terrible/delighted scale
"With the total family income as it is now can you make ends meet:"[b]	Answers on a seven–point very difficulty/very easily scale
"Which of the following categories best describes how you feel about your family income (or your income if you are living with relatives)?"[c]	Answers on a seven–point terrible/delighted scale
"How satisfied are you with the financial situation of your household?"[d]	Answers on a ten–point dissatisfied/satisfied scale
Subjects are asked to evaluate their endowment with seven economic domains (physical needs, government and economy, standard of living, financial security, cost of basic necessities, household income, pay and fringe benefits.[e]	Answers on a seven–point terrible/delighted scale
"In relation to living costs, our family income is:"[f]	Answers on a four–point very insufficient/amply sufficient scale
"How satisfied are you with your household income?"[g]	Answers on a ten–point not satisfied at all/ very satisfied scale

[a] Dubnoff et al. (1981), Vaughan (1984). [b] de Coster et al. (1984). [c] Poulin (1988). [d] Bradbury (1989). [e] Douthitt et al. (1992). [f] Stanovnik (1992). [g] Melenberg et al. (1995).

Especially the significant differences between the equivalence scales in *Poulin* (1988) and *Dubnoff et al.* (1981) are surprising given that both use similar data and models. *Poulin* (1988) gives a possible explanation for partly strange results and high standard errors. *Poulin* (1988, p. 17) observes that "the income levels associated with the extreme levels of satisfaction appear ridiculously high or low" causing ridiculously high or low equivalence–scale values. In the next section, we will deal with this phenomenon in more detail.

Table 2.9. Income Satisfaction Equivalence Scales

Author	Ctr.	Year	AC	ACC	AA	AAC	AACC	AACCC
Dubnoff et al. (1981)[a]	US	1972	1.49	1.57	1.49	1.57	1.72	1.85
Vaughan (1984)	nr	nr	1.28	1.49	1.28	1.49	1.64	1.78
de Coster et al. (1984)[b]	Be	1982	1.37	1.59	1.08	1.45	1.69	1.86
Poulin (1988)[c]	Ca	1983	1.79	2.39	1.79	2.39	2.23	2.88
			1.56	2.03	1.66	2.03	2.45	2.84
Bradbury (1989)	Au	1983	3.91	181.39	1.25	2.48	3.18	3.11
Douthitt et al. (1992)[d]	US	1980	2.00	4.00	2.00	4.00	7.84	15.56
Stanovnik (1992)[d]	Sl	1988	1.47	1.84	1.47	1.84	2.16	2.44
Melenberg and van Soest (1995)	Ne	1984	1.52	1.94	1.51	1.94	2.30	nr

Note: All equivalence scales (re)calculated to the base of a single adult. Notation: Ctr.: Country: Au: Australia; Be: Belgium; Ca: Canada; Ne: Netherlands; Sl: Slovenia; US: United States; nr: not reported. Each A denotes an adult; each C denotes a child. [a] Distinction of family types by family size only. [b] Recalculated from regression coefficients at median welfare level. [c] First row: dummy variables for each household member; second row: log–family size specification. [d] Recalculated from regression coefficients; differentiation of households by number of family members.

Evaluation

The empirical data raise many doubts on whether the *income satisfaction method* is an adequate tool for estimating equivalence scales. Subsequently, we will shed some light on possible reasons.

The proportion of explained variance being rather low, about 25% on average, is common to all studies.[32] One possible interpretation of this finding is that income satisfaction is strongly influenced by random disturbance. If

[32] Coefficients of determination: *Dubnoff et al.* 1981: 0.23; *Vaughan* 1984: 0.26; *de Coster et al.* 1984: n.a.; *Poulin* 1988: 0.19; *Bradbury* 1989: 0.27; *Douthitt et al.* 1992: 0.10; *Stanovnik* 1992: n.a.; *Melenberg* and *van Soest* 1995: n.a.

this were true, strong questions about the reliability of the income satisfaction method would arise. But there also is the possibility of variables with a higher explanatory power having been omitted from the regressions. One of these variables might be the respondents' judgement of their own standard of living. It might be the case that people which are happy express a higher level of satisfaction with their income than unhappy people in objectively similar living conditions: greater happiness improves income satisfaction because happy people distinguish from unhappy people by being more active, optimistic and stress resistant, to give some examples. For Germany, *Headey et al.* (1990) analyse data from four waves of the German *Socio–Economic Panel* (*SOEP*), finding considerable reciprocal effects between "income satisfaction" and "live satisfaction" controlling for household income. However, if "life satisfaction" is omitted from the regressions, then parameter estimates of the influences of income and household size and resulting equivalence scales are biased. Another unconsidered variable that might be particularly important is the standard that people refer to when answering the income satisfaction questions. In the studies cited it is a standard assumption that all respondents use the same average standard when expressing their satisfaction with household income. It is, however, highly probable, that, comparable to the *preference drift* phenomenon, respondents employ different standards which are dependent on their own living standard. Thus, similar biases in equivalence scales to those arising in the income evaluation approach are to be expected.

Moreover, *Vaughan* (1984) turns out to be the only author who includes interactions between explanatory variables in his regression models. He considers an interaction between household income and household size and finds a slightly negative dependence of equivalence scales on income. The impact does, however, not turn out to be stable when other variables are added to the model.

Finally, income satisfaction methods use verbal proxies for household welfare. As the preference–drift phenomenon revealed, such proxies might lead to biased answers and to distorted equivalence scales.

3

The Potential Dependence of Equivalence Scales on Income

In the framework of (neoclassical) demand analysis, the equivalence scale of household type k relative to household type r is that ratio of cost functions $\frac{c(u_k,p_k,s_k)}{c(u_r,p_r,s_r)}$ which equalises the utility of both households. If the utility functions lack interpersonal comparability then any kind of equivalence scales may emerge from analysing household demands. This establishes an *identification problem.* IB and ESE avoid but do not solve the identification problem: relative income needs of different household types are simply assumed to be invariant to the households' utility or income levels at which they are compared. This necessitates a specific form of cost functions, viz. $c(u_r, p_r, s_k) = \sigma(p_r, s_k) * c(u_r, p_r)$. Other authors like *Ray* (1983) and *Jorgenson* and *Slesnick* (1987) implicitly assume in their empirical estimations that the equivalence scales are invariant with respect to income or utility. Thus, given a price vector, equivalence scales in both cases only depend on the demography of the households. Some authors like *Lewbel* (1989) try to make the constancy property the central point in equivalence scale measurement, yet not all authors agree with this idea. According to *Conniffe* (1992, p. 429) this "practice should be changed", justifying his demand by means of an example: *"[...] if a child is taken as equivalent to* 0.5 *of an adult and living standards of a "two adult–four children" household are comparable with a "two adult" household the income of the former would be first divided by two. This implies that the "cost" of a child is* £1,250 *per annum if that household has an income of* £10,000 *per annum and* £125,000 *per annum if the household has an income of* £1m."
According to *Conniffe* (1992), this no longer is plausible, and he criticises that constancy often is assumed without further reflection. Section 3.1 uses a household consumer model to show that IB/ESE only hold for a rather special case of household preferences. Moreover, we will discuss other reasons for income dependent equivalence scales. In Section 3.2, we present the empirical results of previous studies.

3.1 Plausibility of Constant Equivalence Scales

In order to show the restrictions of IB/ESE, we employ a version of the *Brown* and *Heien* (1972) consumer model which turns out to be rather instructive to this purpose. Refering to a working paper of *Koulovatianos et al.*, the following model assumes that a household consumes a variety of commodities $x = (x_i)$ from a continuum $[0, I]$ of commodities,[1] where i is one of these commodities. The number of adults in the household is denoted n_A while n_C denotes the number of children. Let a family with (n_A, n_C) members solve the problem

$$max_{(x_i)} \int_0^I f_i(n_A, n_C) \frac{(x_i + \gamma_i)^{1-\frac{1}{\eta}} - 1}{1 - \frac{1}{\eta}} di \tag{3.1}$$

subject to the budget constraint

$$p'x = \int_0^I p_i x_i di \leq y \tag{3.2}$$

with $x_i \geq max(0, -\gamma_i)$. The vector $p = (p_i)$ is the price vector with $i \in [0, I]$ while y denotes household income. Let $G = f_i(n_A, n_C)$ with $i \in [0, I]$ be a vector of functions that depends on the number of adults n_A and on the number of children n_C in the household. $G = f_i(n_A, n_C)$ transforms household size and composition to a weighting parameter for each commodity $i \in [0, I]$. $f_i(n_A, n_C)$ captures the extent to which commodity i is private or public in the household. If commodity i is purely private within the family (say, clothing), the function f_i might imply no sharing possibilities through a functional form as $f_i(n_A, n_C) = \frac{\varpi_i}{n_A + n_C}$ with $\varpi_i > 0$. On the other hand, an additional household member might not affect congestion costs if the commodity is perfectly public within the household (say, security provided by an alarm system), that is $f_i(n_A, n_C) = \varpi_i$ with $\varpi_i > 0$. For all other types of goods, both derivatives might be positive and lie within these two extreme cases. The vector $\gamma = \gamma_i$ with $i \in [0, I]$ denotes subsistence levels. Thus, we are refering to a Stone–Geary demand system. Under the assumption that y, γ, p and G are such that

$$y \geq \gamma_i \frac{\int_0^I f_i(n_A, n_C)^\eta p_i^{1-\eta} di}{\frac{1}{p_i} f_i(n_A, n_C)^\eta p_i^{1-\eta}} - p'\gamma \tag{3.3}$$

for all $i \in [0, I]$, household demand for commodity i is given by

$$x_i = -\gamma_i + \frac{1}{p_i} \frac{f_i(n_A, n_C)^\eta p_i^{1-\eta}}{\int_0^I f_i(n_A, n_C)^\eta p_i^{1-\eta} di} (y + p'\gamma) \tag{3.4}$$

and the indirect utility function is

[1] It need not be a continuum. To consider both, a continuum as well as a countable set of goods, the integral in Equation 3.1 should be interpreted as a *Riemann–Stieltjes integral*.

$$V(p,y,n_A,n_C) = \frac{(y+p'\gamma)^{1-\frac{1}{\eta}}}{1-\frac{1}{\eta}} \left[\int_0^I f_i(n_A,n_C)^\eta p_i^{1-\eta} di\right]^{\frac{1}{\eta}} - \frac{1}{1-\frac{1}{\eta}}. \quad (3.5)$$

An outline of this argument is given in *Jovanovic* (1995).

Now, let the reference household be of size $(\bar{n}_A, \bar{n}_C)$. Then, the equivalence scale $\sigma(a,c)$ for a household with a more adults and c more children than the reference household should satisfy

$$V(p,\sigma(a,c)y,\bar{n}_A+a,\bar{n}_C+c) = V(p,y,\bar{n}_A,\bar{n}_C). \quad (3.6)$$

Combining equation (3.6) with equation (3.5) and setting $\varphi(G(n_A,n_C),p) = \int_0^I f_i(\bar{n}_A,\bar{n}_C)^\eta p_i^{1-\eta} di$, the equivalence scale for household type $(\bar{n}_A+a,\bar{n}_C+c)$ is

$$\sigma(a,c) = \left(\frac{\varphi(G(\bar{n}_A,\bar{n}_C),p)}{\varphi(G(\bar{n}_A+a,\bar{n}_C+c),p)}\right)^{\frac{1}{\eta-1}}$$

$$+\left[\left(\frac{\varphi(G(\bar{n}_A,\bar{n}_C),p)}{\varphi(G(\bar{n}_A+a,\bar{n}_C+c),p)}\right)^{\frac{1}{\eta-1}} - 1\right]\frac{p'\gamma}{y}. \quad (3.7)$$

Equation (3.7) gives a clear analysis of the determinants of equivalence scales for this demand system. Firstly, the function $\varphi = \int_0^I f_i(\bar{n}_A,\bar{n}_C)^\eta p_i^{1-\eta} di$ should be weakly increasing with respect to n_s with $s \in \{A,C\}$. φ measures how "public" the optimal consumption budget is: in the extreme case that all goods are purely public within the household, then $\varphi_{n_s} = 0$ with $s \in \{A,C\}$ and equation (3.5) implies that all equivalence scales are equal to one. If, on the other hand, $\varphi_{n_s} > 0$ and also $\eta < 1$, then equivalence scales increase with increasing number of family members. Equivalence scales increase at a decreasing rate when more family members are added if $\frac{\partial \varphi_{n_s}}{\partial n_s} \leq 0$, $\eta > 1$, and $p'\gamma > 1$.

The question whether equivalence scales are independent of base or not, depends on $p'\gamma = \int_0^I p_i\gamma_i di$, the *monetary* subsistence levels. In the case that most commodities are "luxuries" such that $p'\gamma > 0$, then equivalence scales depend negatively on reference income. If, by contrast, more commodities are necessities such that $p'\gamma < 0$ then equivalence scales increase as reference income rises. In this demand system, it is not necessary that preferences over all goods are homothetic (γ_i for all $i \in [0,I]$) in order to have $p'\gamma = 0$, which implies IB/ESE. If the subsistence level γ_i is negative, the demand system described above has the interpretation that the household takes away from its budget the amount $p_i\gamma_i$ before starting responding to prices. Moreover, the household responds to prices considering not his overall income y but $y+p'\gamma$. Thus the household corrects for the net value of all subsistence levels. On the contrary, if commodity i is a luxury ($\gamma_i > 0$), the household refrains from consuming i up to the level $p_i\gamma_i$. Again, the household responds to prices by weighting $y+p'\gamma$ with the preference and weight given in equation (3.4). Thus, if $p'\gamma$ is positive with a plausible $\eta > 1$, equivalence scales are decreasing in income y.

Another explanation for income dependencies of equivalence scales may be derived from the study of *Caplovitz* (1967) which shows that prices of goods differ across population subgroups. Especially the members of low income classes are not able to take advantage of favourable purchases because of missing liquidity, technically insufficient possibilities (no freezer, for example), and close quartered living space. Also, there exists discrimination against members of low income classes, for example in the housing market. These observations suggest a negative dependence of equivalence scales on income. Finally, *Nelson* (1993) argues that children weights could decrease as income rises, refering to parents who limit their expenditures on children since they are worried about spoiling them. (*Nelson* 1993, p. 48.) continues that
"it may be that beyond some level of consumption on the part of minor children, parents may be likely to limit their children's current consumption [...] in favor of increasing their welfare through such means as later–in–life investments in higher education, or transfer of assets. If such is the case, so that (loosely speaking) the children's "share" of household consumption drops as income rises, IB is violated (for welfare defined over current consumption)."

3.2 Empirical Picture

A first empirical study dealing with the income dependence of equivalence scales was conducted by *Seneca* and *Taussig* (1971). To define a tax schedule which guarantees horizontal equity, the authors estimate Engel functions for food and other "necessities". Based on observations on individual spending, the authors define sub–samples of different family size groupings. Additionally, each of these sub–sample is divided into 16 income classes. Within each income class, an equivalence scale is computed for a number of different definitions of market baskets containing "necessities". The authors derive equivalence scales which suggest decreasing children weights with increasing income, yet these equivalence scales are rather sensitive with regard to the chosen specification of underlying Engel functions and to the definition of the underlying "necessities".

Van Hoa (1986) proposes an approach which is based on the original Engel method for defining equivalence scales, i.e. the equivalence scale of household k relative to r is given by the income ratio which is connected with an identical expenditure share for food for both households. Based on Engel scales, the author calculates general equivalence scales which solve the primal problem of the household. *Van Hoa* finds that children weights decline from 0.41 for low incomes to 0.14 for a middle income level, but then again increase to 0.21 for high incomes. Unfortunately, the author neither provides any economic argument for this u–shape nor does he mention that the results will be sensitive to the chosen specification of underlying Engel function.

Aaberge and *Melby* (1998) determine income dependent equivalence scales by using Norwegian minimal social security pensions and child allowances. The authors define the equivalence scale of household type k in relation to a single–adult household r as $\sigma_{kr} = 1 + \frac{(y_{min,k} - y_{min,r})}{y_{dis,r}}$ with $\frac{\partial \sigma_{kr}}{\partial y_{dis,r}} < 0$, $y_{min,r}$ being minimal income of household r, and $y_{dis,r}$ its disposable income. $y_{min,k}$ is minimal income of household type k. Unfortunately, the authors do not explain how these incomes are defined. More problematic is that even though the formula may match their empirical findings, its specification is completely arbitrary.

Even *Blundell* and *Lewbel* (1991), the originators of the IB and ESE concept, as well as, for example, *Dickens*, *Fry* and *Pashardes* (1993), find that empirical demand data do not support IB/ESE. However, *Murthi* (1992, pp. 8–9) could not reject IB or ESE empirically in a predominant number of considered cases for different specifications of Engel curves. In their economic approach, *Donaldson and Pendakur* (2003), therefore, suggest non–IB/ESE framework by introducing two different classes of equivalent–income functions that are generalizations of those functions corresponding to IB/ESE equivalence scales. Using Canadian expenditure data, they derive equivalence scales that slightly decrease with increasing household income.

In survey approaches to equivalence scales, income dependencies of equivalence scales have not been of major interest. In general, underlying statistical models imply a constant elasticity of equivalence scales to household size regardless of the income level. This implies that the costs of an additional household member as a proportion of income is constant across incomes. Only few authors consider an interaction term between family size and income in their statistical models. *Kapteyn et al.* (1988) and *Muffels et al.* (1990) find that, in general, the respective coefficient is statistically insignificant or quantitatively small or both. In the rare cases of significance, the estimates are negative, indicating a negative dependence of equivalence scales on reference income, yet high standard errors question the validity of this finding. *Vaughan* (1984) finds a slightly negative dependence of equivalence scales on income. However, the impact does not turn out to be stable when other variables are added to the model.

3.3 Conclusion

The empirical data do not provide an unequivocal picture on whether IB/ESE is an appropriate assumption to describe household preferences.

However, the consumer model outlined above revealed that constant equivalence scales are a correct description of relative household needs only in special cases of household preferences. Many other reasons have been given that raise doubts on the validity of IB and ESE. However, IB/ESE are routinely applied in the empirical estimation of equivalence scales from demand data due to the lack of a more reasonable solution of the *identification problem*. On the other hand, survey approaches seem to be predestinated for testing these assumptions since they directly target on the measurement of household needs. However, only little attention has been paid to the dependence of equivalence scales on income in previous survey approaches and no questionnaire was designed directly addressing to this issue. As outlined above, our surveys herewith attempt to provide the necessarily data to close this gap.

4

Equivalence Scales, Employment and Household Production

The literature of household welfare distinguishes two different arguments in favour of regarding time as a an economic resource, the *earning–capacity* and the *household–production* argument. There exists some confusion about the two arguments, partly because empirical applications often use potential earnings to estimate the value of the time which is spent for household production. Nevertheless, the two arguments are clearly distinct and imply different assumptions and problems.

Garfinkel and *Haveman*'s (1977) earning capacity argument implies that different preferences for work and income versus leisure should not lead to different evaluations of economic status. That is, if individual A does the same kind of work as individual B at the same hourly wage rate, has the same non–wage income, lives in similar circumstances, and voluntarily decides to work less than B, then A should not be regarded as being worse off than B, only because she/he has less monetary income since the individual endowment with economic resources are identical.

The initiator of the household production argument was *Becker* (1965). He argues that a significant number of commodities and services consumed by the households are not bought as such on the market, but are produced within the households using market goods and the time of household members as inputs (*Becker* 1981, pp. 7–8). Though, for instance, take–away food and food services become more and more popular, most meals are still prepared at home combining the inputs food, domestic appliances and time. Moreover, a meal of a given nutritious and culinary value can either be prepared from relatively raw materials by spending a lot of time, or from processed and more expensive ingredients that require less time as input. Thus, to a certain degree market goods and time are substitutes. Given that individuals are not restricted on the labor market, this implies that if household k has – all other things being equal – less time available for household production (or leisure) than household r, then r enjoys a higher living standard.

In the following two sections, we present both arguments, deal with related statistical estimation techniques and available data, and will also discuss whether they are appropriate for the assessment of equivalence scales.

4.1 The Earnings–Capacity Argument

Garfinkel and *Haveman* (1977) and *Haveman* and *Buron* (1993) conducted the main empirical studies based on the earnings capacity approach. The authors argue that measures of economic position should not be affected by differential preferences with respect to leisure and market work. This means that household income is not the adequate measure for household welfare. Instead, they suggest a measure which is based on the earnings capacity of the household. For example, a family is only regarded as poor if full use of its earning capabilities fails to generate enough income to lift the family out of poverty (*Haveman* and *Buron* 1993, p. 144). If, on the other hand, a household's full–time earnings were sufficient to make it reach an agreeable living standard it should not be counted as poor when the household *voluntarily* decides to reduce its working time. Thus, the earnings capacity approach is akin to the *capability concept* (*Sen* 1985, and *Sen* 1993).

However, the earnings–capacity approach suffers from the problem that it is difficult to distinguish whether the labour supply of the household results from a utility maximising decision process in the household or whether it is determined by external constraints. There are a number of such external constraints, like the non–availability of external child care and, above all, the absence of jobs. *Haveman* and *Buron* (1993) turn out to be somewhat ambiguous about this matter and argue that "poor job opportunities for those with few skills" might be one of the reasons why a high percentage of low paid work is not taken up by the low skilled work seekers. In this context it is also interesting to note a methodological weak point in the estimation of earnings capacities. For the earnings capacity approach, it is crucial to be able to distinguish the group of individuals that have voluntarily withdrawn from the labour market from those that are involuntarily unemployed. As long as empirical data do not contain reliable information on that point it turns out to be rather questionable to substitute measures based on disposable income by earnings–capacity measures. Another problem arises if we think of the assessment of household needs if parents change the allocation of their daily routine as soon as they have children. Why shouldn't a family receive a compensation when a parent withdraws from employment in the labour market in order to take care of a new born child, though its potential working capacity is the same as before? Moreover, in most families minor children have to take their parent's decisions as given and it is by no means evident why a child should suffer from the negative financial consequences when its parents (voluntarily) decide to withdraw from the labour market.

The studies of *Garfinkel* and *Haveman* (1977) and *Haveman* and *Buron* (1993) also suffer from a methodological weakness. Earnings capacities for the U.S. are obtained by fitting an earnings function to survey data. These functions are used to attribute potential earnings to persons that have not worked full–time, year round. From a methodological point of view, it is not understandable that for permanently employed individuals corrections should be made for longer periods of being out of work on their part, when on the other hand no corrections are made for those which have completely withdrawn from the labour market.

4.2 The Household–Production Argument

The idea of household production is that households do not simply consume market goods and services, but many of these goods and services are transformed by using time and household appliances as inputs. This means that if household r has more time at its disposal for household production than k, then r can produce more goods for final consumption and therefore needs less cash income to achieve k's living standard. This also implies that the income gain of an additional household member starting to work in the labour market is partly lost since the household ability for household production shrinks such that the income gap between, for example, a one–earner and a two–earner couple systematically overestimates the difference between the two households' living standards (*Homan et al.* 1991). A proper comparison of the two households' situations therefore requires a measure of "compensated" income including the difference in the level of household production.

Two main approaches to define monetary equivalents of household production can be distinguished. A first approach is based on household–production *outputs*. *Gronau* (1988) and *Graham* and *Green* (1984) follow the *output approach* in an *indirect* way by estimating household production functions from time–budget data of private households and from variables that might influence household productivity. However, their results are highly sensitive to the chosen form of the production function as well as to other working assumptions (*Homan et al.* 1991). A *direct* method is applied by *Fitzgerald et al.* (1996). These authors directly measure the time devoted to 49 different types of household–production activities and the resulting quantities. These quantities are valued at market prices which are charged by the sellers of respective services. These studies reveal that the direct measurement of household production is feasible also at a rather disaggregated level. Unfortunately, the availability of such empirical data on household–production activities is exceptional. For example, representative data on time–budgets of

German households are available for 1991/1992 only.

A second approach relies on *inputs*, i.e. the time which is spent for household production.[1] Thus, the *input approach* relies on the number of hours a household spends on household–production activities such that, again, data of time–budget surveys are required. There exist two different versions of the input approach. In the *market cost approach* of *Chadeau* and *Fouquet* (1981), the value of household–production activities per month is defined as the product of monthly working hours in the household and the hourly wage of a domestic servant which would provide the same services. An alternative is to value each household production activity by the market price of the corresponding service. The *opportunity cost approach* argues that the value of one hour of housework is at least as high as the hourly wage which could additionally be earned by the individual in the labour market. For unemployed persons, the reservation wage is considered.

Besides these two main approaches, an *experimental approach* was suggested by *Quah* (1987). He tries to measure the value of household production by *auction bidding*. For instance, subjects are asked for the amount of money that they are willing to pay for a housekeeper which will provide services that correspond to two hours of household production. This question is repeated until the interviewee's willingness–to–pay is zero. Data as derived from such experimental surveys turn out to be a useful standard of comparison for valuations of household production.

There exists an extensive number of empirical and theoretical studies on household production. In these studies, the household member's abilities to provide housework are an important component of household needs. The costs of children, for example, can not only be measured by the household's expenditures for children goods. In fact, children costs to a large extent take the form of parental time and therefore cause opportunity costs by reducing their parents' time for other activities like market work or leisure. Thus, income needs of a single parent with two children might crucially depend on whether the parent is employed or not: an employed single parent is expected to face significantly higher children costs compared to an unemployed parent, especially due to higher expenditures for external child care. These costs are completely unconsidered when household needs are derived from expenditure data as suggested in the economic approach. *Apps* and *Rees* (1995), *Pollak* and *Wales* (1992), and *Gronau* (1988) therefore criticise both, the logic and the relevance of the theoretical basis of the standard economic approach, with its focus on the estimation of demand systems. First attempts that consider the impacts

[1]Studies on household production are surveyed, for example, in *Gronau* 1997, *Widmer* and *Sousa–Poza* 1997, and by the *Organisation for Economic Co–Operation and Development* 1995.

of household production and the non–consumption costs of additional family members (children) are developed by *Apps* and *Rees* (1988, 1995, 1996, 1997). The authors empirically estimate children costs arising from the consumption of market goods and from the parental time that is no longer available for other activities. Their empirical estimations are based on an extended version of the *Becker model* (1965) considering different (multi–person) household types. The model is estimated empirically (*Apps* and *Rees* 1995) using data from the *Australian Bureau of Statistics* 1990 *Income Distribution Survey* and the Australian 1992 *Time Use Survey*. *Apps* and *Rees* (1995, p. 24) find that *"when the value of domestic production and child care is added into the child's consumption, the child's consumption rises to* 146 *per cent of the total consumption (of market and domestically produced goods) of the adult male in traditional households, and* 121 *per cent in non–traditional households."*
A traditional (non–traditional) household is defined as a household in which the female partner works less (more) than 500 hours per year in the market place. Another interesting result refers to the annual market good expenditures for the adult household members comparing traditional and non–traditional households. These expenditures are significantly higher in non–traditional households.

4.3 Conclusion

The last two sections revealed that the earning capacity approach is inappropriate for determining equivalence scales, especially if the household demography is exogenously given and does not result from a utility maximising process within the household. On the contrary, it was shown that household production activities play an important role in the determination of household needs and it is highly probable that the needs of a household are dependent on the employment status of its members. However, most studies neglect these issues completely. This critique holds, in particular, for the standard economic approach which defines the needs of household members exclusively in terms of expenditures on market goods. On condition that the interviewees are able to perform the questionnaire, it is obviously a major advantage of the survey approach to equivalence scales that it can measure the direct costs of a change in the household demography arising from the consumption of market goods and the impacts on the household's time restriction. In our questionnaire, we will ask our interviewees to assess the monetary amounts that compensate for both, differences in expenditures on market goods and for changes in the households' time constraints. These differences result from variations in the stimulus variables that define a set of different hypothetical household types. The stimulus variables comprise the number of ((un)employed) adults and children which are assumed to live in the hypothetical household.

5

A New Consensual Approach

5.1 Introduction

A feature common to all survey approaches suggested in the literature so far is that stimulus and response categories differ: all questionnaire designs either use household income as a stimulus variable and ask for the corresponding level of household welfare or vice versa. As mentioned above, this questionnaire characteristic casts doubts on the reliability of the collected data. We will present a new questionnaire design that overcomes this problem by using household income as the dimension for *both*, stimulus and response. A typical question reads:
"According to your opinion, which family income level can make a household with one adult and two children achieve the same well-being as a household with one adult only and an income of DM 1,000?"
Using hypothetical household types means that we apply a consensual approach. Respondents are asked to use their own knowledge to determine welfare–equalising incomes across different hypothetical household types in comparison to a reference household. The latter is endowed with a pre–defined income which defines its living standard. Opting for a consensual approach means that it is of key relevance to show that the collected data are reliable and that respondents are able to perform the task presented in the questionnaire. Besides this methodological issue, the new survey design is applied to gather insights into the potential dependence of equivalence scales on income and on the employment status of adult household members. As outlined above, previous studies either neglect a possible impact of income on equivalence scales or they rule this possibility out by the IB/ESE assumption. Do our interviewees agree with this constancy assumption? Is there any consensus? To answer this question, we ask our interviewees to assess welfare–equalising incomes of different household types, varying the pre–defined income of a reference household. Moreover, we have shown that households do not simply consume market goods and services, but many of these goods and services are converted before consumption. However, available time for household pro-

duction and leisure varies with the employment status of the adult household members. We are interested in measuring the differences in welfare–equivalent incomes across households that differ in the employment status of adult household members. We analyse what these compensations should be, according to our respondents.

The chapter is organised as follows. Section 5.2 presents the new survey design and works out the differences in comparison to previous survey approaches. A separate section, Section 5.3, is devoted to a discussion of whether household income is an adequate indicator of a household's well–being. Section 5.4 suggests a number of empirical tests to investigate whether our data are biased from personal characteristics of the interviewees and whether the use of hypothetical households is prone to generate errors.

5.2 The New Survey Design

The general structure of the questionnaires was always the same. Section I makes up the *introduction* that explains the stimulus material and illustrates the tasks the respondents are asked to perform in the following two sections. In Section II – the *personal questionnaire* – we ask for some of our subjects' personal characteristics. The personal questionnaire slightly differs across the studies to take country–specific differences and survey specific interests into account. The personal data are collected for two reasons. Firstly, they allow for testing whether the stated equivalence scales of our respondents are biased from their own personal characteristics. The data of previous survey approaches turned out to be strongly dependent upon personal variables, especially upon the personal income of the interviewees, the so–called *preference drift*. Secondly, the collected personal data allow for testing on errors which arise from the use of hypothetical household types in the questionnaires. It is fair to assume that respondents have a better knowledge of income–needs of household types that have a similar demographic composition to their own household. Then, subjects' assessments of household types that are very different from their own might be erroneous. If this were the case, the application of hypothetical household types would be inadequate for the derivation of equivalence scales. The *general questionnaire*, Section III, asks respondents to quantify welfare–equivalent incomes across different hypothetical household types in comparison to a reference household with a given income. As mentioned above, two different sets of stimulus variables are applied to define these households. For both kinds of questionnaires, subjects are asked to assess the welfare–equivalent incomes of different hypothetical households given the monthly after–tax income of the reference household. This task is repeated for different reference–income levels. Each reference–income situation is arranged in a separate table. In such a table, the reference income is given while gaps are left next to the remaining household types. Respondents are asked to assess the welfare–equalising incomes of these remaining households compared to the income situation of the reference household.

5.3 On the Choice of Income as an Indicator of Well–Being

The choice of income as an indicator of a family's well–being is not free of limitations. We already commented on this in the context of the earning–capacity argument and *Sen*'s *capability concept*. Moreover, income–based equivalence scales are only meaningful in the context of a given endowment of non–income based transfer flows, and changes to these patterns (like cuts in government education subsidies) alter the income requirements of different families to meet their needs. It is also important to notice that children themselves contribute to their parents' well–being. *Pollack* and *Wales* (1979) already mentioned that equivalence scales do not take this contribution into account: if parents maximised their own total welfare by having children and they also had complete control over their family structure, then there would be no need to compensate for children costs. Following *Bradbury* (1989), at least three reasons can be given why this is not the case. Firstly, the choice of having children may have been made under circumstances that were different from the present ones. For example, income may be unexpectedly low due to unemployment or illness. A sudden family break–up may also change the perception of a child as a present to one as a burden. Secondly, fertility is sometimes seen as a public good since it is a basic prerequisite for a society's existence and the definition of an appropriate equivalence scale should take this public–good component into account. Thirdly, the definition of a child as a consumption good to its parents completely ignores the needs of the child. To avoid any misunderstandings, we ask our respondents to take the structure of the hypothetical households in the general part of the questionnaires as exogenously given, and to assess the monetary compensations such that all hypothetical household types are equally–well off.

5.4 Validity and Reliability: Test Methods

5.4.1 Validity

We already mentioned that survey methods are frequently charged with providing data that are biased from respondents' personal characteristics. In particular, it is questionable that a single type of subjective–data analysis should be capable of constituting a behavioural or rational rule that corrects for these subjective biases. In this section, we present a model which explains the potential impacts of the interviewees' personal characteristics on their assessments of household needs and thus on equivalence scales derived.[1] The model is used to analyse the *preference drift* phenomenon, and it serves as a basis to develop a number of statistical tests that will be presented later in this section.

Consider that respondents' income levels are mapped to a non–negative real number by the function $H \equiv (h_i)$ with $h_i(y_p) \geq 0$ for all $y_p \geq 0$ and all commodities i ϵ $[0, I]$. Let us assume that *habit persistence* enters the utility function (as defined in Section 3.1) of a person exhibiting habit persistence as

$$\int_0^I f_i(n_A, n_C) \frac{(x_i + \gamma_i - h_i(y_p))^{1-\frac{1}{\eta}} - 1}{1 - \frac{1}{\eta}} di. \tag{5.1}$$

Then, a subject with a fixed income y_p states equivalence scales for reference income y_r according to

$$\sigma(a,c) = \left(\frac{\varphi(G(\bar{n}_A, \bar{n}_C), p)}{\varphi(G(\bar{n}_A + a, \bar{n}_C + c), p)} \right)^{\frac{1}{\eta - 1}}$$
$$+ \left[\left(\frac{\varphi(G(\bar{n}_A, \bar{n}_C), p)}{\varphi(G(\bar{n}_A + a, \bar{n}_C + c), p)} \right)^{\frac{1}{\eta - 1}} - 1 \right] \frac{p'[\gamma - H(y_p)]}{y_r}. \tag{5.2}$$

Equation (5.2) reveals that respondents with a "high" personal income y_p tend to state lower (higher) equivalence scales than their "low" income counterparts if $\eta < 1$ ($\eta > 1$). The reason for this is that for $\eta < 1$ a marginal change in the subsistence level is dominated by a higher marginal increase in (indirect) utility. Consequently, rich (poor) subjects assign a given level of reference income to a lower (higher) living standard. Thus, rich (poor) subjects suggest lower (higher) compensations for additional family members in order to retain the same welfare level and this leads to lower (higher) equivalence scales. The same reasoning holds for the opposite direction when $\eta > 1$. Preference drift, as observed in the Leyden studies, occurs if $\eta > 1$. In this case, equivalence scales are increasing with the level of personal income y_p.

With respect to our survey data, we suggest two tests of *habit persistence* to assess to what extent responses are distorted by the interviewee's personal welfare or income level. Since we did not ask for household welfare we assume that the *adjusted* personal income level y_{adj} is a close proxy for household welfare. These adjusted incomes are derived by converting each respondent's stated personal income to her/his equivalent childless–single–adult household income. For instance, if a respondent with a partner and two children stated a disposable personal income of Euro 3,700, we compared this information with the five income amounts she/he stated for her/his own household type in the general questionnaire (one income amount per

[1] The model is similar to the one used in *Constantinides* 1990.

reference–income level). Then, we assigned her/him to that reference–income level where her/his own personal income was closest to the corresponding equivalent income of her/his own household type. This reference–income level gives the *adjusted* personal income of the respondent. For a fixed demography $\bar{s}$ of the hypothetical households, and a fixed reference–income $\bar{y_r}$, for every adjusted personal income level $y_{adj} > 1.0$, we then run a Mann–Whitney–U test comparing $\sigma(\bar{s}, \bar{y_r}, y_{adj} > 1.0) - \sigma(\bar{s}, \bar{y_r}, y_{adj} = 1.0)$. For example, if $\bar{s} = AAC$ and $\bar{y_r} = 1.0$, we examine whether there is a significant difference in equivalence scales as stated by the respondents assigned to $y_{adj} = 4.0$ and by the respondents assigned to $y_{adj} = 1.0$. Since these two sub–samples are not related and the data turned out to be not normally distributed, a Mann–Whitney–U test of differences between the two sub–samples is appropriate. A weak point of this test is that only two groups of interviewees are attributed to higher adjusted–personal income classes. A first group consists of single adults with high personal incomes since their personal income is equivalent to their adjusted personal income. A second group comprises those interviewees that stated flat equivalence scales for their own household type. Such self–selection is avoided in the second test which is aimed to discover whether equivalence scales are biased from the interviewees' household income level y_p. Equivalently to the test procedure described above, for every personal income level y_p a Mann–Whitney–U test is conducted comparing $\sigma(\bar{s}, \bar{y_r}, y_p > 1.0) - \sigma(\bar{s}, \bar{y_r}, y_p = 1.0)$ for any hypothetical household demography $\bar{s}$ and for any reference–income $\bar{y_r}$ is conducted. The impacts of other personal characteristics such as gender or education on equivalence scales stated are investigated in a number of regressions.

5.4.2 Reliability

Critics of the consensual approach to equivalence scales argue that respondents might not be able to assess "correctly" the needs of household types that differ from their own by demography or living standard. On the contrary, reliability of consensual equivalence scales requires that respondents' insights in household needs are non–trivial which is exactly the assumption of rationality that is underlying most recent economic literature. However, we will examine the possibility of *bounded rationality* or *haziness of knowledge*. This means that respondents have a better knowledge of households that have a comparable income and demographic situation to their own. To analyse such effects, we will restrict the samples in two different ways.

The first restriction takes into account equivalence scales stated for all household types, but only for those where the reference income is closest to the respondent's *adjusted* personal income: we assign each respondent to that reference income for which her/his own personal income is closest to the equivalent income she/he stated for the hypothetical household type that is most similarly to her/his own. This conversion rests upon the assumption that the living standard is about the same within each resulting sub–sample. The second restriction considers only those scale values for which the demographic stimulus variables coincide with – or are closest to – the respondent's actual situation. By evaluating the extent to which the regression coefficients statistically differ between the unrestricted, original sample and the two restricted samples, we form a picture on whether the use of hypothetical households is error–generating or not.

6

Survey I

6.1 Motivation and Outline

Questionnaire V_I was applied in two empirical studies that took place in Germany in 1999 and in the Greek part of Cyprus in 2000. Altogether, about 300 respondents participated in the two surveys.[1] The main aims of these two surveys are threefold. The first aim is to test the IB/ESE assumption. We want to answer the question whether our interviewees' answers lead to equivalence scales that are income dependent or not. Secondly, we want to test the validity of our results and the reliability of our method by examining the following two questions. Firstly, do subjective biases dominate or generate the findings? Secondly, is the use of hypothetical households in our questionnaires error-generating? The third aim is to collect data of two rather different countries to analyse whether our methodology derives similar results.

This chapter is organised as follows: Section 6.2 gives a detailed description of the V_I questionnaire. The sample breakdowns for Germany and Cyprus are given in Section 6.3. In Section 6.4, we shall introduce the regression model, the notation, and the preparation of the data. The results of the two studies are presented in the following Sections 6.5–6.9. Section 6.5 reports the results of a number of regressions that quantify the general impacts of the stimulus variables and the personal characteristics on stated equivalence scales. Country-specific differences between Germany and Cyprus are analysed in Section 6.6. A descriptive analysis of the equivalence scales derived and individual weights follows in Section 6.7. Section 6.8–6.9 deal with the validity and reliability of our method.

[1] In 2002, data of a French sample were collected. The results are presented in *Koulovatianos, Schröder*, and *Schmidt* 2003.

6.2 Questionnaire Design

The country–specific *introductions* of V_I can be taken from the Appendix (Figure A1 and Figure A4). A translation is given in Figure 6.1.

The *personal questionnaire* collects some of the respondents' individual characteristics: gender, whether the respondent lived together with a partner, the number of children in the respondent's household, the household's monthly after–tax income (short: personal income y_p), the respondent's profession and educational level as well as the respondent's number of siblings. The translation is given in Figure 6.2 for Germany and in Figure 6.3 for Cyprus. The country specific originals are depicted in Figure A2 and A5 in the Appendix. We decided not to ask for the number of children in general but for the number of children which are actually living in the household to distinguish respondents that actually raise children from those who do not, since it might be that the former group has a better knowledge about children costs nowadays. The five personal income brackets are defined as follows. In Germany, the first income bracket (y_{p1}) is from zero to 1.75 times the social assistance (P) of a single adult which is about DM 1,000.[2] We interpret the resulting income as the poverty line of an average household. The maxima of the following four income brackets (y_{p2}, ..., y_{p5}) have been obtained by adding increments of DM 1,500 ($1.5 * P$) to the average poverty line ($1.75 * P$). In Cyprus, we adjusted the five German income brackets according to the lower Cypriot per capita GDP and converted these amounts to Cypriot Pounds (CP). Cultural differences across the countries also required to ask Cypriot participants whether they were living with their parents. In Cyprus, it is common that grown–up children still live with their parents and grandparents. Moreover, the questionnaires are adapted to differences in the education systems. In Germany, pupils visit primary school for four years and then, depending on the pupils' marks, there are three options, namely *Hauptschule* (compulsory five additional years), *Realschule* (six additional years), and *Gymnasium* (nine additional years). In Cyprus, the main education levels are the basic compulsory nine years of schooling consisting of six years of elementary school and three years of *Gymnasion* and the next voluntary three years of *Lyceion*.

In the *general questionnaire*, respondents are asked to assess the welfare–equivalent incomes of seven different household types for five reference-income levels of a single–adult household which serves as the reference household. The translated general questionnaire is depicted in Figure 6.4. Again, the originals can be taken from the Appendix (Figures A3 and A6).

---

[2]One Deutschmark is about 0.5 Euros and about 0.33 Cypriot Pounds.

This study deals with the problem that different household types have different needs. These needs (measured in income amounts) depend on the number of adults and children living in the household. For example, you might argue that a two–adult household needs more income as compared to a single adult to be equally well–off.

Therefore, the following question arises: given the income of a specific household type (reference household), what is the income for another household type (differing in the number of children and adults or both) that allows this household to reach an identical living standard as the reference household?

Since there is no correct objective answer, we would like to know your subjective attitude towards this question. Assume that the age of an adult is between 35 and 55, and that it is between 7 and 11 for a child.

Later on, five boxes will be presented to you which look like this.

Single–adult household without children	**Reference income**	Two–adult household without children	
Single–adult household with one child		Two–adult household with one child	
Single–adult household with two children		Two–adult household with two children	
Single–adult household with three children		Two–adult household with three children	

As you see, within the box we vary the number of children and the number of adults. While the number of children ranges between 0 and 3, the number of adults is either 1 (first column of the respective box) or 2 (second column of the respective box). Except for the childless single–adult, gaps are left next to the households.

Later on, you will be asked to fill the gaps of such boxes, putting in the after–tax family income that you believe allows the households differing with respect to the numbers of children and adults the same living standard as the one of the childless single–adult household. Therefore, please take some time to familiarize yourself with the structure of the boxes.

Figure 6.1. Introduction (V_I)

1. Please state your gender here:	[ ]	male
	[ ]	female
2. Are you living together with a partner?	[ ]	yes
	[ ]	no
3. What is the number of children in your household?	[ ]	0
	[ ]	1
	[ ]	2
	[ ]	3 or more
4. What is your total monthly after–tax household income?	[ ]	below DM 1,750
	[ ]	DM 1,750–3,249
	[ ]	DM 3,250–4,749
	[ ]	DM 4,750–6,249
	[ ]	more then DM 6,249
5. Are you	[ ]	social security recipient,
	[ ]	unemployed,
	[ ]	blue–collar worker,
	[ ]	white–collar worker,
	[ ]	civil servant,
	[ ]	pupil, student, trainee,
	[ ]	self–employed,
	[ ]	pensioner,
	[ ]	houseman, housewife?
6. Please state your education level here:	[ ]	unfinished education,
	[ ]	completed Hauptschule,
	[ ]	completed Realschule,
	[ ]	completed Gymnasium,
	[ ]	completed technical school, or university
7. With how many siblings did you live when you were young?	[ ]	0
	[ ]	1
	[ ]	2
	[ ]	3 or more

Figure 6.2. Personal Questionnaire (V_I, Germany)

1. Please state your gender here:	[ ]	male
	[ ]	female
2. Are you living together with a partner?	[ ]	yes
	[ ]	no
3. Are you living together with your parents?[a]	[ ]	yes
	[ ]	no
4. What is the number of children in your household?	[ ]	0
	[ ]	1
	[ ]	2
	[ ]	3 or more
5. What is your total monthly after–tax household income?[b]	[ ]	below CP 275
	[ ]	CP 275–500
	[ ]	CP 501–700
	[ ]	CP 701–925
	[ ]	more then CP 925
6. Are you	[ ]	social security recipient,
	[ ]	unemployed,
	[ ]	blue–collar worker,
	[ ]	white–collar worker,
	[ ]	civil servant,
	[ ]	pupil, student, trainee,
	[ ]	self–employed,
	[ ]	pensioner,
	[ ]	houseman, housewife?
7. Please state your education level here:	[ ]	unfinished education,
	[ ]	completed Gymnasion,
	[ ]	completed Lyceion,
	[ ]	completed technical school, or university
8. With how many siblings did you live when you were young?	[ ]	0
	[ ]	1
	[ ]	2
	[ ]	3 or more

[a] Only for Cyprus. [b] CP denotes Cypriot pounds.

Figure 6.3. Personal Questionnaire (V_I, Cyprus)

Here you see the aforementioned five boxes that vary with respect to the after–tax income level of the childless single-adult. For each box, please state the net family–incomes of the other seven household types such that they reach the same living standard as the childless single–adult.

Single–adult household without children	**1*Minimal Income**	Two–adult household without children	
Single–adult household with one child		Two–adult household with one child	
Single–adult household with two children		Two–adult household with two children	
Single–adult household with three children		Two–adult household with three children	

Single–adult household without children	**2.5*Minimal Income**	Two–adult household without children	
Single–adult household with one child		Two–adult household with one child	
Single–adult household with two children		Two–adult household with two children	
Single–adult household with three children		Two–adult household with three children	

Single–adult household without children	**4.0*Minimal Income**	Two–adult household without children	
Single–adult household with one child		Two–adult household with one child	
Single–adult household with two children		Two–adult household with two children	
Single–adult household with three children		Two–adult household with three children	

Single–adult household without children	**5.5*Minimal Income**	Two–adult household without children	
Single–adult household with one child		Two–adult household with one child	
Single–adult household with two children		Two–adult household with two children	
Single–adult household with three children		Two–adult household with three children	

Single–adult household without children	**7.0*Minimal Income**	Two–adult household without children	
Single–adult household with one child		Two–adult household with one child	
Single–adult household with two children		Two–adult household with two children	
Single–adult household with three children		Two–adult household with three children	

Figure 6.4. General Questionnaire (V_I)

The general questionnaire consists of five boxes. In each box, eight different hypothetical family types are provided, but only for the reference household, the after–tax income (the reference income) was given. The task of our respondents was to fill the gaps next to the remaining seven household types, putting in the after–tax *family* income that, according to their own perception, makes all eight hypothetical household types in the box equally well-off.[3] This task was conducted for five different reference–income levels such that every respondent was asked to complete five of these boxes.

In Germany, the definition of the lowest reference income, denoted *1.0 * Minimal Income* in the general questionnaire, is based on the level of social assistance for a single adult. We interpreted this income as the German poverty line. Starting from this threshold, we add increments of *1.5 * Minimal Income*. According to the lower GDP for Cyprus, all reference incomes for Germany are multiplied by 0.60 and converted and rounded up or down to amounts of hundred Cypriot Pounds. The gradual variation of reference income is the crucial characteristic of the questionnaire and it directly targets on testing the IB/ESE assumption.

6.3 Breakdown of the Samples

Altogether, data from 297 respondents were collected, 167 for Germany and 130 for Cyprus. German data is from August 1999, mainly from the area of Schleswig–Holstein, northern Germany. The Cypriot sample was collected in the Greek part of Nicosia, in Larnaca, and in Limmasol. This data were gathered in June 2000. Though none of the two samples are representative, each of them contains a rather comprehensive set of different personal characteristics.

6.3.1 Demographic Situation

Table 6.1 gives the sample breakdowns by the personal variables that describe the family situation of the respondents. The Cypriot data also comprise information about whether the interviewees are living together with their parents or not.

In both countries, a slight majority of participants is male. Most respondents live together with a partner, overall about 58% in both countries. As expected, a significant share of some 29% of Cypriot interviewees are living together with their parents, especially women, yet all respondents are adults. The majority of German and Cypriot subjects are childless but the average number of children per household is higher for Cyprus. Higher fertility in Cyprus is also reflected by the higher number of siblings in Cyprus: only 7% of Cypriot respondents have no siblings compared to about 19% for Germany. Moreover, about 36% of Cypriot respondents have more than two siblings while respectively for Germany only 20%.

[3] Obviously, the task is different as compared to previous survey methodologies. Instead of choosing different categories for stimulus and response (income *and* well–being), both stimulus and response are measured in terms of income.

Table 6.1. Breakdown by Gender, Partner, Number of Children, and Number of Siblings (V_I)

	All				Females				Males			
	N		%		*N*		%		*N*		%	
	G	C	G	C	G	C	G	C	G	C	G	C
Gender												
Female	71	57	0.425	0.438	71	57	1.000	1.000	0	0	0.000	0.000
Male	96	73	0.575	0.562	0	0	0.000	0.000	96	73	1.000	1.000
Partner												
Yes	97	75	0.581	0.577	48	32	0.676	0.561	49	43	0.510	0.589
No	70	55	0.419	0.423	23	25	0.324	0.439	47	30	0.490	0.411
Living with Prt.s[a]												
Yes	—	37	—	0.285	—	18	—	0.316	—	19	—	0.260
No	—	93	—	0.715	—	39	—	0.684	—	54	—	0.740
Children												
None	123	82	0.737	0.631	54	32	0.761	0.561	69	50	0.719	0.685
One	18	18	0.108	0.138	6	9	0.085	0.158	12	9	0.124	0.123
Two	15	23	0.089	0.177	5	13	0.070	0.228	10	10	0.104	0.137
More than two	11	7	0.066	0.054	6	3	0.085	0.053	5	4	0.052	0.055
Siblings												
None	31	9	0.186	0.070	13	2	0.183	0.035	18	7	0.188	0.096
One	55	34	0.329	0.262	24	18	0.338	0.316	31	16	0.323	0.219
Two	47	40	0.281	0.308	20	19	0.282	0.333	27	21	0.281	0.288
More than two	34	47	0.204	0.362	14	18	0.197	0.316	20	29	0.208	0.397

Notation: G denotes Germany, C Cyprus, and *N* the number of observations; dashes indicate that the data was not collected. [a] "Are you living with parents?" was asked for Cyprus only.

6.3.2 Income, Education, and Employment

In the *personal questionnaires*, we also asked for the household after–tax income per month, the level of education, and the profession. A breakdown of the two samples by income brackets and profession is given in Table 6.2.

In Cyprus we failed our goal to approach respondents from all occupational groups: no Cypriot pensioner participated in the survey, and it was difficult to approach social security recipients and unemployed persons. For Germany, especially the group of housewives and housemen is under–represented. Comparing the occupational data of both nations, we find a significantly higher fraction of white–collar workers for Germany. The relatively large fraction of civil servants for Cyprus may be seen as an explanation for this difference. Since funds and time for data collection in Cyprus were constrained, we decided to accept these shortcomings of the data.

Table 6.2. Breakdown by Income and Occupation (V_I)

	N		y_{p1}		y_{p2}		y_{p3}		y_{p4}		y_{p5}	
	G	C	G	C	G	C	G	C	G	C	G	C
All respondents	167	130	32	9	44	25	37	24	37	31	17	41
Social sec. recipient	7	2	3	1	4	0	0	1	0	0	0	0
Blue–collar worker	10	2	3	0	5	2	2	0	0	0	0	0
White–collar worker	83	40	3	1	24	11	26	13	22	9	8	6
Pupil, student, trainee	34	30	20	7	7	7	2	5	3	5	2	6
Civil servant	13	40	0	0	1	3	4	3	7	15	1	19
Self–employed	7	13	1	0	2	1	1	1	3	1	0	10
Pensioner	10	0	2	0	1	0	2	0	1	0	4	0
Housewife/Houseman	3	3	0	0	0	1	0	1	1	1	2	0

Notation: N denotes the number of observations; G denotes Germany; C denotes Cyprus; $y_{p1}, ..., y_{p5}$ denote personal income brackets.

Comparing the income distributions of both samples, the percentage of high income earners is higher for Cyprus. There are at least three reasons that could explain this finding. Firstly, the fractions of social security recipients, of unemployed interviewees, and of blue–collar workers is higher for Germany. Secondly, the average family size is larger in Cyprus. It is, therefore, not surprising that in Cyprus the average number of employees is higher as well. Thirdly, the Cypriot income classes were specified by multiplying the German classes by 0.60, according to the GDP difference between the two countries. However, Cypriot participants mainly came from two cities with relatively high average income.

Table 6.3. Breakdown by Income and Education (V_I)

	N	y_{p1}	y_{p2}	y_{p3}	y_{p4}	y_{p5}
			Germany			
Unfinished education	1	0	0	0	0	1
Compl. elementary school	21	3	5	5	7	1
Compl. secondary school	39	5	13	10	7	4
Compl. German secondary school	65	20	17	12	11	5
Compl. techn. school or univ.	41	4	9	10	12	6
			Cyprus			
Unfinished education	4	0	2	2	0	0
Compl. Gymnasion	8	2	3	2	0	1
Compl. Lyceion	65	3	11	15	18	18
Compl. techn. school or univ.	53	4	9	5	13	22

Notation: N denotes the number of observations; $y_{p1}, ..., y_{p5}$ denote household personal income brackets.

Table 6.3 gives a breakdown by income brackets and education. Germany and Cyprus being highly educated countries, a predominant number of respondents have at least finished secondary school. However, the fractions of respondents that finished technical school or university is higher than compared with the actual situation in both countries. Personal income is not significantly related positively to the level of education which especially is due to students with low incomes: Spearman's correlation coefficient for two–tailed tests between the variables *personal income* and *pupil, student, or trainee* is −0.387 for Germany and −0.287 for Cyprus.[4]

6.3.3 Conclusion

Altogether, the collected data has some minor shortcomings. However, the data variation is sufficient to investigate the impacts of personal characteristics on the interviewees' assessments of household needs in the *general questionnaire*, that is on equivalence scales. Moreover, respondents are rather well distributed across different family types and income brackets. This means that aforementioned sample restrictions by income and household type and related statistical test procedures (compare Section 5.4) are feasible.

6.4 Regression Model, Notation, and Data Preparation

In this section we run a number of pooled regressions to examine three main issues. Firstly, we analyse whether our interviewees' responses give support to the IB/ESE assumption. Such a test is possible since interviewees were asked to assess household needs for different levels of reference income. Secondly, we compare the income needs of a child with the income needs of an adult, and we analyse whether this relation is tangent to the number of adults or to the level of reference income. Thirdly, the regression results will give a first impression how personal characteristics drive the interviewees' assessments of household needs. Because of restrictions of our data set and the generality of the model in equations (5.1) and (5.2), we cannot estimate this general model. It was only meant to demonstrate the confines of the IB/ESE assumption and should suggest tests for identifying the influences of personal characteristics (Section 5.4.1).

For each country, we have collected 35 equivalence scales from each respondent, 5 equivalence scales for each of the 7 hypothetical households, one for each reference–income level. Remember that subjects did not supply data for the childless single–adult which served as the reference household. These equivalence scales enter the country–specific regressions as dependent variables. Given a sample size of 167 respondents for Germany, the regression for Germany comprises $35 * 167 = 5,845$ observations. Correspondingly, we

[4] Compare also Section 6.4.

have $35 * 130 = 4,550$ observations for Cyprus given a sample size of 130 respondents. The estimated linear equation is

$$\sigma_{i,j} = c_0 + a_1 * Stim_j + a_2 * StimInt_j + a_3 * y_{pi} + a_4 * Pers(I)_i + a_5 * Pers(II)_i + \epsilon_{i,j}, \quad (6.1)$$

where $\sigma_{i,j}$ denotes the equivalence scale stated by respondent i corresponding to the vector of stimulus variables j. $\epsilon_{i,j}$ is the disturbance term. The exogenous variables entered the regression stepwise, that is, an exogenous variable entered the regression if the significance level of its F–to–enter was less than 0.05 and it was removed if the significance level exceeded 0.10.

The coefficient c_0 denotes the regression intercept of the benchmark category, an interviewee for which all dummy variables that define her/his personal characteristics are simultaneously zero.

The conditioning vector of variables denoted $Stim_j$ consists of the three stimulus variables that defined the hypothetical households. Firstly, the five levels of reference income (y_r) of the reference household, a childless single–adult. Equivalence scales are IB if the respective coefficient is zero or insignificant. Secondly, a dummy for the second adult (DA_2). $DA_2 = 0$ in all single–adult households and $DA_2 = 1$ in two–adult households. The respective coefficient can be interpreted as the individual weight of the second adult. The impact of the first adult on equivalence scales is included in the constant c_0. Thirdly, three dummies (DC_i with $i = 1, 2, 3$) for the stimulus number of children, one for each child. $DC_i = 1$ if there is a ith child in the household while else $DC_i = 0$. The respective coefficients can be interpreted as children weights. For an example, for a hypothetical household consisting of two adults and two children, the values of the dummy variables are $DA_2 = DC_1 = DC_2 = 1$ and $DC_3 = 0$.

Furthermore, we include several products between stimulus variables ($StimInt_j$) in the regressions. The square of reference income (y_r^2) quantifies non–linearities in the dependence of equivalence scales on reference income. To capture income dependencies of individual weights, we include the interactions of reference income and the dummy of the second adult, denoted $y_r * DA_2$, as well as the interaction of reference income and the number of children (n_C), denoted $y_r * n_C$. Whether the interviewees' assessments of children costs are contingent on the stimulus number of adults (n_A) is considered by the interaction $n_A * n_C$.

Finally, different vectors of the interviewees' personal characteristics are included in the regressions. These personal characteristics are subdivided into three classes: the first class comprises the personal incomes y_{pi} of each respondent i only. This variable is re–coded from the five after–tax household income brackets in the personal questionnaire: the first four income brackets are represented by their mean values. Since the fifth income class was unrestricted from above, it is included in the regressions by the mean of the fourth income class plus an increment corresponding to the income range for each of the first four income brackets. After–tax household income y_p is distinguished from the other personal characteristics for two reasons. Firstly, the isolated incorporation of y_p in the regressions reveals whether and how the answers of each respondent are affected by her/his own personal income. Thus, the resulting regression coefficient measures the impact of preference drift on equivalence scales. Secondly, personal income is highly correlated with several personal characteristics (compare Table 6.4), and this observation motivates the distinction of two further groups of personal characteristics. *Pers(I)* comprises the personal variables gender, number of siblings, and education. These three variables are only weakly correlated or not correlated with personal family income. *Pers(II)* includes all other personal variables that are correlated with y_p and all variables that describe the interviewee's occupational status. Table 6.4 gives the significant correlation coefficients of personal variables with personal income.

Table 6.4. Correlation Coefficients (V_I)

	Germany	Cyprus
Children	0.460***	0.071+
Education	0.039+	0.223***
Partner	0.548***	0.288***
Siblings	0.214***	0.178**
Blue collar worker	−0.176**	−0.149*
White collar worker	0.263***	−0.203**
Civil servant	0.202**	0.360***
Housewife	0.190**	−0.076+
Self–employed	0.018+	0.275***
Pupil, student, or trainee	−0.392***	−0.257***
Social–sec. rec. or unemployed	−0.204**	−0.136+

Note: Spearman's correlation coeff. for two–tailed test; number of observations: Germany: 167; Cyprus: 130.
Notation: *** rejection of equality at the 1% level; ** rejection of equality at the 5% level; * rejection of equality at the 10% level; + equality cannot be rejected.

The personal data are re–coded according to Table 6.5. Since responses with regard to *gender*, *partner*, *occupational group* and, for Cyprus, *living with parents* are categorical, they are re–coded as 0–1 dummy variables. Correspondingly, we proceed for the variables children and siblings although both variables initially had more than two categories. The initially eight occupational groups are represented by seven dummy variables. Since there are only a few observations for the categories social–security recipient and unemployed person, we combined the two to a single variable. White–collar workers serve as the benchmark category. Personal income is a covariate that considers the means of the five after–tax household income brackets as defined above. Education is also re–coded as a covariate. For Germany, this covariate ranges from zero for unfinished education to 4 if the respondent finished university or technical school. Since there were only four answer categories for Cyprus, the covariate only ranges from 0 to 3.

Table 6.5. Re–coding Personal Characteristics (V_I)

Variable	Type	Values
Household after–tax income	Covariate	Class means of income brackets
Pers(I)		
Gender	Dummy	0: male; 1: female
Siblings	Dummy	0: no; 1: yes
Education	Covariate	0–4[a]; 0–3[b]
Pers(II)		
Partner	Dummy	0: no; 1: yes
Children	Dummy	0: no; 1: yes
Living with parents	Dummy	0: no; 1: yes
Housewife, –man	Dummy	0: no; 1: yes
Pensioner	Dummy	0: no; 1: yes
Pupil, student, or trainee	Dummy	0: no; 1: yes
Social–sec rec. or unemployed	Dummy	0: no; 1: yes
Blue–collar worker	Dummy	0: no; 1: yes
Self–employed	Dummy	0: no; 1: yes
Civil servant	Dummy	0: no; 1: yes

[a] Germany. [b] Cyprus.

Differences across the two countries are discovered by regressions based on the pooled German and Cypriot data. This is analysed by introducing additional conditional variables that capture country specific differences. A dummy variable (*CD*) is defined assigning the value 1.0 to Germany and 0.0 to Cyprus. Then, each and every country specific variable is multiplied with CD. The resulting linear regression model is given by

$$\sigma_{i,j} = c_0 + a_0 * CD + a_1 * Stim_j + a_2 * StimInt_j + a_3 * y_{pi} + a_4 * Pers(I)_i$$
$$+a_5 * CD * Stim_j + a_6 * CD * StimInt_j + a7 * CD * y_{pi} + a_8 * CD * Pers(I)_i + \epsilon_{i,j}. \tag{6.2}$$

We refrained from including *Pers(II)* since these personal variables turned out to possess a negligible explanatory power in the country–specific regressions.

6.5 Country–specific Regression Analysis

Table 6.6 for Germany and Table 6.7 for Cyprus report the results of four different country–specific regressions. Regression (1) only considers the basic set of stimulus variables as conditioning variables. In regressions (2)–(4), we successively add the subsets y_p, *Pers(I)*, and *Pers(II)* of personal characteristics to investigate their impacts on the stimulus variables and how they affect the explanatory power of the regressions. In the text, data for Cyprus will be given in parentheses.

Table 6.6. Regressions 1-4 (V_I, Germany)

Equation	1		2		3		4	
c_0	1.555	(76.73)	1.589	(70.66)	1.436	(53.78)	1.452	(55.11)
y_r	-0.508	(-54.71)	-0.508	(-54.76)	-0.508	(-55.26)	-0.508	(-55.38)
DA_2	0.422	(42.52)	0.422	(42.56)	0.422	(42.95)	0.422	(43.04)
DC_1	0.140	(12.65)	0.140	(12.66)	0.140	(12.77)	0.140	(12.80)
DC_2	0.176	(14.45)	0.176	(14.46)	0.176	(14.59)	0.176	(14.63)
DC_3	0.158	(14.23)	0.158	(14.24)	0.158	(14.37)	0.158	(14.40)
y_p	—		-0.032	(-3.40)	-0.034	(-3.70)	-0.007	(-0.55)
Gender	—		—		0.023	(2.46)	0.025	(2.64)
Siblings	—		—		-0.004	(-0.39)	-0.001	(-0.11)
Education	—		—		0.093	(10.07)	0.079	(8.26)
Partner	—		—		—		-0.031	(-3.03)
Children	—		—		—		-0.030	(-3.00)
Housewife, houseman	—		—		—		0.002	(0.23)
Pensioner	—		—		—		-0.030	(-3.15)
Pupil, student, or trainee	—		—		—		-0.011	(-1.09)
Soc.–sec. rec. or unemployed	—		—		—		0.009	(0.99)
Blue–collar worker	—		—		—		-0.006	(-0.66)
Self–employed	—		—		—		0.000	(-0.03)
Civil servant	—		—		—		0.019	(1.99)
$\bar{R}^2$	0.497		0.498		0.507		0.509	
F statistic	1155.43		966.53		751.48		551.58	

Note: dependent variable: equivalence scale; pooled estimations; N: 5,845.
Notation: t statistics in parentheses; standardised coefficients.

The basic regression (1) already fits the data quite well since it explains 49.7% (44.0%) of total variance (compare the adjusted coefficient of determination $\bar{R}^2$). An F statistic of $1,155.430$ (796.411) strongly rejects the null hypothesis that the true slope coefficients are simultaneously zero. Reference income has a strong negative coefficient for both countries. This means that, according to our subjects, equivalence scales decrease with increasing level of reference income, a result that strongly contrasts the IB/ESE assumption. On the contrary, IB/ESE would require that the coefficients for y_r were zero.[5] Moreover, the data suggest increasing equivalence scales with increasing number of adults and children since the coefficients for both, DA_2 and DC_i for $i = 1, ..., 3$, are positive and significant. The coefficient for the second adult being higher than for a single child means that subjects attribute higher costs to the second adult than to an additional child. However, all four coefficients are lower than 1.0. This finding means that, according to our interviewees, there exists economies of scale in the households. The picture is less clear regarding economies for children. Regression coefficients indicate that the second child is the most expensive one. Quantitative differences, however, are rather small.

Table 6.7. Regressions 1-4 (V_I, Cyprus)

Equation	1	2	3	4
c_0	1.680 (54,73)	1.680 (54,73)	1.647 (33.35)	1.666 (32.56)
y_r	-0.474 (-42.77)	-0.474 (-42.77)	-0.474 (-43.07)	-0.474 (-43.36)
DA_2	0.308 (25.98)	0.308 (25.98)	0.308 (26.16)	0.308 (26.33)
DC_1	0.151 (11.41)	0.151 (11.41)	0.151 (11.49)	0.151 (11.57)
DC_2	0.206 (14.21)	0.206 (14.21)	0.206 (14.31)	0.206 (14.40)
DC_3	0.185 (13.95)	0.185 (13.95)	0.185 (14.05)	0.185 (14.14)
y_p	—	0.003 (0.28)	-0.007 (-0.61)	0.010 (0.82)
Gender	—	—	0.060 (5.33)	0.054 (4.65)
Siblings	—	—	-0.052 (-4.67)	-0.050 (-4.43)
Education	—	—	0.057 (5.15)	0.080 (6.93)
Partner	—	—	—	-0.019 (-1.07)
Children	—	—	—	-0.060 (-5.36)
Parents	—	—	—	-0.023 (-2.00)
Housewife	—	—	—	0.025 (2.183)
Pupil, student or trainee	—	—	—	-0.013 (-1.01)
Soc.–sec. rec. or unemployed	—	—	—	-0.031 (-2.77)
Blue–collar worker	—	—	—	0.003 (0.24)
Self–employed	—	—	—	0.009 (0.74)
Civil servant	—	—	—	-0.059 (-4.904)
R^2	0.440	0.440	0.448	0.455
F statistic	796.41	796.41	462.38	293.47

Note: dependent variable: equivalence scale; pooled estimations; N: 4,550.
Notation: t statistics in parentheses; standardised coefficients.

Regression (2) differs from regression (1) only by a single further variable that is personal income (y_p). As outlined above, its coefficient gives a first impression of whether the interviewees' responses are affected by preference drift. According to the results reported by the *Leyden School* the coefficient

[5]Notice that all coefficients are standardised.

should be positive and quantitatively important. For Germany, the picture is completely inverse. The coefficient is quantitatively small and negative and the inclusion of y_p as a further explanatory variable only slightly alters the explanatory power of regression (2) compared to regression (1). Moreover, all stimulus coefficients are unchanged and their t statistics are hardly affected. The respective coefficient being negative means that "rich" interviewees stated slightly lower equivalence scales than their "poor" counterparts. For Cyprus, preference drift doesn't seem to matter at all.

Regression (3) additionally considers *Pers(I)*, the personal variables *gender*, *siblings* and *education*. The coefficients of all three variables are quantitatively small. In both countries, female respondents stated slightly higher equivalence scales than their male counterparts. The coefficient for *siblings* is significant for Cyprus only: Cypriot respondents that spent their childhood with brothers and sisters stated slightly lower equivalence scales. The impact of *education* is qualitatively the same for Germany and Cyprus: the equivalence scales stated and the education level are positively related. Possibly, high–educated interviewees demand for higher investments in the education of children than low–educated interviewees. To sum it up, the overall impact of *Pers(I)* on equivalence scales is quantitatively minor. Moreover, the stimulus coefficients are the same as in regression (1) and (2) and the explanatory power of the regression increases only slightly.

Regression (4) additionally comprises the vector *Pers(II)*. Its coefficients are small without exception for both countries and the inclusion of *Pers(II)* only marginally increases the explanatory power of regression (4) compared to regressions (1)–(3). Again, none of the stimulus coefficients change and the t statistics stay on high significance levels. For Germany, the impact of the variable *personal income* becomes insignificant though remains insignificant for Cyprus.

In conclusion, regressions (1)–(4) reveal that the personal characteristics of the interviewees have a quantitatively small influence, they do not add much in explaining the variation of equivalence scales, and their inclusion does not change the stimulus coefficients. This result can be interpreted as a first indication that the respondents had taken the required general viewpoint, when they assessed the needs of hypothetical households even if these households differed from their own household type. Another important finding is that the regression results strongly invalidate the IB/ESE assumption. According to our subjects, equivalence scales are a decreasing function of reference income. Moreover, the regression results indicate higher needs for adults than for children and economies of scale in the households. Regarding economies of scale for children, the picture is ambiguous and we will therefore provide a more detailed analysis in Section 6.7. What is left is an analysis of potential interactions between the stimulus variables and possible non–linearities in the dependence of equivalence scales on reference income. Thus, three further regressions, (5)–(7), are conducted. The results are reported in Table 6.8 for Germany and in Table 6.9 for Cyprus.

Table 6.8. Regressions 5-7 (V_I, Germany)

Equ.	5	6	7
c_0	1.889	0.900	1.436
	(65.84)	(37.98)	(53.78)
y_r	-1.702	—	-0.508
	(-43.32)		(-55.26)
DA_2	0.422	0.612	0.422
	(46.37)	(38.02)	(42.95)
DC_1	0.140	0.288	0.140
	(13.79)	(26.12)	(12.77)
DC_2	0.176	0.385	0.176
	(15.76)	(30.82)	(14.59)
DC_3	0.158	0.349	0.158
	(15.52)	(30.60)	(14.37)
y_r^2	1.223	—	—
	(31.13)		
$y_r * DA_2$	—	-0.245	—
		(-14.54)	
$y_r * n_C$	—	-0.625	—
		(-42.20)	
$n_A * n_C$	—	—	0.006
			(0.13)
y_p	-0.034	-0.034	-0.034
	(-3.40)	(-3.89)	(-3.70)
Gender	0.023	0.023	0.023
	(2.66)	(2.59)	(2.46)
Siblings	-0.004	-0.004	-0.004
	(-0.42)	(-0.41)	(-0.39)
Educ.	0.093	0.093	0.093
	(10.88)	(10.58)	(10.07)
R^2	0.577	0.552	0.507
F stat.	886.45	802.35	751.48

Note: dependent variable: equivalence scale; pooled estimations; number of observations: 5,845. t statistics in parentheses; standardised coefficients.

Table 6.9. Regressions 5-7 (V_I, Cyprus)

Equ.	5	6	7
c_0	2.201	1.013	1.647
	(42.74)	(22.34)	(33.35)
y_r	-1.628	—	-0.474
	(-34.08)		(-43.07)
DA_2	0.308	0.488	0.308
	(27.86)	(25.03)	(26.16)
DC_1	0.151	0.290	0.151
	(12.24)	(21.69)	(11.49)
DC_2	0.206	0.402	0.206
	(15.24)	(26.60)	(14.31)
DC_3	0.185	0.364	0.185
	(14.96)	(26.35)	(14.05)
y_r^2	1.181	—	—
	(24.74)		
$y_r * DA_2$	—	-0.232	—
		(-11.35)	
$y_r * n_C$	—	-0.585	—
		(-32.61)	
$n_A * n_C$	—	—	-0.007
			(-0.14)
y_p	-0.007	-0.007	-0.007
	(-0.65)	(-0.63)	(-0.61)
Gender	0.060	0.060	0.060
	(5.68)	(5.55)	(5.33)
Siblings	-0.052	-0.052	-0.052
	(-4.97)	(-4.85)	(-4.67)
Educ.	0.057	0.057	0.057
	(5.16)	(5.04)	5.02)
R^2	0.513	0.489	0.448
F stat.	534.26	485.46	462.38

Note: dependent variable: equivalence scale; pooled estimations. Number of observations: 4,550. t statistics in parentheses; standardised coefficients.

Regression (5) corresponds to regression (3) but additionally considers the square of reference income (y_r^2) capturing non–linearities in the dependence of equivalence scales on this variable. The coefficient for y_r^2 is positive for both Germany and Cyprus. In connection with the negative coefficient for y_r this means that equivalence scales decrease with increasing reference income at a *decreasing* rate. [6]

So far, we estimated the needs for adults and children after conditioning for the effects of reference income. Complementary, regression (6) considers these interactions by the synthetic variables $y_r * DA_2$ and $y_r * n_C$ while y_r is excluded from the set of conditioning variables. Apart from this modification, regression (6) is the same as regression (3). Compared to regression (3), the specification of regression (6) substantially increases the explanatory power of the model for the two countries. Significantly negative coefficients for both, $y_r * DA_2$ and $y_r * n_C$ indicate that both, children weights and the weight for the second adult are decreasing functions of reference income. Moreover, the income dependence of children weights is quantitatively stronger.

In comparison to regression (3), regression (7) includes the interaction $n_A * n_C$. This product captures differences comparing the children weights in single–parent and in two–parent households. For both countries, the respective coefficient is insignificant. However, we will provide a more detailed analysis of this interaction in a later section using descriptive statistics and further statistical tests.

Altogether, regressions (1)–(7) strongly reject the IB/ESE assumption. Instead, our equivalence scales decrease with increasing reference income at a decreasing rate. Moreover, it is likely that children weights are more sensitive to changes in reference income than adult weights. Comparing the weights for adults and children, the coefficients indicate that adult weights are higher. Comparing the explanatory power of the stimulus and of the personal variables, the stimulus variables' explanatory power is significantly stronger. In sum, personal characteristics of the interviewees hardly matter. On the contrary, from all personal characteristics, we observe that only *gender* and *education* have robust impacts on the perception of equivalence scales.

6.6 Cross–country Differences

The country–specific regressions revealed that the influence of the stimulus variables on equivalence scales is *qualitatively* the same in both countries. Moreover, the influences of personal characteristics in Germany and Cyprus turned out to be negligible. In this section, we run four regressions, (3'), (5'),

---

[6] Of course, a positive coefficient for y_r^2 outweighs the negative coefficient for y_r at some critical value. It is, therefore, only meaningful for the given range of reference incomes.

(6'), and (7'), in order to quantify quantitative differences in equivalence scales between the two samples. The structure of these regressions is the same as the structure of the country–specific regressions (3) and (5)–(7). However, the set of explanatory variables is extended by the products of each and every country–specific variable with aforementioned dummy variable *CD*.[7] The linear regression model is given by

$$\sigma_{i,j} = c_0 + a_0 * CD + a_1 * Stim_j + a_2 * StimInt_j + a3 * y_{pi} + a4 * Pers(I)_i +$$

$$a_5 * CD * Stim_j + a_6 * CD * StimInt_j + a_7 * CD * y_{pi} + a_8 * CD * Pers(I)_i + \epsilon_{i,j}. \tag{6.3}$$

To make the data sets of both countries comparable, we had to re–code two explanatory variables. Remember that reference–incomes (y_r) and personal incomes (y_p) for Cyprus were obtained by adjusting each German value with a factor of 0.6. In the following regressions, y_r enters the regressions as a co-variate with values of 1.0, 2.5, 4.0, 5.5 and 7.0. y_p is adjusted correspondingly. Table 6.10 only reports regression coefficients that identify cross-country differences.

First of all, the second adult is assessed about the same by both samples. However, average equivalence scales for Germany are significantly flatter than indicated by the negative coefficient *CD* and by lower weights for children ($CD * DC_i < 0 \; \forall i$). Secondly, the coefficient for $CD * y_r$ is negative which means that the decline of equivalence scales with reference income is stronger for Cyprus. Both results do not come as a great surprise: each reference–income level for Cyprus is only 60% of the corresponding German value. Moreover, most of the data have been collected in urban areas of Cyprus where cost of living is not very different from Germany. Thus it is to be expected, that Cypriot subjects assigned lower spending power to each of the five Cypriot reference income than German respondents evaluating the higher German reference incomes. Given that equivalence scales decrease with increasing spending power of the reference household, it is, therefore, highly plausible that Cypriot respondents would have stated lower equivalence scale values if the German reference incomes had been applied to them.

Figure 6.5 gives a graphical illustration: in the figure, $y_{1.0}$ ($y_{0.6}$) and $y_{2.5}$ ($y_{1.5}$) denote the first two of the five different levels of reference income for Germany (Cyprus). Let us assume that a Cypriot respondent would have stated correspondingly $\sigma_{0.6}$ and $\sigma_{1.5}$, that is decreasing equivalence scales with reference income rising. If we had asked the same subject to state equivalence scales for the corresponding German levels of reference income, $y_{1.0}$ and $y_{2.5}$, we should expect $\sigma_{0.6} > \sigma_{1.0}$ and $\sigma_{1.5} > \sigma_{2.5}$.

[7] A detailed presentation of the regression model is given in Section 6.4.

Table 6.10. Cross–country Differences (V_I)

Equation	3'	5'	6'	7'
CD	-0.102	-0.209	-0.025	-0.102
	(-3.546)	(-5.732)	(-1.035$^+$)	(-3.546)
$CD * y_r$	0.099	0.377	—	0.099
	(5.784)	(5.127)		(5.784)
$CD * DA_2$	0.026	0.026	0.013	0.026
	(1.842$^+$)	(1.973)	(1.123$^+$)	(1.839$^+$)
$CD * DC_1$	-0.079	-0.065	-0.134	-0.079
	(-3.425)	(-2.856)	(-7.108)	(-3.425)
$CD * DC_2$	-0.071	-0.071	-0.110	-0.071
	(-4.068)	(-4.357)	(-6.173)	(-4.068)
$CD * DC_3$	-0.055	-0.055	-0.085	-0.055
	(-3.971)	(-4.254)	(-6.078)	(-3.971)
$CD * y_r^2$	—	-0.226	—	—
		(-3.878)		
$CD * y_r * DA_2$	—	—	0.022	—
			(1.807$^+$)	
$CD * y_r * n_C$	—	—	0.116	—
			(6.475)	
$CD * n_A * n_C$	—	—	—	-0.009
				(-0.391$^+$)
$CD * y_p$	-0.039	-0.039	-0.043	-0.039
	(-3.371)	(-3.611)	(-3.989)	(-3.371)
CD * Gender	-0.031	-0.031	-0.034	-0.031
	(-2.510)	(-2.689)	(-2.963)	(-2.510)
CD * Siblings	0.047	0.047	0.041	0.047
	(3.470)	(3.717)	(3.555)	(3.470)
CD * Education	0.005	0.005	-0.008	0.009
	(0.199$^+$)	(0.213$^+$)	(-0.506$^+$)	(0.416$^+$)
R^2	0.483	0.549	0.525	0.483
F statistic	607.640	667.927	720.302	607.640

Dependent variable: equivalence scale; pooled estimations. Number of observations: 10,395. Standardised coefficients. Notation: t statistics in parentheses; $^+$ insignificant.

Regarding the personal characteristics, differences between the two countries are quantitatively small. The result of Section 6.5 proves to be true: y_p matters only for the German data. On the other hand, the personal variable *siblings* only matters for the Cypriot data. We also find confirmed that females state higher equivalence scales than men. This effect is significantly stronger for Cyprus as the significant and negative coefficient for CD * *gender* reveals. Finally, the impact of the level of education is the same for both countries. Therefore, we can conclude that there are some differences in the assessment of equivalence scales across the two countries, still quantitative deviations are not too large and, more important, quantitative differences in the income dependence of equivalence scales do not come as a surprise.

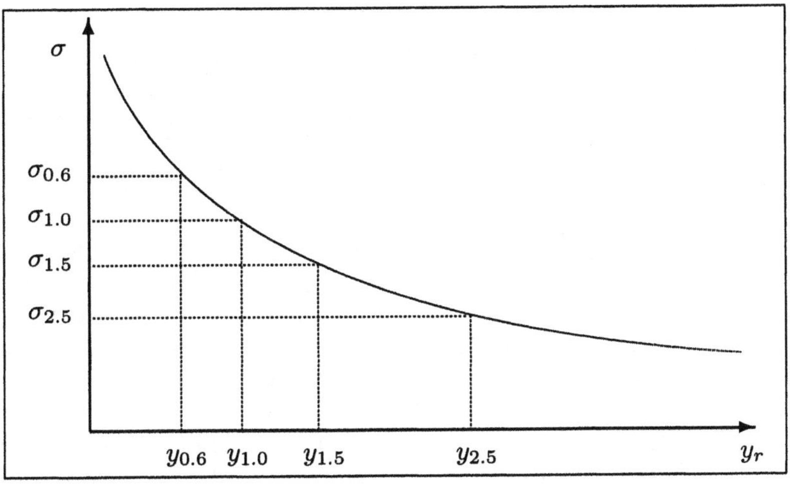

Figure 6.5. Impacts of Cross–country Differences in y_r

6.7 Descriptive Analysis

By providing descriptive statistics and statistical tests, this section will give a picture of how equivalence scales and individual weights for Germany and Cyprus "really" look like. In the following, A denotes an adult, C a child, C_i the ith child in the household ($i = 1, 2, 3$), and individual weights are labelled W. For example, WC_2AA gives the weight for the second child in a two–adult household.

Table 6.11 summarises mean equivalence scales, standard deviations, and deviations in % comparing the equivalence scales between Germany and Cyprus. Holding reference income constant, average equivalence scales are increasing in the number of family members, and average scales are slightly higher for Cyprus, 8.5% on average and 16.8% the most. As outlined in Section 6.6, Cypriot subjects may have assigned lower spending power to each of the five Cypriot reference incomes compared to the corresponding German reference incomes leading to an upward shift of equivalence scales. The decrease of equivalence scales with income rising is substantial: the Cypriot data suggest that the equivalence–scale value of a two–adult household with three children, for instance, almost bisects when moving from the lowest to the highest level of reference income. Thus, average equivalence scales are perfectly in line with the regression results provided in Section 6.5 and 6.6.

Given the average equivalence scales of Table 6.11, individual weights can be calculated as the differences of equivalence scales for each two consecutive household types.

Table 6.11. Descriptive Statistics of Equivalence Scales (V_I)

y_r	1.0		2.5		4.0		5.5		7.0	
	Mean	St.d.	Mean	St.d.	Mean	St.d.	Mean	St.d.	Mean	St.d.
					Germany					
AC	1.570	0.230	1.241	0.114	1.174	0.110	1.128	0.089	1.112	0.088
ACC	2.020	0.398	1.436	0.195	1.315	0.181	1.233	0.150	1.205	0.146
ACCC	2.473	0.612	1.629	0.283	1.451	0.254	1.339	0.210	1.295	0.201
AA	1.753	0.205	1.495	0.266	1.460	0.279	1.387	0.265	1.389	0.272
AAC	2.269	0.325	1.718	0.319	1.612	0.329	1.508	0.311	1.493	0.317
AACC	2.725	0.498	1.919	0.394	1.755	0.373	1.615	0.359	1.587	0.365
AACCC	3.174	0.749	2.115	0.474	1.887	0.435	1.726	0.416	1.677	0.413
					Cyprus					
AC	1.732	0.342	1.330	0.179	1.265	0.161	1.230	0.172	1.199	0.160
	(9.4)		(6.7)		(7.2)		(8.3)		(7.3)	
ACC	2.337	0.590	1.612	0.316	1.488	0.276	1.427	0.300	1.363	0.273
	(13.6)		(10.9)		(11.6)		(13.6)		(11.6)	
ACCC	2.971	0.921	1.888	0.451	1.707	0.398	1.611	0.419	1.524	0.377
	(16.8)		(13.7)		(15.0)		(16.9)		(15.0)	
AA	1.809	0.331	1.483	0.264	1.420	0.276	1.379	0.259	1.341	0.264
	(3.1)		(-0.8)		(-2.8)		(-0.6)		(-3.6)	
AAC	2.442	0.509	1.775	0.352	1.649	0.360	1.581	0.354	1.521	0.356
	(7.1)		(3.2)		(2.2)		(4.6)		(1.8)	
AACC	3.065	0.801	2.063	0.476	1.868	0.459	1.773	0.455	1.684	0.442
	(11.1)		(7.0)		(6.0)		(8.9)		(5.8)	
AACCC	3.676	1.051	2.334	0.585	2.079	0.557	1.953	0.551	1.841	0.521
	(13.7)		(9.4)		(9.2)		(11.6)		(8.9)	

Notation: st.d. denotes standard deviation; data in parentheses is deviation in % compared to Germany; each A denotes an adult, each C a child.

For an example, the average weight for the second child in a two adult household (WC_2AA) for $y_r = 1.0$ is calculated by taking the difference of the average equivalence scales of household type $AACC$ and AAC for $y_r = 1.0$. These weights are reported in Table 6.12.[8] All individual weights are decreasing functions of reference income. Moreover, the data suggest higher weights for children in single–adult households than in two–adult households ($WC_iA > WC_iAA \; \forall i$) given the same level of reference income. Finally, average weights for children behave differently compared with the children coefficients derived in the regressions of Section 6.5: while the regression coefficients

[8] Individual costs per household member are the product of its individual weight and the level of reference income. The children costs can be taken from Table A1 in the Appendix.

did not confirm economies of scale for children, now the picture is different: the average weight for each further child is less than the weight for the preceding child: $WC_1A > WC_2A > WC_3A$ and $WC_1AA > WC_2AA > WC_3AA$.

Table 6.12. Descriptive Statistics of Individual Weights (V_I)

y_r	1.0		2.5		4.0		5.5		7.0	
	Mean	St.d.	Mean	St.d.	Mean	St.d.	Mean	St.d.	Mean	St.d.
					Germany					
WC_1A	0.570	0.230	0.241	0.114	0.174	0.110	0.128	0.089	0.112	0.088
WC_2A	0.451	0.223	0.195	0.097	0.141	0.081	0.105	0.068	0.094	0.065
WC_3A	0.453	0.270	0.193	0.106	0.136	0.084	0.106	0.069	0.089	0.063
WAA	0.753	0.205	0.495	0.266	0.460	0.279	0.387	0.265	0.389	0.272
WC_1AA	0.516	0.225	0.223	0.119	0.153	0.107	0.121	0.087	0.104	0.083
WC_2AA	0.456	0.254	0.201	0.126	0.143	0.084	0.107	0.078	0.094	0.070
WC_3AA	0.449	0.317	0.196	0.114	0.132	0.088	0.112	0.091	0.091	0.067
					Cyprus					
WC_1A	0.732	0.342	0.330	0.179	0.265	0.161	0.230	0.172	0.199	0.160
WC_2A	0.605	0.309	0.281	0.161	0.223	0.134	0.197	0.139	0.164	0.124
WC_3A	0.634	0.399	0.276	0.160	0.219	0.142	0.183	0.130	0.161	0.123
WAA	0.809	0.331	0.483	0.264	0.420	0.276	0.379	0.259	0.341	0.264
WC_1AA	0.633	0.345	0.291	0.149	0.229	0.140	0.201	0.154	0.180	0.143
WC_2AA	0.623	0.395	0.288	0.189	0.219	0.144	0.192	0.133	0.162	0.113
WC_3AA	0.611	0.355	0.271	0.155	0.210	0.136	0.180	0.126	0.157	0.104

Notation: st.d. denotes standard deviation; each *A* denotes an adult; each *C* denotes a child; *W* denotes weight.

Of course, the descriptive statistics in isolation do not guarantee that the observed patterns are statistically significant as well. The statistical tests provided below will close this gap. We start with a test of reference–income dependence of individual weights. If the individual weights pass this test, then equivalence scales pass as well since a household's equivalence scale is the sum of its members' weights. Since data is not normally distributed[9] and since data across the vectors are related, we conduct a Wilcoxon test comparing the vector of responses of the respective sample for $y_r = 1.0$ with the corresponding responses for $y_r = 2.5$. Table 6.13 states the absolute differences of each individual weight comparing any two levels of reference income and the Z values of the Wilcoxon test. The entries in column $t(1.0 - 2.5)$ row WC_2AA for Germany, for instance, mean that the absolute decrease ($\triangle$) of the weight for the second child in a two–adult household (WC_2AA) is 0.254 comparing the first and the second level of reference income (1.0–2.5) and that the Z value of this comparison is -10.758. The test statistics are convincing: except for a single observation, all test statistics are significant at the 1% level which means that the null hypothesis of constant weights for all levels of reference income has

[9]For none of the 35 hypothetical household types equivalence scales were normally distributed according to a Kolmogorov–Smirnov test on normality.

to be rejected. On the contrary, negative Z values indicate that individual weights are decreasing functions of reference income.

Table 6.13. Influence of Reference Income on Weights (V_I)

	1.0–2.5		2.5–4.0		4.0–5.5		5.5–7.0	
	△	Z	△	Z	△	Z	△	Z
				Germany				
WC_1A	0.328	-11.036	0.067	-9.101	0.046	-9.360	0.016	-6.254
WC_2A	0.256	-10.953	0.054	-8.878	0.036	-9.119	0.012	-5.603
WC_3A	0.260	-10.864	0.057	-9.174	0.030	-8.821	0.017	-7.019
WAA	0.258	-9.687	0.035	-3.282	0.073	-7.522	-0.002	-0.302$^+$
WC_1AA	0.293	-10.976	0.070	-10.130	0.031	-8.288	0.017	-6.847
WC_2AA	0.254	-10.758	0.059	-9.382	0.036	-9.033	0.013	-5.581
WC_3AA	0.253	-10.921	0.063	-9.056	0.021	-6.139	0.021	-5.571
				Cyprus				
WC_1A	0.402	-9.690	0.065	-5.963	0.035	-5.079	0.031	-5.332
WC_2A	0.323	-9.589	0.058	-5.325	0.026	-4.422	0.033	-5.863
WC_3A	0.358	-9.434	0.057	-5.391	0.036	-4.958	0.022	-4.073
WAA	0.326	-8.638	0.063	-5.204	0.041	-4.247	0.038	-4.344
WC_1AA	0.342	-9.293	0.063	-5.600	0.027	-4.792	0.022	-3.482
WC_2AA	0.335	-9.263	0.069	-6.000	0.027	-4.152	0.030	-3.795
WC_3AA	0.340	-9.221	0.061	-5.170	0.030	-5.170	0.023	-3.354

Note: Z values of Wilcoxon test; all results are significant at the 1% level except for $^+$ denoting insignificance; Germany: N = 167; df = 166; Cyprus: N = 130; df = 129.

Notation: each A denotes an adult; each C denotes a child; W denotes weight; △ denotes difference in individual weights.

Are economies of scale for children statistically significant? We attempt to answer this question by again conducting aforementioned Wilcoxon tests of differences comparing, for the same reference income, the vector of weights of the first and of the second child denoted $C_1 - C_2$, of the second and the third child denoted $C_2 - C_3$, and of the first and the third child denoted $C_1 - C_3$. The test statistics are reported in Table 6.14. For Germany, the first child is significantly more expensive than the two other as indicated by negative test statistics for $C_1 - C_2$ and for $C_1 - C_3$. For Cyprus, this pattern is not consistent in all cases. For both countries, insignificant statistics in a predominant number of cases indicate that the weights for the second and for the third child are about the same. In total, the first child is the most expensive one, while the other two show little difference. In the △ columns, Table 6.14 also states differences in the costs assigned to the first and second child, and to the second and third child. The basic information of the children costs can be taken from Table A1 in the Appendix.

Table 6.14. Economies of Scale for Children (V_I)

		$C_1 - C_2$		$C_2 - C_3$		$C_1 - C_3$
	y_r	$\triangle$	Z	$\triangle$	Z	Z
			Germany			
	1.0	118.683	-6.904***	-2.156	-0.771$^+$	-6.015***
	2.5	116.168	-6.969***	5.539	-0.757$^+$	-6.060***
A	4.0	131.976	-6.803***	19.880	-1.975**	-6.443***
	5.5	122.515	-5.639***	-1.647	-0.477$^+$	-4.884***
	7.0	127.844	-3.969***	31.018	-2.442**	-5.168***
	1.0	60.419	-4.684***	6.886	-1.549$^+$	-5.317***
	2.5	53.743	-4.288***	14.072	-1.291$^+$	-4.309***
AA	4.0	39.042	-3.473***	41.437	-3.939***	-4.333***
	5.5	78.383	-5.326***	-26.018	-0.654$^+$	-3.727***
	7.0	70.419	-3.791***	20.120	-1.736*	-4.011***
			Cyprus			
	1.0	25.515	-5.037***	-5.838	-1.054$^+$	-3.458***
	2.5	24.438	-4.074***	2.585	-0.424$^+$	-4.220***
A	4.0	33.515	-4.162***	3.238	-1.095$^+$	-4.207***
	5.5	35.977	-3.902***	15.508	-2.043**	-5.149***
	7.0	48.346	-4.729***	4.746	-0.730$^+$	-3.915***
	1.0	1.992	-1.489$^+$	2.546	-0.106$^+$	-1.215$^+$
	2.5	1.508	-1.729*	8.608	-1.093$^+$	-1.981**
AA	4.0	7.546	-1.932*	7.146	-0.966$^+$	-2.510***
	5.5	10.277	-1.299$^+$	13.262	-2.081**	-2.066**
	7.0	24.200	-1.996**	7.492	-1.102$^+$	-2.088**

Note: absolute differences in children costs; data for Germany in DM; data for Cyprus in CP; Z values of Wilcoxon tests. Germany: N = 167; df = 166; Cyprus: N = 130; df = 129. Notation: *** rejection of equality at the 1% level; ** rejection of equality at the 5% level; * rejection of equality at the 10% level; $^+$ equality cannot be rejected; $\triangle$ absolute difference.

A final test refers to the question whether the assessment of children costs depends on the number of adults in the hypothetical households. Positive differences of children costs in single–adult and in two–adult households can be interpreted as a bonus for single parents. For each reference income, Table 6.15 states these differences in DM for Germany and in Cypriot Pounds for Cyprus separately for each child. Moreover, Z values of Wilcoxon tests are provided testing the stated income amounts for children in single–parent and two–parent families on significance. The picture is the same across the two countries: for the first child, respondents state significantly higher costs for children in single– than in two–parent households. The average increments ("boni") are rather stable across the different levels of reference income. For the second and the third child, differences are insignificant.

Table 6.15. Single–parent Boni (V_I)

	C_1		C_2		C_3	
y_r	△	Z	△	Z	△	Z
			Germany			
1.0	53.293	-3.830***	-4.970	-0.054+	4.072	-0.995+
2.5	45.808	-3.145***	-16.617	-0.659+	-8.084	-0.162+
4.0	86.227	-5.139***	-6.707	-0.171+	14.850	-1.626+
5.5	35.899	-2.578***	-8.233	-0.653+	-32.605	-0.005+
7.0	56.587	-2.004**	-0.838	-0.988+	-11.736	-0.030+
			Cyprus			
1.0	19.792	-3.869***	-3.730	-0.164+	4.654	-0.756+
2.5	19.439	-2.927***	-3.493	-0.190+	2.531	-0.693+
4.0	28.746	-3.632***	2.777	-1.163+	6.684	-1.257+
5.5	31.477	-3.502***	5.777	-0.437+	3.531	-0.397+
7.0	26.754	-2.279**	2.608	-0.072+	5.354	-0.079+

Note: Z values of Wilcoxon tests.
Notation: *** rejection of equality at the 1% level; ** rejection of equality at the 5% level; + insignificant; △ absolute difference; Germany in DM; Cyprus in CP.

6.8 Validity

This section will examine in more detail how personal income (y_p) and adjusted personal income (y_{adj}) affect the respondents' assessments of household needs. These two personal variables rise so much attention as they revealed a substantial impact on *Leyden School* equivalence scales, the preference drift phenomenon. For our surveys we hope that choosing income as the dimension for both, stimulus and response, helps eliminating such undesirable habit effects. The impacts of personal income and adjusted personal income on stated equivalence scales will be identified by Mann–Whitney–U tests since data across the vectors are not related.

We comment on the impacts of personal income first. For each country, the test is based on a decomposition of the sample according to the personal household income of the respondents. For Germany (Cyprus), the distribution of household income can be taken from column three (N) of Table 6.16 (Table 6.17). For each of the five personal–income groups, these tables report average equivalence scales for each hypothetical household type and for each reference–income level. For example, 1.63 is the average equivalence scale for a single adult with one child (AC) at the lowest level of reference income ($y_r = 1.0$) that was stated by German respondents belonging to the second personal income bracket ($y_p = 3.0$). Given a specific hypothetical household type and the reference–income level, the test procedure is as follows.

Table 6.16. Impacts of Personal Income (V_I, Germany)

y_r	y_p	N	AC	ACC	ACCC	AA	AAC	AACC	AACCC
	1.0	32	1.53	1.98	2.40	1.78	2.25	2.76	3.21
	2.0	44	1.55$^+$	2.03$^+$	2.52$^+$	1.71*	2.21$^+$	2.70$^+$	3.19$^+$
1.0	3.0	37	1.63*	2.08$^+$	2.58$^+$	1.78$^+$	2.35$^+$	2.80$^+$	3.30$^+$
	4.0	37	1.61$^+$	2.07$^+$	2.51$^+$	1.77$^+$	2.31$^+$	2.75$^+$	3.16$^+$
	5.0	17	1.50$^+$	1.84$^+$	2.18$^+$	1.73$^+$	2.17$^+$	2.52$^+$	2.85*
	1.0	32	1.22	1.42	1.60	1.52	1.72	1.94	2.14
	2.0	44	1.26$^+$	1.47$^+$	1.68$^+$	1.47$^+$	1.70$^+$	1.92$^+$	2.13$^+$
2.5	3.0	37	1.27*	1.48*	1.70**	1.51$^+$	1.77$^+$	1.97$^+$	2.18$^+$
	4.0	37	1.22$^+$	1.41$^+$	1.58$^+$	1.54$^+$	1.75$^+$	1.92$^+$	2.11$^+$
	5.0	17	1.19$^+$	1.35$^+$	1.49$^+$	1.41$^+$	1.60$^+$	1.76$^+$	1.91$^+$
	1.0	32	1.16	1.29	1.43	1.52	1.66	1.79	1.92
	2.0	44	1.18$^+$	1.32$^+$	1.47$^+$	1.45$^+$	1.60$^+$	1.75$^+$	1.90$^+$
4.0	3.0	37	1.20$^+$	1.36*	1.50$^+$	1.47$^+$	1.64$^+$	1.80$^+$	1.94$^+$
	4.0	37	1.17$^+$	1.31$^+$	1.44$^+$	1.45$^+$	1.60$^+$	1.74$^+$	1.86$^+$
	5.0	17	1.14$^+$	1.26$^+$	1.37$^+$	1.38*	1.52*	1.64$^+$	1.74$^+$
	1.0	32	1.12	1.22	1.32	1.43	1.55	1.66	1.77
	2.0	44	1.13$^+$	1.24$^+$	1.35$^+$	1.39$^+$	1.51$^+$	1.61$^+$	1.73$^+$
5.5	3.0	37	1.13$^+$	1.25$^+$	1.36$^+$	1.37$^+$	1.50$^+$	1.61$^+$	1.72$^+$
	4.0	37	1.13$^+$	1.23$^+$	1.33$^+$	1.39$^+$	1.51$^+$	1.61$^+$	1.72$^+$
	5.0	17	1.11$^+$	1.21$^+$	1.30$^+$	1.34$^+$	1.45$^+$	1.55$^+$	1.66$^+$
	1.0	32	1.09	1.18	1.26	1.47	1.56	1.65	1.73
	2.0	44	1.11$^+$	1.20$^+$	1.30$^+$	1.39$^+$	1.49$^+$	1.58$^+$	1.67$^+$
7.0	3.0	37	1.12$^+$	1.22$^+$	1.32$^+$	1.37$^+$	1.49$^+$	1.59$^+$	1.69$^+$
	4.0	37	1.13$^+$	1.22$^+$	1.30$^+$	1.37$^+$	1.47$^+$	1.57$^+$	1.66$^+$
	5.0	17	1.10$^+$	1.19$^+$	1.27$^+$	1.34$^+$	1.44$^+$	1.53$^+$	1.62$^+$

Note: Average scales and significance levels of Mann–Whitney–U tests. Notation: each A denotes an adult, each C a child; y_p denotes personal income; y_r denotes the reference–income level; *** rejection of equality at the 1% level; ** rejection of equality at the 5% level; ** rejection of equality at the 10% level; $^+$ insignificant.

Mann–Whitney–U tests are conducted comparing the responses of the $y_p = 1.0$ sub–sample with the responses for any $y_p > 1.0$ sub–sample. For instance, the asterisk in Table 6.16 for ($y_r = 2.5$, $y_p = 3.0$, AC) means that the $y_p = 3.0$ sub–sample gave equivalence scales for a single adult with one child (AC) at a reference–income level $y_r = 2.5$ which significantly differed from the answers of the $y_p = 1.0$ sub–sample. Thus, we do not report any significance levels in entries of personal–income level $y_p = 1.0$. Insignificant differences across the sub–samples are marked by a "+". For both countries, the impact of personal income on the respondents' assessments of household needs hardly matters. Except for some exceptions, equivalence scales are the same across the five sub–samples. For Germany, there is no indication of any systematic bias in the interviewees' assessments arising from personal income. With the exception of nine cases, all 140 test statistics are insignificant.

Table 6.17. Impacts of Personal Income (V_I, Cyprus)

y_r	y_p	N	AC	ACC	ACCC	AA	AAC	AACC	AACCC
	1.0	9	1.62	2.10	2.65	1.68	2.24	2.72	3.24
	2.0	25	1.71^+	2.31^+	2.93^+	1.79^+	2.41^+	2.99^+	3.60^+
1.0	3.0	24	1.72^+	2.35^+	3.05^+	1.80^+	2.46^+	3.07^+	3.66^+
	4.0	31	1.72^+	2.29^+	2.84^+	1.74^+	2.34^+	3.01^+	3.52^+
	5.0	41	1.79^+	2.44^+	3.12^+	1.91^{**}	2.56^{**}	3.23^+	3.95^+
	1.0	9	1.40	1.68	1.99	1.50	1.81	2.11	2.40
	2.0	25	1.30^+	1.58^+	1.88^+	1.40^+	1.67^+	2.00^+	2.30^+
2.5	3.0	24	1.35^+	1.65^+	1.93^+	1.48^+	1.77^+	2.02^+	2.29^+
	4.0	31	1.34^+	1.60^+	1.85^+	1.47^+	1.77^+	2.03^+	2.27^+
	5.0	41	1.31^+	1.60^{**}	1.87^{**}	1.54^{*}	1.84^+	2.14^+	2.41^{**}
	1.0	9	1.28	1.53	1.76	1.47	1.78	2.04	2.27
	2.0	25	1.26^+	1.49^+	1.71^+	1.36^+	1.61^{*}	1.84^{*}	2.08^+
4.0	3.0	24	1.30^+	1.53^+	1.75^+	1.40^+	1.62^{*}	1.83^{*}	2.04^+
	4.0	31	1.27^+	1.51^+	1.73^+	1.42^+	1.65^+	1.87^+	2.07^+
	5.0	41	1.24^{*}	1.44^{*}	1.65^+	1.46^+	1.66^+	1.87^+	2.07^{*}
	1.0	9	1.34	1.63	1.88	1.47	1.76	2.02	2.21
	2.0	25	1.25^+	1.48^+	1.68^+	1.32^+	1.55^+	1.76^+	1.96^+
5.5	3.0	24	1.23^+	1.42^+	1.61^{*}	1.31^+	1.50^+	1.70^+	1.89^+
	4.0	31	1.25^+	1.46^+	1.65^+	1.38^+	1.60^+	1.80^+	1.97^+
	5.0	41	1.18^+	1.33^+	1.48^+	1.43^+	1.59^+	1.75^+	1.92^+
	1.0	9	1.29	1.52	1.74	1.46	1.75	1.95	2.12
	2.0	25	1.22^+	1.39^+	1.58^+	1.29^+	1.49^+	1.66^+	1.82^+
7.0	3.0	24	1.22^+	1.39^+	1.54^+	1.29^+	1.47^+	1.64^+	1.79^+
	4.0	31	1.21^+	1.38^+	1.55^+	1.34^+	1.54^+	1.71^+	1.86^+
	5.0	41	1.15^+	1.28^+	1.41^{*}	1.38^+	1.51^+	1.65^+	1.81^+

Note: Average scales and significance levels of Mann–Whitney–U tests. Notation: each A denotes an adult, each C a child; y_p denotes personal income; y_r denotes the reference–income level; *** rejection of equality at the 1% level; ** rejection of equality at the 5% level; ** rejection of equality at the 10% level; $^+$ insignificant.

For Cyprus, we find 15 cases of significant differences and there are some robust differences for higher reference incomes where richer respondents state significantly lower equivalence scales for single parents relative to poorer ones. A possible interpretation is that interviewees with low personal incomes overestimate the needs of single parents with a high living standard. But even in these cases, the quantitative differences of the stated equivalence scales are not too large. To sum up, personal–income level of our respondents hardly matters for their assessments of household needs. On the contrary, the interviewees were able to take a rather general viewpoint: "richer" respondents had about the same understanding of the needs of a "poorer" household and vice versa.

Table 6.18. Impacts of Adjusted Personal Income (V_I Germany)

y_r	y_{adj}	N	AC	ACC	ACCC	AA	AAC	AACC	AACCC
	1.0	50	1.56	2.03	2.46	1.80	2.30	2.80	3.26
	2.0	64	1.57^{+}	2.06^{+}	2.57^{+}	1.73^{*}	2.29^{+}	2.76^{+}	3.24^{+}
1.0	3.0	33	1.57^{+}	1.98^{+}	2.44^{+}	1.73^{+}	2.23^{+}	2.64^{+}	3.10^{+}
	4.0	16	1.58^{+}	1.97^{+}	2.29^{+}	1.72^{+}	2.21^{+}	2.58^{+}	2.88^{*}
	5.0	4	1.58^{+}	1.88^{+}	2.23^{+}	1.80^{+}	2.18^{+}	2.53^{+}	2.88^{+}
	1.0	50	1.25	1.44	1.64	1.55	1.76	1.98	2.18
	2.0	64	1.27^{+}	1.49^{+}	1.69^{+}	1.52^{+}	1.77^{+}	1.99^{+}	2.20^{+}
2.5	3.0	33	1.22^{+}	1.40^{+}	1.59^{+}	1.45^{+}	1.66^{+}	1.84^{+}	2.03^{+}
	4.0	16	1.19^{*}	1.35^{*}	1.49^{*}	1.38^{**}	1.55^{**}	1.69^{**}	1.84^{**}
	5.0	4	1.12^{**}	1.23^{**}	1.32^{**}	1.33^{+}	1.46^{*}	1.57^{*}	1.69^{*}
	1.0	50	1.17	1.30	1.44	1.51	1.66	1.80	1.92
	2.0	64	1.19^{+}	1.35^{+}	1.50^{+}	1.51^{+}	1.67^{+}	1.83^{+}	1.98^{+}
4.0	3.0	33	1.18^{+}	1.33^{+}	1.46^{+}	1.38^{**}	1.54^{+}	1.69^{+}	1.81^{+}
	4.0	16	1.13^{+}	1.24^{+}	1.34^{+}	1.34^{**}	1.45^{**}	1.55^{**}	1.66^{**}
	5.0	4	1.06^{**}	1.13^{*}	1.18^{**}	1.25^{*}	1.31^{**}	1.40^{**}	1.44^{**}
	1.0	50	1.12	1.23	1.33	1.41	1.52	1.63	1.74
	2.0	64	1.14^{+}	1.26^{+}	1.38^{+}	1.43^{+}	1.57^{+}	1.68^{+}	1.80^{+}
5.5	3.0	33	1.13^{+}	1.23^{+}	1.34^{+}	1.33^{+}	1.45^{+}	1.57^{+}	1.68^{+}
	4.0	16	1.10^{+}	1.19^{+}	1.27^{+}	1.30^{+}	1.40^{+}	1.49^{+}	1.60^{+}
	5.0	4	1.04^{**}	1.06^{**}	1.10^{**}	1.19^{+}	1.23^{*}	1.26^{**}	1.31^{**}
	1.0	50	1.10	1.19	1.27	1.44	1.53	1.62	1.70
	2.0	64	1.13^{*}	1.23^{+}	1.34^{+}	1.43^{+}	1.54^{+}	1.64^{+}	1.74^{+}
7.0	3.0	33	1.12^{+}	1.21^{+}	1.30^{+}	1.31^{**}	1.43^{+}	1.53^{+}	1.62^{+}
	4.0	16	1.09^{+}	1.16^{+}	1.24^{+}	1.32^{+}	1.41^{+}	1.48^{+}	1.57^{+}
	5.0	4	1.03^{**}	1.06^{**}	1.09^{**}	1.14^{*}	1.17^{**}	1.20^{**}	1.23^{*}

Note: Average scales and significance levels of Mann–Whitney–U tests. Notation: each A denotes an adult, each C a child; y_p denotes personal income; y_r denotes the reference–income level; *** rejection of equality at the 1% level; ** rejection of equality at the 5% level; ** rejection of equality at the 10% level; $^{+}$ insignificant.

Now, we shall turn to the impacts of adjusted personal income y_{adj}. Adjusted personal income can be interpreted as a proxy for household welfare and the aim is to investigate whether the individual level of household welfare, as described by the level of y_{adj}, affects the interviewees' assessments of household needs. For each country, the analysis is based on a decomposition of the sample according to the adjusted personal–income level of the respondents. The adjusted personal–income distributions of the two samples can be taken from column three (N) of Table 6.18 for Germany and Table 6.19 for Cyprus.

Table 6.19. Impacts of Adjusted Personal Income (V_I Cyprus)

y_r	y_{adj}	N	AC	ACC	ACCC	AA	AAC	AACC	AACCC
	1.0	29	1.67	2.24	2.85	1.77	2.39	2.98	3.53
	2.0	40	1.75**	2.35*	2.99*	1.85+	2.43*	3.02+	3.61+
1.0	3.0	31	1.76+	2.42+	3.10+	1.78+	2.50+	3.24+	3.91+
	4.0	24	1.75*	2.36*	2.89+	1.74+	2.39+	2.98+	3.58+
	5.0	6	1.67+	2.23+	2.92+	2.08+	2.64+	3.23+	3.88+
	1.0	29	1.34	1.62	1.89	1.47	1.77	2.07	2.35
	2.0	40	1.36+	1.67*	1.96**	1.60**	1.86**	2.16*	2.45**
2.5	3.0	31	1.32+	1.61+	1.89+	1.51+	1.82+	2.10+	2.35+
	4.0	24	1.28+	1.52+	1.75+	1.31+	1.56+	1.84+	2.08+
	5.0	6	1.30+	1.57+	1.82+	1.58+	1.87+	2.13+	2.30+
	1.0	29	1.27	1.52	1.74	1.42	1.70	1.94	2.16
	2.0	40	1.32*	1.58+	1.85*	1.51+	1.77+	2.02+	2.26+
4.0	3.0	31	1.25+	1.46+	1.67+	1.44+	1.66+	1.87+	2.05+
	4.0	24	1.20+	1.36+	1.52+	1.23+	1.39*	1.56*	1.74+
	5.0	6	1.21+	1.34**	1.48**	1.46+	1.60+	1.74+	1.86+
	1.0	29	1.27	1.54	1.76	1.40	1.66	1.88	2.08
	2.0	40	1.30+	1.53+	1.76+	1.44+	1.68+	1.92+	2.13+
5.5	3.0	31	1.19+	1.36+	1.51+	1.44+	1.62+	1.79+	1.96+
	4.0	24	1.14**	1.26***	1.38***	1.20**	1.31**	1.44**	1.56**
	5.0	6	1.12***	1.22***	1.35***	1.30*	1.42**	1.52**	1.67**
	1.0	29	1.25	1.45	1.65	1.38	1.61	1.81	1.99
	2.0	40	1.26+	1.46+	1.65+	1.40+	1.62+	1.81+	1.99+
7.0	3.0	31	1.16+	1.31+	1.45+	1.38+	1.54+	1.68+	1.81+
	4.0	24	1.11**	1.22**	1.32**	1.17+	1.27**	1.39**	1.52**
	5.0	6	1.08***	1.17***	1.27***	1.29*	1.36**	1.43**	1.58**

Note: Average scales and significance levels of Mann–Whitney–U tests. Notation: each A denotes an adult, each C a child; y_p denotes personal income; y_r denotes the reference–income level; *** rejection of equality at the 1% level; ** rejection of equality at the 5% level; ** rejection of equality at the 10% level; + insignificant.

For each of the five adjusted personal–income groups, the two tables report five average equivalence scales for each of the seven hypothetical household types, one for each reference income. For example, 50 (4) German respondents are assigned to the lowest (highest) level of adjusted personal income which is denoted $y_{adj} = 1.0$ ($y_{adj} = 5.0$) and on average these respondents state an equivalence scale of 1.44 (1.23) for a single parent with two children (ACC) at a reference income of $y_r = 2.5$. For each hypothetical household type and reference–income level, a Mann–Whitney–U tests is conducted comparing the responses of the $y_{adj} = 1.0$ sub–sample with the responses for any $y_{adj} > 1.0$

sub–sample, such that no significance levels are reported in row $y_{adj} = 1.0$. Again, a "+" indicates that the hypothesis of the scales differing across the respective sub–samples is to be rejected while asterisks indicate significant differences. In our example, we test whether the 50 equivalence scales for ACC at $y_r = 2.5$ stated by the $y_{adj} = 1.0$ sub–sample are different compared with the corresponding 4 responses of the $y_{adj} = 5.0$ sub–sample. Two asterisks indicate that the responses of the two sub–samples are significantly different at the 5% level.

For Germany, differences across the sub samples are significant in 41 out of 140 cases. It turns out that respondents with a high living standard partly state significantly lower equivalence scales compared to those respondents with a low standard of living. The same pattern is visible for Cyprus, especially for the two highest levels of reference income. As argued in Section 5.4.1, these observations should not be over–emphasised since these results, at least partly, are driven by the classification procedure that assigns the respondents according to a specific level of adjusted personal income. Moreover, for both countries there are only few observations for the highest level of adjusted personal income and we are able to control for the impacts adjusted personal income on equivalence scales.

6.9 Reliability

The use of *hypothetical* households is suited for deriving equivalence scales only if subjects "correctly" judge the needs of household types that differ from their own regarding at least one category, i.e. living standard or household size. Reliability of our method requires that respondents are not too rationally bounded to make general judgements about household needs, especially if these households are different from their own. As outlined in Section 5.4.2, we analyse such effects by restricting the two samples in two different ways: the first restriction takes into account equivalence scales stated for all household *types*. However, responses are considered for that level of reference income only which is closest to the respondents' *adjusted* personal incomes (y_{adj}). This conversion rests upon the assumption that the living standard is about the same in each of the resulting sub–samples. The resulting joint distributions of respondents' demographic compositions and adjusted personal incomes are reported in Table 6.20. For example, altogether 59 German respondents live in two–adult households without children. This represents 35.3%. From these respondents, 13 are assigned to $y_{adj} = 1.0$, thus 7.8% of the overall sample. The second restriction considers the stated equivalence scale only if the respondent's own household type coincides or is closest to the demography of the hypothetical household.[10]

[10]For the distribution of respondents across household types compare Table 6.1.

Table 6.20. Joint Distribution of Demography and Adjusted Personal Income (V_I)

y_{adj}	1.0		2.0		3.0		4.0		5.0		Sum	
	N	%	N	%	N	%	N	%	N	%	N	%
					Germany							
A	30	17.9	21	12.6	10	6.0	2	1.2	1	0.6	64	38.3
AC	0	0.0	1	0.6	1	0.6	3	1.8	0	0.0	5	3.0
ACC	0	0.0	0	0.0	0	0.0	0	0.0	0	0.0	0	0.0
ACCC	0	0.0	1	0.6	0	0.0	0	0.0	0	0.0	1	0.6
AA	13	7.8	25	14.9	11	6.6	10	6.0	0	0.0	59	35.3
AAC	2	1.2	6	3.6	2	1.2	1	0.6	2	1.2	13	7.8
AACC	4	2.4	4	2.4	6	3.6	0	0.0	1	0.6	15	9.0
AACCC	1	0.6	6	3.6	3	1.8	0	0.0	0	0.0	10	6.0
Sum	50	29.9	64	38.3	33	19.8	16	9.6	4	2.4	167	100.0
					Cyprus							
A	5	3.8	6	4.6	3	2.3	0	0.0	4	3.1	18	13.8
AC	0	0.0	0	0.0	0	0.0	0	0.0	0	0.0	0	0.0
ACC	0	0.0	0	0.0	1	0.8	0	0.0	0	0.0	1	0.8
ACCC	0	0.0	0	0.0	0	0.0	0	0.0	0	0.0	0	0.0
AA	10	7.7	17	13.1	19	14.6	16	12.3	2	1.5	64	49.2
	(7)	(5.4)	(9)	(6.9)	(4)	(3.1)	(5)	(3.8)	(0)	(0.0)	(25)	
AAC	4	3.1	8	6.2	4	3.1	2	1.5	0	0.0	18	13.8
	(2)	(1.5)	(6)	(4.6)	(0)	(0.0)	(0)	(0.0)	(0)	(0.0)	(8)	
AACC	8	6.2	8	6.2	2	1.5	4	3.1	0	0.0	22	16.9
	(1)	(0.8)	(3)	(2.3)	(0)	(0.0)	(0)	(0.0)	(0)	(0.0)	(4)	
AACCC	2	1.5	1	0.8	2	1.5	2	1.5	0	0.0	7	5.4
	(0)	(0.0)	(0)	(0.0)	(0)	(0.0)	(0)	(0.0)	(0)	(0.0)	(0)	
Sum	29	22.3	40	30.8	31	23.8	24	18.5	6	4.6	130	100.0

Notation: number of respondents out of the particular group who were living with parents in parentheses; y_{adj} denotes adjusted personal income; each A denotes an adult; each C denotes a child.

A regression analysis is conducted for each restriction, and, by evaluating the extent to which regression coefficients of the sub–sample statistically differ from the regression coefficients of the overall sample, we ascertain whether the use of hypothetical households is error–generating or not.

Considering the first restriction, for each reference income the regression equation

$$\sigma_{i,j} = c_0 + a_1 * Stim'_j + a_2 * Dy_{adji} + a_3 * Dy_{adji} * Stim'_j + a_4 * Pers(I)_i + \epsilon_{i,j} \quad (6.4)$$

is estimated. $\sigma_{i,j}$ is the equivalence scale stated by respondent i corresponding to the stimulus vector $Stim'_j$. $Stim'_j$ comprises dummies for the second adult (DA_2) and for each child (DC_1, DC_2, DC_3), but for obvious reasons not the reference–income vector. The number of observations for Germany

(Cyprus) amounts to $167 * 7 = 1.169$ ($130 * 7 = 910$), seven observations per interviewee, one for each hypothetical household type (except for the reference household). $Dy_{adj} * Stim'$ denotes the products of the sample–restricting dummy (Dy_{adj}) and the vector $Stim'$, thus the interactions $Dy_{adj} * DA_2$, $Dy_{adj} * DC_1$, $Dy_{adj} * DC_2$, $Dy_{adj} * DC_3$. If the respective coefficients are significant, there exist differences in the assessments of equivalence scales comparing the overall sample and the respective sub–sample obtained from the Dy_{adj}–restriction. *Pers(I)* again comprises the personal variables *gender*, *siblings*, and *education*. We refrain from including the vector *Pers(II)* since its explanatory power proved to be negligible. Of course, we do not consider personal household incomes y_p either.

Table 6.21. Regressions with Sample Restricted by Adjusted Personal Income (V_I)

y_r	1.0	2.5	4.0	5.5	7.0
			Germany		
Dy_{adj}	0.014	0.112	-0.002	-0.093	-0.036
	(0.474)$^+$	(5.177)***	(-0.053)$^+$	(-4.017)***	(-0.980)$^+$
Dy_{adj}	0.061	0.041	-0.097	-0.053	-0.099
$*DA_2$	(2.833)***	(1.115)$^+$	(-4.027)***	(-1.451)$^+$	(-4.114)***
Dy_{adj}	0.016	0.048	0.000	0.000	-0.038
$*DC_1$	(0.632)$^+$	(0.811)$^+$	(-0.001)$^+$	(0.000)$^+$	(-1.272)$^+$
Dy_{adj}	0.026	0.045	0.001	-0.017	-0.041
$*DC_2$	(1.063)$^+$	(1.230)$^+$	(0.037)$^+$	(-0.466)$^+$	(-1.478)$^+$
Dy_{adj}	0.018	0.031	-0.003	-0.013	-0.033
$*DC_3$	(0.770)$^+$	(1.046)$^+$	(-0.130)$^+$	(-0.467)$^+$	(-1.304)$^+$
$\bar{R}^2$	0.557	0.462	0.401	0.370	0.353
F statistic	245.477	144.235	112.627	98.955	91.981
			Cyprus		
Dy_{adj}	-0.037	0.112	-0.009	-0.194	-0.134
	(-0.591)$^+$	(5.177)***	(-0.338)$^+$	(-6.765)***	(-4.683)***
Dy_{adj}	-0.030	0.041	0.008	-0.050	-0.023
$*DA_2$	(-1.038)$^+$	(1.115)$^+$	(0.258)$^+$	(-1.128)$^+$	(-0.522)$^+$
Dy_{adj}	-0.061	0.048	-0.018	-0.076	-0.075
$*DC_1$	(-1.452)$^+$	(0.811)$^+$	(-0.648)$^+$	(-1.021)$^+$	(-0.990)$^+$
Dy_{adj}	-0.106	0.045	-0.024	-0.078	-0.061
$*DC_2$	(-4.288)***	(1.230)$^+$	(-0.797)$^+$	(-1.761)*	(-1.393)$^+$
Dy_{adj}	-0.024	0.031	-0.025	-0.056	-0.037
$*DC_3$	(-1.471)$^+$	(1.046)$^+$	(-0.808)$^+$	(-1.596)$^+$	(-1.069)$^+$
$\bar{R}^2$	0.499	0.462	0.335	0.315	0.262
F statistic	114.048	144.235	92.460	60.811	54.777

Note: dependent variable: equivalence scale. Number of observations: Germany 1,169; Cyprus: 910.

Notation: t statistics in parentheses; *** significant at the 1% level; ** significant at the 5% level; * significant at the 10% level; $^+$ insignificant.

Table 6.21 states regression coefficients regarding those variables (Dy_{adj} and $Dy_{adj} * Stim'$) that measure differences between the restricted and the unrestricted sample. For Germany, significant coefficients for Dy_{adji} in column $y_r = 2.5$ and $y_r = 5.5$ indicate that subjects whose adjusted personal income corresponds to the respective level of reference income stated significantly different equivalence scales than the overall sample. Compared with the overall sample, equivalence scales of the sub–sample are higher for $y_r = 2.5$ and lower for $y_r = 5.5$. Also, there are significant differences regarding the assessment of the second adult. However, all differences are quantitatively minor. Moreover, there are no differences regarding children needs comparing the overall sample and the y_{adj}–restricted sub–sample. Thus, for Germany there is no serious indication that respondents are too rationally bounded to make general judgements about the needs of households with living standards differing from their own. This conclusion can be equally applied to Cyprus: here, equivalence scales for the sub–sample are higher for $y_r = 2.5$ and lower for $y_r = 5.5$ and $y_r = 7.0$. Additionally, a significant difference is also identified for the second child for $y_r = 1.0$ and for $y_r = 5.5$. However, all other stimulus coefficients are the same for both, the overall sample and the sub–sample.

The second restriction aims at discovering whether differences in the demographic composition of an interviewee's household and the hypothetical households are error–generating. To attach our interviewees to different sub–samples, we define a new dummy variable (DHC) that is set equal to 1.0 if the interviewee's household demography is the same as the demography of the hypothetical household, while else it is zero. Unfortunately, not all hypothetical household types find their correspondence in the samples. In Germany, no respondent was a single parent with two children. The Cypriot sample does not contain a single parent with two or more children. Thus, we have to exclude these hypothetical household types from our regression analysis. For each hypothetical household type we regress equivalence scales on the conditioning variables which comprise reference–income (y_r), DHC, the product of the sample–restricting dummy and reference income ($DHC * y_r$), and *Pers(I)*. Thus, the regression equation takes on the form

$$\sigma_i = c_0 + a_1 * y_r + a_2 * DHC + a_3 * DHC * y_r + a_4 * Pers(I)_i + \epsilon_i. \quad (6.5)$$

The number of observations for Germany (Cyprus) amounts to $167 * 5 = 835$ ($130 * 5 = 650$), i.e. five observations per interviewee, one for each reference income. Again, Table 6.22 states regression coefficients regarding only those variables (DHC and $DHC * y_r$) that measure differences between the restricted and the unrestricted sample. We comment on Germany first. For the hypothetical household types *AC*, *AA*, and *AACCC* the regression coefficients are insignificant, pointing out that there are no differences between the restricted and the unrestricted sample. Compared with the unrestricted sample, interviewees who are singles with three children state higher equivalence scales for their respective household type ($DHC > 0$), yet this effect vanishes/inverts with an increasing level of reference income. Moreover, there was only a single respondent who stated to live in an *ACCC* household (compare Table 6.20), such that this pattern should not be overrated. Finally, interviewees with a partner and one or two children state slightly lower equivalence scales ($DHC < 0$) for their own household type (*AAC*, *AACC*) compared with the unrestricted sample. In Cyprus, differences are identified for *AC* and *AAC*, but these coefficients are quantitatively small and significant at the 10% level only. For *ACC*, *AACC*, and *AACCC* responses do not depend on whether the respondents' household characteristics match with those of the hypothetical household type or not. Thus, even though there are some significant differences in the assessment of equivalence scales, we can conclude that in all cases differences are minor. Moreover, except for *ACCC* in Germany, insignificant coefficients for $DHC * y_r$ reveal that there are no differences in the assessment of income dependencies of equivalence scales comparing the restricted with the unrestricted sample.

Table 6.22. Regressions with Sample Restricted by Household Type (V_I)

	AC	ACC	ACCC	AA	AAC	AACC	AACCC
			Germany				
DHC	-0.028	—	0.147	-0.018	-0.087	-0.080	-0.018
	(-1.21)+	—	(2.94)***	(-0.59)+	(-3.30)***	(-3.19)***	(-0.70)+
DHC	-0.017	—	-0.102	-0.009	-0.042	-0.003	-0.007
$*y_r$	(-0.72)+	—	(-2.04)**	(-0.28)+	(-0.73)+	(-0.05)+	(-0.29)+
$\bar{R}^2$	0.553	—	0.542	0.210	0.421	0.474	0.471
F stat.	258.424	—	198.701	74.997	152.585	189.180	248.441
			Cyprus				
DHC	-0.062	0.027	—	—	0.058	0.040	-0.037
	(-1.96)*	(0.78)+	—	—	(1.78)*	(0.58)+	(-1.18)+
DHC	-0.032	0.024	—	—	0.050	-0.006	-0.018
$*y_r$	(-1.01)+	(0.63)+	—	—	(1.53)+	(-0.09)+	(-0.58)+
$\bar{R}^2$	0.355	0.218	—	—	0.330	0.365	0.377
F stat.	120.076	90.106	—	—	107.625	75.542	99.357

Note: dependent variable: equivalence scale; number of observations: Germany 835; Cyprus: 650.

Notation: each *A* denotes an adult; each *C* denotes a child; t statistics in parentheses; *** significant at the 1% level; ** significant at the 5% level; * significant at the 10% level; + insignificant.

Summarising the results of both restrictions, cross–country evidence shows that respondents are not too rationally bounded to make judgements about the needs of households even if these households differ from their own by demography or by living standard. Therefore, our conclusion is that neither the use of hypothetical reference incomes describing welfare levels of the reference household nor the use of hypothetical household types is error–generating. On the contrary, the empirical results indicate that the use of different reference incomes and hypothetical household types in our questionnaires is reliable.

7

Survey II

7.1 Motivation and Outline

This chapter presents the data of two more empirical surveys which have been conducted in Germany (2001) and Belgium (2002). In comparison with the V_I surveys outlined in the preceding chapter, a first difference arises with regard to the set of stimulus variables which is extended by a further variable, the *number of employees* in the household. The V_{II}–questionnaire describes the hypothetical households not only by the number of adults and children, but in addition by the employment status of the adults and distinguishing among full–time employed and unemployed adults. This additional dimension reflects a new focal point, the sensitivity of equivalence scales with regard to differences in household-production abilities arising from different household time–constraints. In the questionnaires we now ask our subjects questions such as:
"In your opinion, which family–income level can make a household with one employed adult and two children achieve the same welfare level as a household with one unemployed adult and two children and a monthly after–tax family income of DM 1,000?"
Secondly, we have chosen another survey medium. In V_I, we employed written questionnaires. Instead of this, V_{II} data has been collected in the world–wide web, in the "*internet*". The internet is a rather new and interesting survey medium which makes new demands on both, the researcher conducting the survey, and the interviewee dealing with the questionnaire.

The chapter is organised as follows: Section 7.2 deals with the internet as a new survey medium. Section 7.3 gives a detailed description of the V_{II} questionnaire. The sample breakdowns for Germany and Belgium are given in Section 7.4. In Section 7.5, we introduce the regression model, the notation, and the preparation of the data. The results of the two studies are presented in the following Sections 7.6–7.10. Section 7.6 reports the results of a number of regressions that quantify the general impacts of the stimulus variables and the personal characteristics on the equivalence scales stated. Section 7.7 deals with country–specific differences between equivalence scales for Germany and for Belgium. A descriptive analysis of the equivalence scales and individual weights derived follows in Sections 7.8, while Sections 7.9 and 7.10 again address to the issues of validity and reliability.

7.2 On Internet Surveys

Besides the traditional verbal or written survey methods, there exists a variety of computer based interviews, in particular *computer assisted telephone interviewing* (CATI) and *computer assisted personal interviewing* (compare *Nicholls* and *de Leeuw* 1996). Further technological innovations like fully digital telephone interviews (*touchtone data entry*) or *voice recognition* (*O'Connell et al.* 1996) mark a further step in the automation of interview techniques. The present state of this evolution are internet surveys. The internet has several features that make it an interesting alternative in comparison to other media. On the other hand, the realisation of internet surveys is far from being "standard" and raises a number of practical and methodological questions.

The programming of the questionnaire and its installation on a *server* are the first two hurdles to be taken. We will not address these technical issues here, since there are a multitude of software–hardware options. A description of these options would go beyond the scope of this thesis.

An important question is whether the internet allows to collect representative sample data. Data is representative if there is no systematic selection processes: respondents are determined via random selection. Internet surveys rarely conform with this request. Firstly, an unknown base–set and self selection of respondents cause substantial restrictions. Such self selection processes are of less importance in standard survey techniques where interviewers can directly address to potential respondents such that the researcher can (partially) steer the selection process (*Breiter* and *Batinic* 1997). Secondly, potential participants have to find the questionnaire sheet's internet address, which is normally subject to their independent search and chance. This hurdle is not easily solved since the survey's internet address is aimed to be distributed across the relevant target group *before* the participants themselves can call up the questionnaire sheet's internet address. There is a large range of possibilities to pass the information on the questionnaire's internet address to the target group of internet users: registration of the survey in an *internet–search engine*, *linking* the internet address of the survey with other web pages, installation of *advertising banners* on well–known web pages, and promoting the survey in *news groups*, *mailing lists*, or other media. The choice of the "spreading technique" crucially determines the sample structure and, thus, the collected data. If, for instance, a survey on the assessment of nuclear electricity was conducted and it was made public in an ecological *news group* only, then it is highly probable that the assessment of nuclear electricity in the sample will not coincide with the assessment in the entire population. For our two surveys in Germany and Belgium, we have chosen the following "spreading technique". For Germany, the questionnaire's internet address was boosted via three channels. Firstly, interested parties were directly led to the internet address via a link on the homepage of the *Institute of Public Economics* at the *Christian–Albrechts–University*, Kiel. Secondly, we supplied information about the survey using the internet pages of two internet agencies (*geizkragen.de* and *kostenlos.de*) which publish all kinds of online games and surveys. Thirdly, we sent emails to internet users whose surnames matched the ones of the faculty members *Schmidt* and *Schröder*. Both surnames are widespread in Germany. Our strategy was slightly different for Belgium since there do not exist Belgium internet agencies that are comparable to the ones mentioned above. Again, invitation emails were sent to internet users whose surnames were the same as those of faculty members (*Renthergem*, *Bosmans*, *de Coster* and *van Camp*). Moreover, we advertised the survey in the *E-Nieuwsbrief*, a virtual gratis magazine of the *Catholic University of Leuven* which has about 7,000 readers. Section 7.4 will identify none of the two samples as representative, yet the set of socio–demographic characteristics is rather comprehensive.

Another source of systematic distortions arises if opinions differ between the subjects who participated and those who refused participation. Yet, this is a general problem of surveys with voluntary participation. Nevertheless, one should be aware that, for example, the costs of private internet surfing might incite only highly interested subjects (*Hauptmanns* 1999) or subjects with free online access or subjects with a flat–rate to participate in the survey. Moreover, *Hauptmanns* (1999, Chapter 4.5) observes different surfing behaviour in different population subgroups like women and men. He suggests that variables affecting the surfing behaviour should be included in the questionnaire. We are confident that the set of personal variables collected in our questionnaires are sufficient to control for such biases.

A further crucial question is whether the data quality of internet surveys comes up to standard survey techniques. In general, the data quality of surveys depends on a variety of factors like the motivation and concentration of the respondents, errors in data input, missing values, distortions of the answers by *interview effects*, *scale effects*, *tendencies of agreement*, and the ordering and formulation of the survey questions. Internet surveys offer a variety of options to reduce the frequency of faulty or incomplete responses. In our surveys, *fade–ins* called the participants' attention to incomplete and inconsistent responses. A first fade–in prevented subjects from switching to the *general questionnaire* before completing the *personal questionnaire*. *Reips* (1997) and *Gräf* and *Heidingsfelder* (1999) observed a computer specific source of distortion: if answer categories are arranged as pop–up menus, the pre–selection of one category in these pop–up menus might make respondents choose the alternative. We avoided this source of error by using a blank field as pre–selected answer category. In the *general questionnaire* fade–ins appeared whenever the income amounts stated by our respondents decreased with increasing size of the hypothetical households, when the income stated for a given hypothetical household type was higher for a lower level of reference income compared with a higher level of reference income, and when entries did not consist of figures only. In all three cases the fade–ins asked the respondents to correct their answers.

Layout, format and structure of the questionnaire highly influence the data quality and the willingness to participate in the survey. Therefore, the questionnaire should be self–explanatory and it should convince the participant of the survey's importance (*Schnell et al.* 1995, *Gräf* and *Heidingsfelder* 1999). Besides an attractive design, financial rewards are a further possibility to reach the desired sample size. Though *Theobald* (1998) reports on positive experiences even with low value donations, the impacts of such rewards on the participation rate are still a topic of open debate.

What are the (dis)advantages of internet surveys compared to surveys in other media? As a first advantage, the physical absence of an interviewer guarantees that responses are unbiased by the interviewer or by misunderstandings in the communication between interviewer and respondent. Moreover, response errors resulting from mistakes or carelessness of the interviewer can be avoided. The situation's anonymity also diminishes the probability that subjects refuse to answer on delicate topics or choose answer categories only to conform with social norms (*Will* and *Daburger* 1996). Help menus providing additional information make check–backs superfluous and guarantee identical information on the side of the respondents. However, anonymity leaves the researcher out of control of the investigation situation. Especially, since one can neither observe the respondent's identity nor can one assess whether the respondent is influenced by other subjects. Moreover, misunderstandings might arise if the design of the questionnaire is affected by the participant's hard– and software or both. For example, testing our virtual questionnaire we found that computers with obsolete software could not read the Euro currency sign so that we had to replace it by the abbreviation *EUR*. Compared to other survey media, another important advantage of internet surveys is their fast and cheap realisation. Except for donations, costs are fixed and do not impose any constraints on the sample size. Of course, a large sample size does not guarantee that it is representative since self selection behaviour can not be ruled out and might bias the collected data. An advantage of standard survey media is that on principle a random sample can be defined. Yet, it is very likely that a significant fraction of subjects will refuse participation. If these absences were systematical, the self–selection problem would also arise for standard survey media. In sum, internet surveys, therefore, can be seen as a powerful alternative to standard survey methods, especially for testing hypotheses as well as for explorative and international studies.

7.3 Questionnaire Design

The V_{II} questionnaire structure is the same as for V_I, comprising an *introduction*, a *personal questionnaire*, and a *general questionnaire*. Exemplary for Germany, the original computer screens are given in Figures A7–A10 in the Appendix. The *introduction* was arranged on two computer screens. The translation of the first screen can be taken from Figure 7.1.

> This study deals with the problem that different household types have different needs. These needs (measured in income amounts) depend on the number of adults and children living in the household. Furthermore, household needs might vary with respect to the occupational status of the adults (unemployed or full–time employee) since the employment status might affect the ability of the adults to provide services in the household. Therefore, the following question arises: given the income of a specific household type (reference household), what is the income for another household type (differing with respect to the number of children and/or adults and/or employees) that allows this household to reach an identical living standard as the reference household?
>
> Since there is no correct objective answer, we would like to know your subjective attitude towards this question. Assume that each adult's age is between 35 and 55, the age of each child is between 7 and 11.

Figure 7.1. Introduction Page 1 (V_{II})

The similarity to V_I is obvious and adjustments have only been made to include the additional dimension, the adults' *employment status*. Pressing on a virtual "click button" leads the respondents to the second part of the introduction (Figure 7.2). Text and structure of V_I again were adjusted to include the additional stimulus variable. The *personal questionnaire* asked for several of the subjects' personal characteristics. Answer categories were given in pop–up menus, yet there was no answer category pre–specified to avoid pre–selection biases. Compared to V_I, the personal questionnaire comprised three further personal variables. First, we asked how much time the interviewees and their partner spend in the labour market. The interviewees could choose among the categories *not working*, *working irregularly*, *working* $\frac{1}{2}$ *a day*, *working* $\frac{1}{1}$ *day*. Moreover, we asked for the interviewees' age. Three answer categories, $<$ 20 *years*, *20–40 years*, and $>$ *40 years* were distinguished. The website was controlled by a routine program controlling device for completeness and consistency of the answers. If necessary, a fade–in asked for corrections.

Later on, three boxes will be presented to you that ask you to evaluate three different situations which only differ with respect to the after–tax income of the unoccupied and childless single–adult household.

Subsequently, we give you an example of such a box. Please take some time to familiarise yourself with the structure of the table.

	1 adult, unemployed	1 adult, full–time employed	2 adults, both un–employed	2 adults, 1 unempl., 1 full-time employed	2 adults, both full–time employed
0 children	after–tax income				
1 child					
2 children					
3 children					

As you see, we vary the number of children, the number of adults and the employment status of the adults. All these characteristics might affect the needs of the resulting household types. The number of children varies between 0 and 3. Moreover, we distinguish among households with 1 and with 2 adults. Each of these adults is either unemployed or is a full–time employee.

Later on, you will be asked to fill the gaps of these boxes, putting in the after–tax family income that you believe allows all household the same living standard as the one of the unemployed and childless single–adult household.

Figure 7.2. Introduction Page 2 (V_{II})

The translation of the *general questionnaire* is given in Figure 7.3 and asked the respondents to evaluate three different situations displayed by three separate tables providing 20 different hypothetical family types. Yet for only one household type, a childless and unemployed single adult, the reference household, the after–tax income per month was given. Gaps were left to the remaining 19 household types and interviewees were asked to assess the welfare-equalising after–tax family incomes for these 19 household types. This examination was conducted for three reference–income levels. For Germany, we distinguish reference incomes of DM 1,000, DM 4,000, and DM 7,000. Due to the introduction of the Euro, corresponding amounts in Belgium are given in Belgian Francs and in Euro. Compared to V_I, we skipped two level of reference income to limit time costs for our V_{II} interviewees which had to assess welfare-equalising incomes across 19 hypothetical household types instead of 7 in survey V_I.

Here you see the aforementioned three boxes that vary with respect to the net–income level of the childless single-adult. For each box, please state the net family–incomes of the other nineteen household types such that they reach the same living standard as the childless and unemployed single–adult.

	1 adult, unemployed	1 adult, full–time employed	2 adults, both un–employed	2 adults, 1 unempl., 1 full-time employed	2 adults, both full–time employed
0 children	**1⋆Minimal income**				
1 child					
2 children					
3 children					

	1 adult, unemployed	1 adult, full–time employed	2 adults, both un–employed	2 adults, 1 unempl., 1 full-time employed	2 adults, both full–time employed
0 children	**4⋆Minimal income**				
1 child					
2 children					
3 children					

	1 adult, unemployed	1 adult, full–time employed	2 adults, both un–employed	2 adults, 1 unempl., 1 full-time employed	2 adults, both full–time employed
0 children	**7⋆Minimal income**				
1 child					
2 children					
3 children					

Figure 7.3. General Questionnaire (V_{II})

7.4 Breakdown of the Samples

The German sample consists of 101 respondents which participated in the survey from March – June 2001. The data of 149 Belgian interviewees were collected in April 2002. In the text, the Belgian numbers will be given in parentheses.

7.4.1 Demographic Situation

Table 7.1 gives a breakdown of the two samples by *gender*, *partner*, number of *children* and *siblings*, and *age*.

Table 7.1. Breakdown by Gender, Partner, Number of Children, Number of Siblings, and Age (V_{II})

	All Respondents				Females				Males			
	N		%		*N*		%		*N*		%	
	G	B	G	B	G	B	G	B	G	B	G	B
Gender												
Female	29	69	0.287	0.463	29	69	1.000	1.000	0	0	0.000	0.000
Male	72	80	0.713	0.537	0	0	0.000	0.000	72	80	1.000	1.000
Partner												
Yes	49	109	0.485	0.732	12	53	0.414	0.768	37	56	0.514	0.700
No	52	40	0.515	0.268	17	16	0.586	0.232	35	24	0.486	0.300
Children												
None	81	80	0.802	0.537	26	37	0.897	0.536	55	43	0.764	0.538
One	14	17	0.139	0.114	1	9	0.034	0.130	13	8	0.181	0.100
Two	5	31	0.049	0.208	2	15	0.069	0.217	3	16	0.042	0.200
More than two	1	21	0.010	0.141	0	8	0.000	0.116	1	13	0.014	0.163
Siblings												
None	13	1	0.129	0.007	3	0	0.103	0.000	10	1	0.139	0.013
One	28	10	0.277	0.067	8	2	0.276	0.029	20	8	0.278	0.100
Two	39	69	0.386	0.463	13	32	0.448	0.464	26	37	0.361	0.463
More than two	21	69	0.208	0.463	5	35	0.172	0.507	16	34	0.222	0.425
Age												
$<$ 20 Years	0	1	0.000	0.007	0	1	0.000	0.014	0	0	0.000	0.000
20 - 40 Years	84	108	0.832	0.725	25	54	0.862	0.783	59	54	0.819	0.675
$>$ 40 Years	17	40	0.168	0.268	4	14	0.138	0.203	13	26	0.181	0.325

Notation: *N*: number of observations; G denotes Germany, B Belgium.

The gender distribution for Germany is distorted in favour of the male share: only 28.7 percent of the interviewees were females. This finding might be due to the user structure of the internet. A study of the *GfK* (2001) for Germany finds that only about 42% of internet users are female. For Belgium, we find almost equal fractions of male and female respondents. About 49% (73%) of our interviewees had a partner living in the household. In both countries, the majority of interviewees were childless, about 80% (54%). The low number of children is somewhat astonishing considering the age distribution of our samples: about 83% (73%) are in their twenties to forties. Possibly, this finding results from rather restricted time budgets of respondents with dependent children in the household which prevented their participation in our survey. The structure among internet users is similar: in Germany, 67% of internet users are in their twenties to forties (GfK, 2001). Finally, during their childhood the vast majority of German and Belgian respondents lived together with siblings.

7.4.2 Income, Education, and Employment

In the personal questionnaire we also asked what *level of education* was reached, the *occupational status*, the *occupational status of the partner* (if applicable), and the *monthly after–tax household income* (short: *personal income*, y_p). The respective country–specific breakdowns are given in Table 7.2.

As to the distribution across the education levels, we find a rather high fraction of highly educated respondents for both samples. This concentration is even more pronounced for Belgium: about 90% of the Belgian respondents completed a technical school or university. These responses mainly came from university members which reacted to the note in the university newsletter. This fraction of respondents also biases the Belgian sample's income distribution and its distribution across occupation categories.

For both countries, the distribution of occupational status reveals a difficulty in approaching unemployed subjects, social–security recipients as well as blue–collar workers, pensioners, and housewives/–men. Interviewees were predominantly white–collar workers, civil servants, pupils, students, or trainees. 28.8% (34.2%) of the interviewees' partners were unemployed. About 16% (0.0%) of the partners were working irregularly, about 22% (11%) had a half–time job, and 62% (54%) were full–time employees.

Data on *personal income* was arranged in five income brackets. The income distribution of the German sample is similar to the overall German income distribution. 23.8% of the participants stated a personal income below DM 1,750. About 30% of German subjects can be assigned to the second income bracket, 19.8% to the third, and 15.8% to the fourth. About 11% of German respondents disposed of more than DM 6,249. For Belgium, the sample is distorted in favour of high income recipients: more than 26% of the interviewees disposed of a personal income that exceeds EUR 3,195 (DM 6,249). This bias is mainly driven by the large fraction of white–collar workers with high incomes.

Table 7.2. Breakdown by Education, Occupation, Employment Status, and Household Income (V_{II})

	N		%	
	G	B	G	B
Education				
Unfinished education	1	0	0.010	0.000
Compl. element. school	1	1	0.010	0.007
Compl. second. school	3	10	0.030	0.067
Mittlere Reife	1	—	0.010	—
Compl. German second. school	42	—	0.416	—
Compl. techn. School or univ.	53	138	0.525	0.926
Occupational group				
Social–sec. rec. or unemployed	1	1	0.010	0.007
Blue–collar worker	1	3	0.010	0.020
White–collar worker	45	118	0.446	0.792
Civil servant	8	11	0.079	0.074
Pupil, student, trainee	39	12	0.386	0.081
Self–employed	5	2	0.050	0.013
Pensioner	1	2	0.010	0.013
Housewife, houseman	1	0	0.010	0.000
Own working time				
Not working	7	3	0.069	0.020
Working irregularly	25	6	0.248	0.040
Working $\frac{1}{2}$ day	21	3	0.208	0.020
Working $\frac{1}{1}$ day	48	137	0.475	0.919
Working time of partner				
Not working	15	51	0.288	0.342
Working irregularly	6	0	0.115	0.000
Working $\frac{1}{2}$ day	8	17	0.154	0.114
Working $\frac{1}{1}$ day	23	81	0.442	0.544
After–tax household–income				
$y_p < 1.75P$	24	4	0.238	0.027
$1.75P \leq y_p < 3.25P$	30	36	0.297	0.242
$3.25P \leq y_p < 4.75P$	20	28	0.198	0.188
$4.75P \leq y_p < 6.25P$	16	41	0.158	0.275
$y_p \geq 6.25P$	11	40	0.109	0.268

Notation: G denotes Germany; B denotes Belgium; y_p denotes personal household after–tax income per month; P denotes social assistance for a single adult for Germany.

7.4.3 Conclusion

Especially, the Belgian data are distorted by the "spreading technique" of the questionnaire. A substantial sample fraction comes from the Catholic University of Leuven which means that the Belgian sample contains a huge fraction of respondents with rather homogeneous characteristics regarding the variables *education*, *monthly after–tax income*, and *profession*. Yet, the data variation is still sufficient for measuring the impacts of personal characteristics on the collected equivalence scales. Moreover, the main bias refers to the distribution across the levels of education which did not turn out to be an important explanatory variable in the V_I surveys. Finally, respondents of both samples are well distributed across different family types and income brackets. This means that the tests on validity and reliability remain possible.

7.5 Regression Model, Notation, and Data Preparation

We run country–specific pooled regressions across 57 equivalence–scale values $\sigma_{i,j}$ for each respondent i taking the unemployed and childless single–adult as the reference household. Given a sample size of 101 German participants, the number of observations amounts to $57 * 101 = 5,757$. For Belgium, the corresponding number is $57 * 149 = 8,493$. The structure of the regression model is the same as for V_I and is given by

$$\sigma_{i,j} = c_0 + a_1 * Stim_j + a_2 * StimInt_j + a_3 * y_{pi} + a_4 * Pers(I)_i + a_5 * Pers(II)_i + \epsilon_{i,j}. \tag{7.1}$$

Again, $\sigma_{i,j}$ denotes the equivalence scale of respondent i corresponding to the vector of stimulus variables j. The regression intercept of the benchmark category, that is, a interviewee for whom all dummy variables are zero, is denoted c_0; $\epsilon_{i,j}$ is the disturbance term. The exogenous variables entered the regression stepwise, that is, an exogenous variable entered the regression if the significance level of its F–to–enter was less than 0.05 and it was removed if the significance level exceeded 0.10.

As explanatory variables we distinguish four different variable vectors plus a single variable, *personal income*. *Stim* is a vector of stimulus variables comprising the three levels of reference income $y_r = (1.0, 4.0, 7.0)$, the dummies for the second adult (DA_2) and for children (DC_i), and the number of employed adults $n_E = (0, 1, 2)$. *StimInt* is a vector of stimulus interactions which is the same as for V_I, yet extended by the product $(y_r * n_E)$ to reveal whether the impacts of employment on equivalence scales are sensitive to the level of y_r, and by $(n_C * n_E)$ which captures the dependence of children needs on the employment status of their adults. The personal variable *personal income* (y_p) is considered separately for the reasons outlined in Section 6.4. *Pers(I)* is a vector of personal characteristics that are not correlated with personal income, comprising *gender*, *siblings*, and *education*. *Pers(II)* are personal characteristics that reflect the occupational status of the respondent, or that are significantly correlated with *monthly after–tax household income* or both. Table 7.3 provides an overview of those personal variables that turned out to be correlated with personal income. Interestingly, the correlation coefficient is positive for the personal variable *children*. Possibly, this finding results from children–related tax deductions and transfers.

Table 7.3. Correlation Coefficients (V_{II})

	Germany	Belgium
Working time	0.359***	0.133+
Working time partner	0.636***	0.615***
Children	0.417***	0.599***
Partner	0.659***	0.671***
White–collar worker	0.266***	0.265***
Civil servant	0.331***	0.070+
Pupil, student, trainee	−0.550***	−0.350***
Self-employed	0.220**	−0.009+
Age	0.326***	0.348***

Note: Spearman's correlation coefficient for two–tailed test. Number of observations: Germany: 101; Belgium: 149.

Notation: *** rejection of equality at the 1% level; ** rejection of equality at the 5% level; + equality cannot be rejected.

The personal variables *personal income*, *gender*, *siblings*, *level of education*, *occupational status*, and *children* are re–coded as in V_I. The new variables *working time*, *working time of partner*, and *age* are re–coded as covariates that can be taken from Table 7.4.

Table 7.4. Re–coding Personal Characteristics (V_{II})

Variable	Type	Values
Working time	Covariate	0: not working
		1: working irregularly
		2: working $\frac{1}{2}$ day
		3: working $\frac{1}{1}$ day
Age	Covariate	0: $<$ 20 years
		1: 20–40 years
		2: $>$ 40 years

Differences in equivalence scales between Germany and Belgium will be quantified by running cross–country regressions using the pooled data of both countries. Since the regression equation and the notation are the same as for V_I, we refer to the model and explanations given in Section 6.6.

7.6 Country–specific Regression Analysis

The impacts of the stimulus variables and the personal data on equivalence scales are analysed by the set of country–specific pooled regressions (1)–(4) and (5)–(7) which are reported in Tables 7.5–7.8. In the text, results for Belgium are given in parentheses.

Table 7.5. Regressions 1-4 (V_{II}, Germany)

Equation	1	2	3	4[a]
c_0	1.845	1.986	1.731	0.933
	(52.607)	(50.539)	(35.091)	(8.818)
y_r	-0.462	-0.462	-0.462	-0.462
	(-46.982)	(-47.225)	(-47.591)	(-48.067)
DA_2	0.269	0.269	0.269	0.269
	(26.155)	(26.290)	(26.494)	(26.759)
DC_1	0.122	0.122	0.122	0.122
	(10.348)	(10.402)	(10.483)	(10.587)
DC_2	0.126	0.126	0.126	0.126
	(9.278)	(9.326)	(9.398)	(9.492)
DC_3	0.100	0.100	0.100	0.100
	(8.348)	(8.391)	(8.456)	(8.541)
n_E	0.258	0.258	0.258	0.258
	(25.114)	(25.244)	(25.440)	(25.694)
y_p	—	-0.076	-0.067	0.000
		(-7.781)	(-6.888)	(-0.001)
Gender	—	—	0.058	0.068
			(5.987)	(6.889)
Siblings	—	—	0.070	0.097
			(7.174)	(9.859)
Education	—	—	0.009	0.062
			(0.930)	(5.589)
$\bar{R}^2$	0.443	0.448	0.457	0.467
F statistic	762.447	668.945	538.572	389.549

Note: dependent variable: equivalence scale; pooled estimations. Number of observations: 5,757.
Notation: t statistics in parentheses; standardised coefficients.
[a] Partner: -0.019 (-1.812); working time partner: 0.020 (1.708); working time: 0.024 (1.859); Children: 0.020 (1.692); unemployed: 0.010 (1.012); blue–collar worker 0.004 (0.436); civil servant: -0.002 (-0.233); pupil, student, trainee: 0.130 (11.552); self–employed: -0.039 (-3.602); pensioner: 0.005 (0.468); houseman/–wife : -0.036 (-3.567); age 0.045 (3.659).

For both countries, regression (1) only includes the basic vector *Stim* as conditioning variables. The adjusted coefficient of determination ($\bar{R}^2$) reveals that this basic regression already fits the data quite well: about 44.3% (41.1%) of total variance is explained and an F statistic of 762.447 (1,042.006) strongly rejects the null hypothesis that the true slope coefficients are zero simultaneously.

Table 7.6. Regressions 1-4 (V_{II}, Belgium)

Equation	1	2	3	4a[a]	4b
c_0	1.615	1.615	0.818	1.094	1.074
	(64.393)	(64.393)	(6.047)	(7.876)	(7.669)
y_r	-0.364	-0.364	-0.364	-0.364	-0.364
	(-45.225)	(-45.225)	(-45.377)	(-46.179)	(45.991)
DA_2	0.252	0.252	0.252	0.252	0.252
	(29.507)	(29.507)	(29.607)	(30.130)	(30.007)
DC_1	0.134	0.134	0.134	0.134	0.134
	(13.533)	(13.533)	(13.578)	(13.818)	(13.762)
DC_2	0.131	0.131	0.131	0.131	0.131
	(11.519)	(11.519)	(11.558)	(11.762)	(11.714)
DC_3	0.114	0.114	0.114	0.114	0.114
	(11.532)	(11.532)	(11.571)	(11.775)	(11.727)
n_E	0.286	0.286	0.286	0.286	0.286
	(33.526)	(33.526)	(33.639)	(34.234)	(34.094)
y_p	—	-0.016	-0.019	0.112	—
		(-1.942)	(-2.318)	(8.551)	
Gender	—	—	0.017	-0.025	-0.026
			(2.145)	(-2.824)	(-2.942)
Siblings	—	—	0.020	0.020	0.023
			(2.484)	(2.524)	(2.866)
Education	—	—	0.059	0.026	0.039
			(7.266)	(3.016)	(4.583)
R^2	0.420	0.420	0.424	0.444	0.439
F statistic	1,079.628	1,079.628	658.588	397.052	438.387

Note: dependent variable: equivalence scale; pooled estimations. Number of observations: 8,493.

Notation: t statistics in parentheses; standardised coefficients.

[a] Partner: -0.134 (-9.735); working time partner: 0.053 (4.170); working time: -0.004 (-0.444); children: -0.031 (-2.991); unempl.: -0.028 (-3.461); blue–collar worker: 0.059 (6.973); civil servant:-0.008 (-1.013); pupil, student, trainee: 0.093 (10.707); self–employed-0.020 (-2.451); pensioner: 0.016 (1.891); age: -0.041 (-4.450)

[b] partner: -0.098 (-7.920); working time partner: 0.077 (6.197); working time: 0.010 (1.119); children: -0.010 (-0.970); unempl.: -0.029 (-3.648); blue–collar worker: 0.057 (6.799); civil servant:-0.003 (-0.414); pupil, student, trainee: 0.073 (8.701); self–employed: -0.032 (-3.930); pensioner: 0.009 (1.023); age: -0.024 (-2.836)

The explanatory power of the regression is rather similar to regression (1) for the V_I surveys. The impacts of the stimulus coefficients on equivalence scales are rather similar as well: first of all, equivalence scales stated again decrease with an increasing level of reference income. Moreover, equivalence scales increase with increasing number of adults and children, and this increase is stronger for an additional adult. Economies of scale are more pronounced compared to V_I: regression coefficients for V_{II} indicate economies of scale for both, adults *and* children. The new stimulus number of employed adults (n_E) has a significant impact on equivalence scales stated. For both countries, we observe a quantitatively rather similar and positive dependence of equivalence scales on n_E. The respective coefficient can be interpreted as a compensation subjects attribute to those households in which less time can be spent on household production activities or leisure.

Regression (2) differs from regression (1) by the inclusion of the personal variable *personal income*. Remember, that according to the *Leyden School* we should expect a positive and rather strong influence of this variable on the stated scale values. On the opposite, V_I data revealed a slightly negative dependence for Germany and no significant pattern for Cyprus. The results for V_{II} are comparable. For Germany the coefficient again is negative and quantitatively small. Thus, "rich" interviewees again stated slightly lower equivalence scales than "poor" interviewees. However, the inclusion of y_p only slightly alters the explanatory power of the regression and leaves all stimulus coefficients unchanged. For Belgium, y_p is insignificant.

Compared to regression (2), regression (3) also considers the vector *Pers(I)*. Its inclusion does not affect any of the stimulus coefficients of both samples and also hardly changes their t statistics. For both countries, the V_I result of higher equivalence scales for female respondents is confirmed. The same holds for respondents that spent their childhood with siblings. While the level of *education* does not matter for Germany, there exists a slightly positive correlation between the education level and equivalence scales for Belgium. However, the overall quantitative and qualitative effects of *Pers(I)* just for V_I are rather small and do not add much to the explanatory power of the regression.

In regression (4) for Germany and (4a) for Belgium, the set of explanatory variables is extended by the vector *Pers(II)*. The corresponding coefficients are small without exception for both countries and the inclusion of this vector only slightly increases the percentage of explained variance. Again, the stimulus effects remain very robust for the two countries: none of their coefficients changes and their t statistics keep their high significance levels. For Germany, y_p becomes insignificant while its impact is inverted for Belgium: now, there is a significantly positive effect of y_p on the equivalence scales stated. In order to avoid potential problems of collinearity between y_p and *Pers(II)* for Belgium,

y_p is excluded in regression (4b).

With respect to the personal characteristics, regressions (1)–(4) confirm the findings for V_I: respondents' personal characteristics only marginally affect the equivalence scales stated, and their explanatory power is minor. Once more, the influence of *all* stimulus coefficients turns out to be very robust. As for V_I, adult weights are higher than children weights and both are decreasing with an increasing level of reference income. Moreover, the V_{II} results suggest economies of scale for both, adults and children while the picture was somewhat ambiguous for V_I. Beyond that, the regressions give a preliminary picture of the monetary compensations the interviewees demanded for employed adults. For both samples, the corresponding coefficient indicates a very robust upward shift of equivalence scales with an increasing number of employed adults.

As for V_I, regressions (5) to (7) consider interactions of stimulus variables. Regression (5) corresponds to regression (3) but additionally comprises y_r^2 to capture non–linearities in the dependence of equivalence scales on this variable. That equivalence scales are decreasing with increasing level of reference income at a *decreasing* rate is confirmed by both V_{II} samples: the regression coefficient is negative for y_r, while the one for y_r^2 is positive. Regression (6) considers the stimulus interactions $y_r * DA_2$, $y_r * n_C$ and $y_r * n_E$. All interactions are negative and highly significant indicating decreasing weights with an increasing reference income for further adults, children, and employees. Regression (7) includes the interactions $(n_A * n_C)$ and $(\frac{n_E}{n_A} * n_C)$. The interaction $(n_A * n_C)$ quantifies the impact of the number of adults on children needs (the "single–adult bonus"). As for V_I, this variable turns out to be insignificant. The second interaction $(\frac{n_E}{n_A} * n_C)$ captures whether the needs of children depend on their parents employment status. It is likely that the respondents assess higher children needs if parents are employed compared to if they are not. Considering the *percentage* of employed adults $(\frac{n_E}{n_A})$ seems to be more reasonable than the alternative specification $n_E * n_C$ since, intuitively, it is more relevant for children needs that there is a parent who stays at home or not rather than the absolute number. For both samples, the corresponding regression coefficient indicates increasing children needs with an increasing percentage of employed parents.

In conclusion, regressions (5)–(7) confirm the V_I findings: again, equivalence scales and individual weights for adults and children decrease with an increasing reference income at a decreasing rate. Beyond this, the data indicate that the weights of additional employees are positive and depend negatively on reference income. Moreover, children weights increase significantly with the fraction of employed adults.

Table 7.7. Regressions 5-7 (V_{II}, Germany)

Equ.	5	6	7
c_0	2.155	0.913	1.731
	(40.04)	(20.38)	(35.09)
y_r	-1.228	—	-0.462
	(-27.46)		(-47.59)
DA_2	0.269	0.403	0.269
	(27.19)	(23.41)	(26.49)
DC_1	0.122	0.219	0.122
	(10.76)	(18.10)	(10.48)
DC_2	0.126	0.244	0.126
	(9.65)	(17.45)	(9.40)
DC_3	0.100	0.204	0.100
	(8.68)	(16.55)	(8.46)
n_E	0.258	0.426	0.258
	(26.11)	(23.86)	(25.44)
y_r^2	0.784	—	—
	(17.52)		
$y_r * DA_2$	—	-0.190	—
		(-9.48)	
$y_r * n_C$	—	-0.380	—
		(-22.34)	
$y_r * n_E$	—	-0.229	—
		(-11.27)	
$\frac{n_E}{n_A} * n_C$	—	—	0.025
			(1.38)
$n_A * n_C$	—	—	-0.013
			(-0.35)
y_p	-0.067	-0.067	-0.067
	(-7.07)	(-7.11)	(-6.89)
Gender	0.058	0.058	0.058
	(6.14)	(6.18)	(5.99)
Siblings	0.070	0.070	0.070
	(7.36)	(7.41)	(7.17)
Educ.	0.009	0.009	0.009
	(0.96)	(0.96)	(0.93)
R^2	0.484	0.490	0.457
F stat.	541.20	504.32	538.57

Note: dependent variable: equivalence scale; pooled estimations; umber of observations: 5,757.

Notation: t statistics in parentheses; standardised coefficients.

Table 7.8. Regressions 5-7 (V_{II}, Belgium)

Equ.	5	6	7
c_0	1.146	0.189	0.837
	(8.50)	(1.45)	(6.18)
y_r	-0.971	—	-0.364
	(-25.98)		(-45.39)
DA_2	0.252	0.331	0.260
	(30.06)	(22.57)	(28.63)
DC_1	0.134	0.218	0.125
	(13.79)	(21.21)	(12.07)
DC_2	0.131	0.229	0.121
	(11.74)	(19.28)	(10.15)
DC_3	0.114	0.198	0.105
	(11.75)	(19.29)	(10.16)
n_E	0.286	0.475	0.259
	(34.15)	(31.40)	(19.77)
y_r^2	0.620	—	—
	(16.60)		
$y_r * DA_2$	—	-0.111	—
		(-6.57)	
$y_r * n_C$	—	-0.312	—
		(-21.75)	
$y_r * n_E$	—	-0.255	—
		(-14.91)	
$\frac{n_E}{n_A} * n_C$	—	—	0.041
			(2.73)
$n_A * n_C$	—	—	0.008
			(0.28)
y_p	-0.019	-0.019	-0.019
	(-2.35)	(-2.40)	(-2.32)
Gender	0.017	0.017	0.017
	(2.18)	(2.22)	(2.15)
Siblings	0.020	0.020	0.020
	(2.52)	(2.57)	(2.49)
Educ.	0.059	0.059	0.059
	(7.38)	(7.51)	(7.27)
R^2	0.441	0.460	0.424
F stat.	642.20	636.63	599.83

Note: dependent variable: equivalence scale; pooled estimations; number of observations: 8,493.

Notation: t statistics in parentheses; standardised coefficients.

7.7 Cross–country Differences

In the country–specific regressions the main influences of the stimulus variables on equivalence scales turned out to be *qualitatively* similar across the two countries. Now, we will investigate whether the regression coefficients are quantitatively similarly as well. We therefore proceed by running the well–known cross–country regressions (3'), (5'), (6') and (7') of Section 6.6. The linear regression model is the same as in Section 6.6, thus given by

$$\sigma_{i,j} = c_0 + a_0 * CD + a_1 * Stim_j + a_2 * StimInt_j + a_3 * y_{pi} + a_4 * Pers(I)_i$$

$$+a_5 * CD * Stim_j + a_6 * CD * StimInt_j + a_7 * CD * y_{pi} + a_8 * CD * Pers(I)_i + \epsilon_{i,j}. \tag{7.2}$$

$\sigma_{i,j}$ is the equivalence scale stated by respondent i corresponding to the vector j of stimulus variables. CD denotes the dummy variable that distinguishes the two samples: CD takes a value of 1.0 for Belgium and 0.0 for Germany. The vectors *Stim*, *StimInt*, *Pers(I)*, and the variable y_p are defined correspondingly to Section 7.6.

Table 7.9 lists the regression coefficients that are related to those variables that quantify country–specific differences between Belgium and Germany. Regression (3') reveals that the downward influence of increasing reference income on equivalence scales – as indicated by the positive coefficient for $y_r * CD$ – is significantly stronger for Germany compared with Belgium. A possible reason for this observation is that average Belgian scales are slightly flatter (compare the negative coefficient for CD), and that the costs of the second adult are slightly lower for Belgium as well. While CD indicates flatter scales for Belgium, this result is almost compensated by the positive coefficient of *Education* $*$ *CD*. Remember, most Belgian respondents are highly educated. Taking this observation into account, there are almost no quantitative differences in the assessment of equivalence scales across the two countries. Moreover, children costs and compensations for employed household members are assessed equally across the two countries, a result that prevails in the further regressions.

In the country–specific regressions, equivalence scales decreased with an increasing reference income at a *decreasing* rate. Regression (5') indicates that both effects are qualitatively stronger for Germany. This finding is also reflected by weights for adult and children being less sensitive to the level of reference income in Belgium as indicated by the positive coefficients for $y_r * DA_2 * CD$, $y_r * n_C * CD$, and for $y_r * DA_2 * n_E$ in regression (6'). Finally, regression (7') shows that across the two countries there are no quantitative differences in the variation of children weights with the number and the occupational status of adults: $\frac{n_E}{n_A} * n_C * CD$ and $n_A * n_C * CD$ are insignificant.

Table 7.9. Cross–country Differences (V_{II})

Equation	3'	5'	6'	7'
CD	-0.369	-0.405	-0.341	-0.405
	(-9.128)	(-9.588)	(-8.315)	(-9.676)
$y_r * CD$	0.100	0.261	—	0.100
	(6.892)	(7.372)		(6.906)
$DA_2 * CD$	-0.023	-0.023	-0.084	-0.023
	(-1.725)	(-1.759)	(-4.357)	(-1.728)
$DC_1 * CD$	0.010	0.010	-0.027	0.010
	$(0.645)^+$	$(0.658)^+$	$(-1.436)^+$	$(0.646)^+$
$DC_2 * CD$	0.011	0.011	-0.025	0.011
	$(0.883)^+$	$(0.900)^+$	$(-1.568)^+$	$(0.884)^+$
$DC_3 * CD$	0.013	0.013	-0.009	0.013
	$(1.199)^+$	$(1.223)^+$	$(-0.661)^+$	$(1.201)^+$
$n_E * CD$	0.011	0.011	0.020	0.011
	$(0.925)^+$	$(0.943)^+$	$(1.635)^+$	$(0.927)^+$
$y_r^2 * CD$	—	-0.029	—	—
		(-2.405)		
$y_r * DA_2 * CD$	—	—	0.081	—
			(4.548)	
$y_r * n_C * CD$	—	—	0.037	—
			(2.862)	
$y_r * n_E * CD$	—	—	0.015	—
			$(1.125)^+$	
$\frac{n_E}{n_A} * n_C * CD$	—	—	—	0.022
				$(1.935)^+$
$n_A * n_C * CD$	—	—	—	0.006
				$(0.485)^+$
$y_p * CD$	-0.029	-0.029	0.065	0.065
	(-2.358)	(-2.405)	(3.619)	(3.517)
*Gender * CD*	-0.054	-0.054	-0.054	-0.054
	(-3.894)	(-3.972)	(-4.015)	(-3.902)
*Siblings * CD*	0.013	0.013	0.021	0.021
	$(0.241)^+$	$(0.245)^+$	$(0.413)^+$	$(0.401)^+$
*Education * CD*	0.277	0.277	0.283	0.283
	(7.227)	(7.372)	(7.594)	(7.381)
R^2	0.420	0.443	0.455	0.423
F statistic	862.101	810.338	660.864	696.460

Note: dependent variable: equivalence scale; pooled estimations; number of observations: 14,250; standardised coefficients.
Notation: t statistics in parentheses; $^+$ insignificant.

In conclusion, the cross–country regressions indicate that equivalence scales are assessed very similar by German and Belgian respondents. Section 7.8 will provide even more evidence on this issue. Equivalence scales being so similar is not a great surprise given that socio–economic conditions in the two countries are not too different. On the other hand, empirical applications of previous survey designs show inexplicably and unexpectedly high differences in equivalence scales across very similar countries.[1] Thus, the similarity of the German and Belgian data can be seen as a further mark that our method is in fact an improvement over other survey methodologies.

7.8 Descriptive Analysis

This section presents descriptive statistics of equivalence scales and individual weights for both samples. Moreover, we will scrutinise the regression outcomes of the previous two sections by a number of statistical tests.

Table 7.10. Descriptive Analysis of Equivalence Scales (V_{II}, Germany)

y_r	1.0			4.0			7.0		
	Median	Mean	St.d.	Median	Mean	St.d.	Median	Mean	St.d.
UC	1.550	1.598	0.217	1.150	1.255	0.284	1.114	1.145	0.130
UCC	2.000	2.127	0.418	1.275	1.438	0.437	1.200	1.276	0.269
UCCC	2.500	2.591	0.671	1.375	1.614	0.609	1.286	1.400	0.408
E	1.500	1.661	0.485	1.250	1.324	0.409	1.143	1.208	0.260
EC	2.000	2.253	0.512	1.400	1.576	0.556	1.286	1.383	0.340
ECC	2.500	2.741	0.636	1.550	1.772	0.682	1.414	1.523	0.436
ECCC	2.950	3.176	0.825	1.750	1.958	0.834	1.543	1.659	0.551
UU	1.900	2.004	0.558	1.500	1.588	0.415	1.429	1.464	0.322
UUC	2.400	2.553	0.580	1.725	1.803	0.600	1.500	1.614	0.420
UUCC	2.850	3.034	0.724	1.850	1.971	0.703	1.586	1.739	0.516
UUCCC	3.100	3.419	0.885	2.000	2.146	0.905	1.686	1.868	0.650
EU	2.200	2.500	0.877	1.750	1.817	0.576	1.486	1.647	0.462
EUC	2.700	3.028	0.909	1.900	2.048	0.769	1.643	1.809	0.554
EUCC	3.100	3.513	1.030	2.025	2.217	0.859	1.814	1.936	0.635
EUCCC	3.500	3.882	1.142	2.200	2.394	1.027	1.857	2.069	0.748
EE	2.500	3.048	1.173	2.000	2.109	0.843	1.714	1.907	0.714
EEC	3.400	3.692	1.209	2.125	2.387	1.067	1.857	2.095	0.812
EECC	3.800	4.224	1.318	2.275	2.580	1.159	2.014	2.242	0.894
EECCC	4.250	4.658	1.474	2.500	2.793	1.334	2.200	2.389	0.987

Notation: each C denotes a child; each E denotes an employed adult; each U denotes an unemployed adult; y_r denotes reference income.

The notation is similar to Section 6.7. Each C denotes a child, each E denotes an employed adult, and each U denotes an unemployed adult. In the text, Belgian data are given in parentheses. Table 7.10 (Table 7.11) report medians, means, and standard deviations of equivalence scales for Germany (Belgium) taking the unemployed and childless single adult (U) as the reference

[1] Compare the data provided in Section 2.3.

household. The results are perfectly in line with our regression results. Firstly, at a given level of reference income, average and median equivalence scales are increasing in the number of adults, children, and employees. Secondly, for each household type, equivalence scales are a decreasing function of reference income. This decrease is quantitatively substantial: the German (Belgian) data suggest that the equivalence–scale value of two employed adults with three children, for instance, drops from a value of 4.250 (4.200) for $y_r = 1.0$ to a value of 2.389 (2.487) for $y_r = 7.0$. Moreover, Belgian and German equivalence scales are quantitatively very similar. Table 7.12 gives the relative deviations of mean equivalence scales for Belgium compared with the German values. The average deviations is 3.7% only. However, a specific pattern can be observed: while Belgian equivalence scales are always flatter compared with the German values for $y_r = 1.0$, they are about the same for $y_r = 4.0$, and they are generally steeper for $y_r = 7.0$.

Table 7.11. Descriptive Analysis of Equivalence Scales (V_{II}, Belgium)

y_r	1.0			4.0			7.0		
	Median	Mean	St.d.	Median	Mean	St.d.	Median	Mean	St.d.
UC	1.500	1.517	0.231	1.200	1.233	0.182	1.114	1.171	0.178
UCC	1.900	1.940	0.410	1.375	1.431	0.334	1.200	1.326	0.333
UCCC	2.300	2.359	0.606	1.500	1.624	0.481	1.286	1.482	0.495
E	1.500	1.607	0.567	1.200	1.311	0.395	1.143	1.224	0.353
EC	2.000	2.180	0.605	1.450	1.579	0.478	1.286	1.427	0.442
ECC	2.500	2.655	0.745	1.600	1.801	0.593	1.371	1.597	0.560
ECCC	3.000	3.122	0.971	1.750	2.024	0.752	1.457	1.774	0.725
UU	1.700	1.758	0.336	1.500	1.548	0.313	1.429	1.459	0.336
UUC	2.200	2.268	0.488	1.700	1.771	0.435	1.571	1.627	0.448
UUCC	2.600	2.701	0.654	1.900	1.968	0.587	1.714	1.793	0.590
UUCCC	3.000	3.141	0.853	2.050	2.167	0.774	1.800	1.958	0.743
EU	2.000	2.280	0.762	1.700	1.784	0.543	1.514	1.661	0.566
EUC	2.600	2.786	0.825	1.885	2.021	0.644	1.714	1.830	0.648
EUCC	3.000	3.229	0.913	2.000	2.225	0.775	1.836	1.992	0.751
EUCCC	3.500	3.653	1.030	2.235	2.446	0.989	1.943	2.164	0.897
EE	2.400	2.900	1.299	1.950	2.089	0.886	1.686	1.908	0.859
EEC	3.100	3.530	1.385	2.163	2.372	0.961	1.886	2.110	0.950
EECC	3.700	4.030	1.535	2.350	2.600	1.065	2.029	2.296	1.058
EECCC	4.200	4.511	1.743	2.500	2.840	1.236	2.200	2.487	1.201

Notation: each C denotes a child; each E denotes an employed adult; each U denotes an unemployed adult; y_r denotes reference income.

In the regressions, we gave a first impression on the impacts of the stimulus variables, *number of adults*, *number of employees*, and *reference income*, on children weights. Table 7.13 gives the average weight and standard deviation for each child dependent on these three variables. The three mean values in row WC_2E, for instance, give the weights for the second child (C_2) for a single parent being a full–time employee (E), one weight for each reference–income level (y_r). The underlying absolute income amounts for each additional child can be taken from Table A2 in the Appendix.

Table 7.12. Cross–country Deviations in % (V_{II})

y_r	1.0	4.0	7.0
	Δ in %	Δ in %	Δ in %
UC	-5.4	-1.8	2.2
UCC	-9.6	-0.5	3.8
UCCC	-9.8	0.6	5.6
E	-3.4	-1.0	1.3
EC	-3.4	0.2	3.0
ECC	-3.2	1.6	4.6
ECCC	-1.7	3.3	6.5
UU	-1.4	-2.6	-0.3
UUC	-12.6	-1.8	0.8
UUCC	-12.3	-0.2	3.0
UUCCC	-8.8	1.0	4.6
EU	-9.6	-1.9	0.9
EUC	-8.7	-1.3	1.1
EUCC	-8.8	0.4	2.8
EUCCC	-6.3	2.1	4.4
EE	-5.1	-1.0	0.0
EEC	-4.6	-0.6	0.7
EECC	-4.8	0.8	2.3
EECCC	-3.3	1.7	3.9

Note: mean equivalence scales for Belgium relative to the mean equivalence scales for Germany. Notation: each C denotes a child; each E denotes an employed adult; each U denotes an unemployed adult; y_r denotes reference income; Δ denotes difference.

First of all, average weights for children decrease with increasing reference income. For example, in Germany (Belgium) the average weight for the first child in a two adult household with one employed adult (WC_1EU) drops from 0.533 (0.505) for the lowest level of reference income $y_r = 1.0$ to about a third of its value for $y_r = 7.0$, namely 0.162 (0.168). Secondly, in most cases children weights increase as the number/percentage of employees increases. In Germany, the weight of the first child in a two adult household at a reference income of $y_r = 4.0$, for example, increases from 0.212 if both adults are unemployed to 0.232 (0.275) if one (two) adult is (are) employed. The corresponding Belgian values are 0.223, 0.238, and 0.283. Thirdly, average weights for children seem to be slightly higher in single parent households compared with two–parent households given the same percentage of employed adults for both households. In a household without employees at a reference–income level of $y_r = 1.0$, for example, the weight for the first child is 0.602 (0.517) in a single–parent household for Germany (Belgium) and drops to a value of 0.551 (0.509) in a two–parent household. Finally, the data indicate economies of scale for children. For instance, given a single employed parent at $y_r = 1.0$, the inequality $WC_1E > WC_2E > WC_3E$ holds for Germany and Belgium.

Table 7.13. Children Weights (V_{II})

y_r	1.0		4.0		7.0	
	Mean	St.d.	Mean	St.d.	Mean	St.d.
			Germany			
WC_1U	0.602	0.217	0.246	0.284	0.136	0.130
WC_2U	0.534	0.246	0.176	0.184	0.125	0.141
WC_3U	0.458	0.312	0.180	0.189	0.118	0.142
WC_1E	0.589	0.253	0.251	0.262	0.182	0.180
WC_2E	0.486	0.254	0.199	0.176	0.137	0.137
WC_3E	0.432	0.270	0.190	0.193	0.144	0.144
WC_1UU	0.551	0.212	0.212	0.283	0.153	0.185
WC_2UU	0.477	0.271	0.166	0.138	0.132	0.128
WC_3UU	0.392	0.267	0.165	0.231	0.129	0.161
WC_1EU	0.533	0.217	0.232	0.355	0.162	0.212
WC_2EU	0.488	0.309	0.172	0.145	0.133	0.129
WC_3EU	0.371	0.251	0.183	0.220	0.131	0.153
WC_1EE	0.639	0.296	0.275	0.426	0.187	0.238
WC_2EE	0.527	0.322	0.188	0.148	0.149	0.143
WC_3EE	0.426	0.282	0.211	0.242	0.152	0.154
			Belgium			
WC_1U	0.517	0.231	0.233	0.182	0.171	0.178
WC_2U	0.424	0.213	0.198	0.165	0.155	0.163
WC_3U	0.419	0.224	0.193	0.163	0.156	0.169
WC_1E	0.573	0.351	0.269	0.279	0.203	0.216
WC_2E	0.476	0.296	0.222	0.192	0.170	0.176
WC_3E	0.467	0.333	0.223	0.204	0.178	0.205
WC_1UU	0.509	0.302	0.223	0.221	0.168	0.182
WC_2UU	0.434	0.271	0.197	0.205	0.166	0.194
WC_3UU	0.440	0.327	0.200	0.218	0.165	0.190
WC_1EU	0.505	0.317	0.238	0.272	0.168	0.183
WC_2EU	0.443	0.288	0.204	0.221	0.162	0.180
WC_3EU	0.424	0.262	0.221	0.285	0.172	0.210
WC_1EE	0.630	0.533	0.283	0.313	0.203	0.221
WC_2EE	0.500	0.411	0.228	0.226	0.186	0.206
WC_3EE	0.481	0.411	0.240	0.267	0.191	0.221

Notation: C_i denotes child i; each E denotes an employed adult; each U denotes an unemployed adult; W denotes weight; y_r denotes reference income.

Tests of significance regarding these observations will be provided below. We start with a test of economies of scale for children: keeping all other stimulus variables constant, we test whether the weight of the first child is different from the weight of the second (third) child and whether the respondents stated different weights for the second child compared with the third child. Results for Germany and Belgium are reported in Table 7.14. In Germany, the first child is always more expensive than the second and third child. This finding, in general, also holds for Belgium. The picture is less clear comparing the weights of the second and third child. In Germany, the second child is significantly more expensive than the third child only at the lowest level of reference income while else the difference is insignificant. For Belgium, the weights for the second and third child are assessed about the same. To sum it up, the test results are very similar and can be seen as a further confirmation of the V_I findings.

Table 7.14. Economies of Scale for Children (V_{II})

		Germany			Belgium		
	y_r	$C_1 - C_2$	$C_2 - C_3$	$C_1 - C_3$	$C_1 - C_2$	$C_2 - C_3$	$C_1 - C_3$
	1.0	-4.186***	-4.131***	-5.256***	-6.547***	-0.492+	-5.686***
U	4.0	-4.815***	-2.570***	-4.986***	-5.391***	-0.623+	-4.730***
	7.0	-3.837***	-2.594***	-4.698***	-3.801***	-0.395+	-2.936***
	1.0	-5.032***	-3.695***	-6.165***	-5.547***	-1.671*	-4.929***
E	4.0	-5.395***	-2.531**	-5.844***	-5.426***	-0.495+	-4.606***
	7.0	-5.376***	-1.575+	-5.489***	-4.976***	-0.859+	-3.904***
	1.0	-4.085***	-6.144***	-6.619***	-4.802***	-0.510+	-4.087***
UU	4.0	-5.316***	-2.412**	-5.677***	-4.451***	-0.599+	-3.560***
	7.0	-4.364***	-1.376+	-4.103***	-2.015**	-0.008+	-1.687*
	1.0	-3.507***	-6.147***	-7.022***	-4.216***	-1.161+	-3.716***
EU	4.0	-5.279***	-1.873+	-5.032***	-4.638***	-0.231+	-3.726***
	7.0	-4.290***	-0.816+	-3.773***	-2.561***	-0.043+	-1.925*
	1.0	-4.814***	-5.029***	-7.616***	-5.852***	-1.325+	-5.329***
EE	4.0	-5.479***	-1.043+	-5.023***	-5.989***	-0.377+	-4.477***
	7.0	-4.671***	-1.331+	-4.210***	-3.877***	-0.173+	-3.356***

Note: Z values of Wilcoxon tests; number of observations: Germany: 101; Belgium: 149.

Notation: *** rejection of equality at the 1% level; ** rejection of equality at the 5% level; * rejection of equality at the 10% level; + equality cannot be rejected; C_i denotes child i; each E denotes an employed adult; each U denotes an unemployed adult; W denotes weight; y_r denotes reference income.

We proceed with a Wilcoxon test comparing children weights varying the number of adults and/or employees. Results for Germany (Belgium) are given in Table 7.15 (Table 7.16). For example, the entry -4.799^{***} (-5.530^{***}) in row ($UU - EE$), $y_r = 7.0$ and column C_1 for Germany (Belgium) gives the

Z value of the Wilcoxon test comparing the weights for the first child (C_1) living with two unemployed adults (UU) with the respective weights if both parents are employed (EE) at the highest level of reference income.

Table 7.15. Impacts of Employment and the Number of Adults on Children Weights (V_{II}, Germany)

y_r		C_1	C_2	C_3
	U–E	-0.511^{+}	-1.700*	-2.386**
	U–UU	-3.269***	-3.285***	-4.057***
	U–EU	-4.470***	-3.401***	-4.714***
	U–EE	-1.262^{+}	-0.046^{+}	-2.092**
1.0	E–UU	-2.433**	-1.611^{+}	-3.404***
	E–EU	-2.871***	-1.705*	-3.965***
	E–EE	-2.145**	-1.183^{+}	-0.290^{+}
	UU–EU	-2.225**	-0.495^{+}	-1.370^{+}
	UU–EE	-4.109***	-3.617***	-3.630***
	EU–EE	-5.343***	-3.570***	-4.417***
	U–E	-2.159**	-2.226**	-1.342^{+}
	U–UU	-2.324**	-2.411**	-1.105^{+}
	U–EU	-0.432^{+}	-1.591^{+}	-0.532^{+}
	U–EE	-2.733***	-2.461**	-4.283***
4.0	E–UU	-4.423***	-4.005***	-2.795***
	E–EU	-3.108***	-3.172***	-1.550^{+}
	E–EE	-1.645^{+}	-0.412^{+}	-4.113***
	UU–EU	-2.102**	-0.449^{+}	-0.761^{+}
	UU–EE	-5.330***	-3.937***	-4.630***
	EU–EE	-5.038***	-4.019***	-5.003***
	U–E	-4.243***	-2.397**	-3.599***
	U–UU	-0.723^{+}	-1.382^{+}	-1.102^{+}
	U–EU	-0.799^{+}	-0.126^{+}	-2.795***
	U–EE	-4.440***	-2.594***	-4.041***
7.0	E–UU	-3.880***	-3.319***	-2.210**
	E–EU	-2.574***	-2.566***	-0.787^{+}
	E–EE	-1.261^{+}	-1.444^{+}	-2.520**
	UU–EU	-2.481**	-1.434^{+}	-2.103**
	UU–EE	-4.799***	-4.464***	-3.943***
	EU–EE	-4.544***	-4.241***	-3.301***

Note: Z values of Wilcoxon tests; number of observations: 101. Notation: *** rejection of equality at the 1% level; ** rejection of equality at the 5% level; * rejection of equality at the 10% level; $^{+}$ equality cannot be rejected; C_i denotes child i; each E denotes an employed adult; each U denotes an unemployed adult; W denotes weight; y_r denotes reference income.

The value is significant at the 1% level and indicates that the weight in a two–parent household where both parents are unemployed is *lower* than in a two–parent household where both parents are full–time employees.

Table 7.16. Impacts of Employment and the Number of Adults on Children Weights (V_{II}, Belgium)

y_r		C_1	C_2	C_3
	U–E	-3.523***	-3.863***	-3.194***
	U–UU	-1.091+	-0.149+	-0.371+
	U–EU	-0.822+	-0.916+	-0.194+
	U–EE	-4.071***	-3.770***	-2.901***
1.0	E–UU	-4.099***	-4.102***	-2.649***
	E–EU	-3.953***	-2.769***	-2.931***
	E–EE	-1.836*	-0.717+	-1.052+
	UU–EU	-0.529+	-1.150+	-0.836+
	UU–EE	-4.958***	-4.055***	-3.115***
	EU–EE	-5.028***	-3.436***	-3.700***
	U–E	-4.092***	-3.800***	-4.811***
	U–UU	-2.422**	-1.513+	-0.472+
	U–EU	-1.346+	-0.757+	-0.897+
	U–EE	-3.759***	-3.464***	-4.416***
4.0	E–UU	-5.063***	-4.572***	-5.010***
	E–EU	-4.643***	-3.996***	-3.448***
	E–EE	-0.786+	-0.474+	-0.729+
	UU–EU	-1.454+	-1.347+	-2.265**
	UU–EE	-5.612***	-4.819***	-5.109***
	EU–EE	-5.752***	-4.502***	-4.276***
	U–E	-5.721***	-4.009***	-3.863***
	U–UU	-1.079+	-0.175+	-1.148+
	U–EU	-0.385+	-0.667+	-0.989+
	U–EE	-4.398***	-4.420***	-5.048***
7.0	E–UU	-5.220***	-4.047***	-2.598***
	E–EU	-5.093***	-3.566***	-2.860***
	E–EE	-0.287+	-1.862*	-2.289**
	UU–EU	-1.075+	-0.130+	-0.162+
	UU–EE	-5.530***	-4.054***	-4.648***
	EU–EE	-5.250***	-5.084***	-5.014***

Note: Z values of Wilcoxon tests; number of observations: 149. Notation: *** rejection of equality at the 1% level; ** rejection of equality at the 5% level; * rejection of equality at the 10% level; + equality cannot be rejected; C_i denotes child i; each E denotes an employed adult; each U each denotes an unemployed adult; W denotes weight; y_r denotes reference income.

Holding all other variables constant, negative and significant Z values for the comparisons $(U-E)$, $(UU-EU)$, $(UU-EE)$, and for $(EU-EE)$ indicate that children weights are increasing in the number of employed adults. Respondents obviously had thought of additional costs arising, for instance, for external child care as soon as a parent would be employed and commence working in the labour market. Concerning the impacts of the number of adults on children weights, the picture is less clear. While significant and negative test statistics comparing the children weights for $(U-UU)$ and for $(E-EE)$ in Germany confirm the "single–parent bonus" observed for V_I, the Belgian data does not reveal any stable pattern.

Finally, mean weights for children are negatively related to the level of reference income as can be taken from Table 7.17 for Germany and from Table 7.18 for Belgium. Besides mean children weights and corresponding standard deviations, both tables contain test statistics of Wilcoxon tests comparing children weights for each two consecutive levels of reference income. All test statistics are significant at the 1% level which means that the null hypothesis of children weights being constant has to be rejected. On the opposite, negative Z values show that the weight for each child is a decreasing function of reference income.

Table 7.17. Dependence of Children Weights on y_r (V_{II}, Germany)

y_r	1.0		4.0			7.0		
	Mean	St.d.	Mean	St.d.	Z.	Mean	St.d.	Z
WC_1U	0.602	0.217	0.246	0.284	-6.964***	0.136	0.130	-7.520***
WC_2U	0.534	0.246	0.176	0.184	-7.881***	0.125	0.141	-6.565***
WC_3U	0.458	0.312	0.180	0.189	-7.192***	0.118	0.142	-6.552***
WC_1E	0.589	0.253	0.251	0.262	-7.851***	0.182	0.180	-7.438***
WC_2E	0.486	0.254	0.199	0.176	-7.877***	0.137	0.137	-6.231***
WC_3E	0.432	0.270	0.190	0.193	-7.143***	0.144	0.144	-5.963***
WC_1UU	0.551	0.212	0.212	0.283	-8.073***	0.153	0.185	-7.238***
WC_2UU	0.477	0.271	0.166	0.138	-8.172***	0.132	0.128	-5.872***
WC_3UU	0.392	0.267	0.165	0.231	-7.005***	0.129	0.161	-5.741***
WC_1EU	0.533	0.217	0.232	0.355	-7.958***	0.162	0.212	-6.087***
WC_2EU	0.488	0.309	0.172	0.145	-7.974***	0.133	0.129	-5.383***
WC_3EU	0.371	0.251	0.183	0.220	-6.820***	0.131	0.153	-5.128***
WC_1EE	0.639	0.296	0.275	0.426	-7.928***	0.187	0.238	-6.394***
WC_2EE	0.527	0.322	0.188	0.148	-7.973***	0.149	0.143	-5.700***
WC_3EE	0.426	0.282	0.211	0.242	-6.406***	0.152	0.154	-5.930***

Note: Z values of Wilcoxon tests; number of observations: 101.
Notation: *** rejection of equality at the 1% level; C_i denotes child i; each E denotes an employed adult; each U denotes an unemployed adult; W denotes weight; y_r denotes reference income.

Table 7.18. Dependence of Children Weights on y_r (V_{II}, Belgium)

y_r	1.0		4.0			7.0		
	Mean	St.d.	Mean	St.d.	Z	Mean	St.d.	Z
WC_1U	0.517	0.231	0.233	0.182	-9.524***	0.171	0.178	-7.760***
WC_2U	0.424	0.213	0.198	0.165	-9.509***	0.155	0.163	-7.543***
WC_3U	0.419	0.224	0.193	0.163	-9.501***	0.156	0.169	-7.302***
WC_1E	0.573	0.351	0.269	0.279	-9.316***	0.203	0.216	-7.213***
WC_2E	0.476	0.296	0.222	0.192	-9.594***	0.170	0.176	-7.485***
WC_3E	0.467	0.333	0.223	0.204	-8.764***	0.178	0.205	-7.047***
WC_1UU	0.509	0.302	0.223	0.221	-9.334***	0.168	0.182	-6.740***
WC_2UU	0.434	0.271	0.197	0.205	-9.289***	0.166	0.194	-6.821***
WC_3UU	0.440	0.327	0.200	0.218	-9.294***	0.165	0.190	-6.608***
WC_1EU	0.505	0.317	0.238	0.272	-9.058***	0.168	0.183	-7.182***
WC_2EU	0.443	0.288	0.204	0.221	-9.038***	0.162	0.180	-6.765***
WC_3EU	0.424	0.262	0.221	0.285	-8.833***	0.172	0.210	-7.267***
WC_1EE	0.630	0.533	0.283	0.313	-9.107***	0.203	0.221	-6.961***
WC_2EE	0.500	0.411	0.228	0.226	-9.088***	0.186	0.206	-7.059***
WC_3EE	0.481	0.411	0.240	0.267	-8.928***	0.191	0.221	-6.849***

Note: Z values of Wilcoxon tests; number of observations: 149.
Notation: *** rejection of equality at the 1% level; C_i denotes child i; each E denotes an employed adult; each U denotes an unemployed adult; W denotes weight; y_r denotes reference income.

In the following, we will comment on the influences of employment and of reference income on adult weights. In Table 7.19, we have listed average adult weights for all reference incomes taking a childless and unemployed single adult (U) as the reference household. For example, the entry 0.592 (0.548) in column three (five), row WUU $y_r = 4.0$ is the weight for a second unemployed adult at the second level of reference income for Germany (Belgium). Corresponding to the regression results, average weights for employed adults are higher compared to unemployed adults and both are a decreasing function of reference income. We conduct two different Wilcoxon tests to confirm these patterns.

Are the needs of adults dependent on their employment status? For each reference–income level separately, we investigate this issue by testing whether our respondents stated a positive compensation for a childless and employed single adult (E) compared to a childless unemployed adult (U), given by the Z value for ($U - E$), and whether they stated positive compensations whenever the employment status of a further adult changed from unemployed to employed, given by the Z values for ($UU - EU$) and for ($EU - EE$). The Wicoxon–test statistics are reported in Table 7.20. For both samples, all test statistics are negative and highly significant. This means that the needs of adults increase if their status changes from unemployed to employed. A second test investigates the impact of reference income on adult weights.

Given the number and employment status of the adults, a Wilcoxon test is conducted comparing the vector of weights for adults for any two consecutive levels of reference income. The results can be taken from Table 7.21. All test statistics are negative and highly significant indicating that adult weights are a decreasing function of reference income.

Table 7.19. Weights for Adults (V_{II})

		G		B	
	y_r	Mean	St.d.	Mean	St.d.
	1.0	0.661	0.485	0.607	0.567
WE	4.0	0.318	0.409	0.311	0.395
	7.0	0.207	0.260	0.224	0.353
	1.0	1.001	0.558	0.758	0.336
WUU	4.0	0.592	0.415	0.548	0.313
	7.0	0.456	0.322	0.459	0.336
	1.0	1.502	0.877	1.280	0.762
WEU	4.0	0.821	0.576	0.784	0.543
	7.0	0.649	0.462	0.661	0.566
	1.0	2.053	1.173	1.900	1.299
WEE	4.0	1.107	0.843	1.089	0.886
	7.0	0.912	0.714	0.908	0.859

Notation: G denotes Germany, B Belgium, each E an employed adult, each U an unemployed adult, W weight.

Table 7.20. Adult Weights and Employment (V_{II})

y_r		G	B
1.0		-8.610***	-9.794***
4.0	U-E	-7.987***	-9.600***
7.0		-7.974***	-9.374***
1.0		-6.312***	-3.718***
4.0	UU-EU	-7.496***	-9.162***
7.0		-7.441***	-9.029***
1.0		-8.598***	-9.714***
4.0	EU-EE	-7.929***	-9.600***
7.0		-7.969***	-9.397***

Note: Z values of Wilcoxon tests; number of observations: Germany: N = 101; Belgium: N = 149.
Notation: G denotes Germany, C Cyprus, W weight, each E an employed adult, each U an unemployed adult, *** rejection of equality at the 1% level.

Table 7.21. Income Dependence of Adult Weights (V_{II})

		G	B
WE	1.0 – 4.0	-6.254***	-7.805***
	4.0 – 7.0	-6.129***	-6.982***
WUU	1.0 – 4.0	-5.904***	-6.876***
	4.0 – 7.0	-5.533***	-5.593***
WEU	1.0 – 4.0	-6.581***	-8.359***
	4.0 – 7.0	-5.773***	-6.190***
WEE	1.0 – 4.0	-6.639***	-8.617***
	4.0 – 7.0	-5.288***	-6.714***

Note: Z values of Wilcoxon tests; number of observations: Germany: N = 101; Belgium: N = 149.
Notation: G denotes Germany, C Cyprus, W weight; each E an employed adult, each U an unemployed adult, *** rejection of equality at the 1% level.

7.9 Validity

How does (adjusted) personal income affect our interviewees' assessments of household needs? We conduct two tests of differences which are based on the decomposition of the two samples by the criteria level of *personal income* (y_p) and *adjusted personal income* (y_{adj}). Concerning the latter, only three instead of five different sub–samples can be distinguished since the general V_{II} questionnaire considered only three reference–income levels compared to five in V_I.

We comment on the impacts of personal income y_p first. For each country, the test is based on a decomposition of the sample according to the personal–income levels of the respondents. The personal–income distributions can be taken from Table 7.2. For each of the five personal–income groups separately, Table 7.22 (Table 7.23) report average equivalence scales for each hypothetical household type and for each reference–income level as stated for each of the five respective German (Belgian) sub–samples. Given a specific hypothetical household type and reference income level, the test procedure is the same as outlined in Section 6.8: a Mann–Whitney-U test is conducted comparing the responses of the y_p = 1.0 sub–sample with the responses for any y_p > 1.0 sub–sample.

Table 7.22. Impacts of Personal Income (V_{II}, Germany)

	y_p	1.0	2.0	3.0	4.0	5.0
y_r	N	24	30	20	16	11
	UC	1.606	1.613$^+$	1.610$^+$	1.616$^+$	1.491$^+$
	UCC	2.135	2.152$^+$	2.105$^+$	2.281$^+$	1.855$^+$
	UCCC	2.585	2.700$^+$	2.563$^+$	2.725$^+$	2.159$^+$
	E	1.598	1.778*	1.608$^+$	1.700$^+$	1.523$^+$
	EC	2.177	2.387**	2.258$^+$	2.294*	1.986$^+$
	ECC	2.715	2.857$^+$	2.725$^+$	2.822$^+$	2.395$^+$
	ECCC	3.156	3.290$^+$	3.153$^+$	3.350$^+$	2.695$^+$
	UU	2.031	2.070$^+$	2.015$^+$	2.022$^+$	1.718**
1.0	UUC	2.563	2.658$^+$	2.565$^+$	2.600$^+$	2.159**
	UUCC	3.048	3.187$^+$	3.025$^+$	3.109$^+$	2.491*
	UUCCC	3.458	3.552$^+$	3.383$^+$	3.597$^+$	2.777*
	EU	2.485	2.648$^+$	2.468$^+$	2.581$^+$	2.068$^+$
	EUC	3.021	3.175$^+$	2.993$^+$	3.191$^+$	2.468$^+$
	EUCC	3.467	3.707$^+$	3.468$^+$	3.759*	2.809$^+$
	EUCCC	3.865	4.082$^+$	3.778$^+$	4.209$^+$	3.086*
	EE	3.006	3.238$^+$	2.923$^+$	3.288$^+$	2.495$^+$
	EEC	3.635	3.895$^+$	3.588$^+$	4.009$^+$	2.986$^+$
	EECC	4.175	4.450$^+$	4.078$^+$	4.628$^+$	3.395$^+$
	EECCC	4.617	4.887$^+$	4.460$^+$	5.188$^+$	3.714*

Table continues

Continuation of Table 7.22

	y_p	1.0	2.0	3.0	4.0	5.0
y_r	N	24	30	20	16	11
	UC	1.297	1.288^{**}	1.184^{***}	1.281^{+}	1.164^{**}
	UCC	1.563	1.476^{**}	1.304^{***}	1.419^{+}	1.332^{**}
	UCCC	1.834	1.653^{***}	1.409^{***}	1.548^{*}	1.498^{**}
	E	1.373	1.291^{+}	1.284^{+}	1.381^{+}	1.294^{+}
	EC	1.682	1.572^{**}	1.452^{+}	1.622^{+}	1.518^{+}
	ECC	1.968	1.763^{**}	1.580^{**}	1.771^{+}	1.722^{+}
	ECCC	2.250	1.945^{***}	1.691^{***}	1.907^{+}	1.911^{+}
	UU	1.664	1.606^{+}	1.474^{*}	1.654^{+}	1.489^{+}
4.0	UUC	1.914	1.876^{+}	1.621^{**}	1.835^{+}	1.650^{+}
	UUCC	2.161	2.032^{+}	1.746^{**}	1.971^{+}	1.800^{+}
	UUCCC	2.407	2.222^{*}	1.853^{**}	2.101^{+}	1.964^{+}
	EU	1.985	1.784^{+}	1.676^{+}	1.895^{+}	1.683^{+}
	EUC	2.257	2.079^{*}	1.828^{**}	2.091^{+}	1.847^{*}
	EUCC	2.516	2.239^{**}	1.951^{**}	2.211^{+}	1.997^{*}
	EUCCC	2.775	2.418^{+}	2.073^{**}	2.344^{+}	2.156^{**}
	EE	2.332	2.095^{+}	1.896^{+}	2.148^{+}	1.991^{+}
	EEC	2.657	2.443^{**}	2.085^{**}	2.383^{+}	2.201^{*}
	EECC	2.931	2.623^{+}	2.231^{**}	2.538^{+}	2.395^{*}
	EECCC	3.280	2.824^{***}	2.369^{***}	2.677^{***}	2.590^{*}
	UC	1.196	1.138^{**}	1.116^{*}	1.129^{+}	1.127^{+}
	UCC	1.375	1.262^{**}	1.225^{*}	1.231^{*}	1.255^{+}
	UCCC	1.560	1.376^{**}	1.317^{*}	1.321^{**}	1.385^{+}
	E	1.238	1.173^{+}	1.184^{+}	1.246^{+}	1.223^{+}
	EC	1.460	1.346^{***}	1.322^{*}	1.409^{*}	1.388^{+}
	ECC	1.663	1.467^{***}	1.432^{**}	1.521^{**}	1.537^{+}
	ECCC	1.861	1.593^{***}	1.532^{**}	1.619^{**}	1.686^{+}
	UU	1.582	1.439^{+}	1.346^{**}	1.506^{+}	1.434^{+}
7.0	UUC	1.767	1.597^{+}	1.467^{**}	1.641^{+}	1.553^{+}
	UUCC	1.950	1.701^{+}	1.567^{**}	1.750^{+}	1.675^{+}
	UUCCC	2.135	1.830^{+}	1.661^{**}	1.846^{+}	1.803^{+}
	EU	1.778	1.610^{+}	1.520^{*}	1.737^{+}	1.568^{+}
	EUC	1.983	1.777^{*}	1.643^{**}	1.876^{+}	1.718^{+}
	EUCC	2.171	1.879^{**}	1.748^{**}	1.988^{+}	1.844^{+}
	EUCCC	2.361	2.008^{**}	1.849^{**}	2.088^{+}	1.975^{+}
	EE	2.037	1.870^{+}	1.713^{*}	1.984^{+}	1.969^{+}
	EEC	2.266	2.071^{*}	1.855^{**}	2.154^{+}	2.142^{+}
	EECC	2.473	2.193^{*}	1.981^{**}	2.279^{+}	2.288^{+}
	EECCC	2.686	2.335^{*}	2.091^{**}	2.381^{*}	2.439^{+}

Note: average equivalence scales and significance levels of Mann–Whitney–U tests.

Notation: each E denotes an employed adult; each U denotes an unemployed adult; ** significance at the 5% level; ** significance at the 10% level; $^{+}$ insignificant.

Table 7.23. Impacts of Personal Income (V_{II}, Belgium)

y_r	y_p / N	1.0 / 4	2.0 / 36	3.0 / 28	4.0 / 41	5.0 / 40
	UC	1.450	1.528$^+$	1.486$^+$	1.529$^+$	1.522$^+$
	UCC	1.800	1.972$^+$	1.910$^+$	1.944$^+$	1.943$^+$
	UCCC	2.088	2.412$^+$	2.344$^+$	2.355$^+$	2.354$^+$
	E	1.275	1.556$^+$	1.700$^+$	1.498$^+$	1.732*
	EC	1.813	2.099$^+$	2.241$^+$	2.138$^+$	2.289$^+$
	ECC	2.225	2.572$^+$	2.702$^+$	2.644$^+$	2.753$^+$
	ECCC	2.513	3.027$^+$	3.172**	3.144*	3.211$^+$
	UU	1.675	1.727$^+$	1.764$^+$	1.751$^+$	1.798$^+$
1.0	UUC	2.100	2.263$^+$	2.213$^+$	2.275$^+$	2.319$^+$
	UUCC	2.425	2.725$^+$	2.648$^+$	2.707$^+$	2.739$^+$
	UUCCC	2.713	3.148$^+$	3.094$^+$	3.118$^+$	3.235$^+$
	EU	1.850	2.221*	2.398$^+$	2.142$^+$	2.437$^+$
	EUC	2.275	2.742$^+$	2.878$^+$	2.666$^+$	2.934$^+$
	EUCC	2.600	3.191$^+$	3.336*	3.129*	3.352$^+$
	EUCCC	2.888	3.622$^+$	3.797*	3.528*	3.784$^+$
	EE	2.100	2.735*	3.268$^+$	2.615$^+$	3.162*
	EEC	2.588	3.301*	3.823$^+$	3.405$^+$	3.753*
	EECC	3.050	3.749$^+$	4.287$^+$	3.997$^+$	4.234$^+$
	EECCC	3.413	4.186$^+$	4.772$^+$	4.535*	4.705**
	UC	1.200	1.289$^+$	1.177$^+$	1.249$^+$	1.208$^+$
	UCC	1.444	1.528$^+$	1.340$^+$	1.444$^+$	1.392$^+$
	UCCC	1.688	1.756$^+$	1.492$^+$	1.636$^+$	1.580$^+$
	E	1.201	1.342$^+$	1.253$^+$	1.272$^+$	1.373$^+$
	EC	1.435	1.667$^+$	1.454$^+$	1.599$^+$	1.582$^+$
	ECC	1.757	1.932$^+$	1.613$^+$	1.841$^+$	1.778$^+$
	ECCC	2.066	2.196$^+$	1.764$^+$	2.077$^+$	1.994$^+$
	UU	1.463	1.634$^+$	1.419$^+$	1.563$^+$	1.554$^+$
4.0	UUC	1.656	1.923$^+$	1.593$^+$	1.799$^+$	1.740$^+$
	UUCC	1.963	2.157$^+$	1.743$^+$	2.016$^+$	1.906$^+$
	UUCCC	2.253	2.401$^+$	1.884$^+$	2.228$^+$	2.084$^+$
	EU	1.551	1.932$^+$	1.626$^+$	1.778$^+$	1.789$^+$
	EUC	1.844	2.218$^+$	1.795$^+$	2.056$^+$	1.986$^+$
	EUCC	2.226	2.452$^+$	1.946$^+$	2.287$^+$	2.153$^+$
	EUCCC	2.591	2.698$^+$	2.091$^+$	2.515$^+$	2.382$^+$
	EE	1.676	2.291$^+$	1.916$^+$	2.033$^+$	2.125$^+$
	EEC	2.142	2.613$^+$	2.113$^+$	2.374$^+$	2.357$^+$
	EECC	2.570	2.857$^+$	2.291$^+$	2.642$^+$	2.545$^+$
	EECCC	3.092	3.121$^+$	2.453$^+$	2.901$^+$	2.772$^+$

Table continues

Continuation of Table 7.23

y_r	y_p / N	1.0 / 24	2.0 / 30	3.0 / 20	4.0 / 16	5.0 / 11
	UC	1.254	1.240^+	1.108^+	1.170^+	1.146^+
	UCC	1.457	1.449^+	1.214^+	1.319^+	1.289^+
	UCCC	1.718	1.658^+	1.325^+	1.463^+	1.431^+
	E	1.200	1.304^+	1.175^+	1.201^+	1.211^+
	EC	1.538	1.570^+	1.303^+	1.418^+	1.382^+
	ECC	1.793	1.790^+	1.425^+	1.595^+	1.525^+
	ECCC	2.038	2.014^+	1.545^+	1.765^+	1.702^+
	UU	1.589	1.600^+	1.361^+	1.440^+	1.406^+
7.0	UUC	1.932	1.831^+	1.470^+	1.600^+	1.552^+
	UUCC	2.129	2.030^+	1.581^+	1.779^+	1.709^+
	UUCCC	2.389	2.242^+	1.693^+	1.954^+	1.848^+
	EU	1.750	1.859^+	1.517^+	1.647^+	1.590^+
	EUC	2.104	2.074^+	1.630^+	1.807^+	1.745^+
	EUCC	2.300	2.283^+	1.741^+	1.987^+	1.881^+
	EUCCC	2.554	2.491^+	1.852^+	2.159^+	2.055^+
	EE	2.051	2.174^+	1.716^+	1.871^+	1.825^+
	EEC	2.510	2.430^+	1.850^+	2.060^+	2.017^+
	EECC	2.822	2.665^+	1.962^+	2.270^+	2.171^+
	EECCC	3.202	2.895^+	2.086^+	2.472^+	2.345^+

Note: average equivalence scales and significance levels of Mann–Whitney–U tests.
Notation: each E denotes an employed adult; each U denotes an unemployed adult; ** significance at the 5% level; ** significance at the 10% level; $^+$ insignificant.

For both countries, differences in equivalence scales across the five different personal–income groups are insignificant in the majority of cases, namely in about 64% (Belgium: 94%). In cases of significance, the quantitative differences in equivalence scales in most cases are minor such that our conclusion is the same as for V_I: the personal–income levels of our respondents hardly matter for their assessments of household needs.

Does adjusted personal income (y_{adj}), which we interpret as a measure of household welfare, affect the interviewees' assessments of household needs? The analysis is based on samples decomposed according to the criterion adjusted personal–income. The adjusted personal–income distributions for Germany (Belgium) can be taken from row three (N) of Table 7.24 (Table 7.25). For each of the three adjusted personal–income levels, these tables report average equivalence scales for each hypothetical household type and for each reference–income level. A Mann–Whitney–U test is conducted comparing the responses of the $y_{adj} = 1.0$ sub–sample with the responses of the other two $y_{adj} > 1.0$ sub–samples. A $^+$ indicates that the hypothesis of different scales across the respective sub–samples has to be rejected while asterisks indicate significant differences.

Table 7.24. Impacts of Adjusted Personal Income (V_{II}, Germany)

y_r	1.0			4.0			7.0		
y_{adj}	1.0	4.0	7.0	1.0	4.0	7.0	1.0	4.0	7.0
N	76	20	5	76	20	5	76	20	5
UC	1.60	1.61^{+}	1.52^{+}	1.21	1.16^{+}	1.17^{+}	1.16	1.12^{+}	1.10^{+}
UCC	2.13	2.17^{+}	1.96^{+}	1.48	1.29*	1.36^{+}	1.30	1.22^{+}	1.21^{+}
UCCC	2.58	2.70^{+}	2.33^{+}	1.67	1.42*	1.54^{+}	1.43	1.31^{+}	1.32^{+}
E	1.69	1.52^{+}	1.73^{+}	1.38	1.14***	1.15^{+}	1.24	1.10***	1.09^{+}
EC	2.28	2.19^{+}	2.11^{+}	1.65	1.36**	1.31*	1.43	1.26**	1.17**
ECC	2.76	2.73^{+}	2.55^{+}	1.86	1.51**	1.52^{+}	1.58	1.36**	1.27*
ECCC	3.18	3.24^{+}	2.87^{+}	2.06	1.64**	1.69^{+}	1.73	1.47**	1.39^{+}
UU	2.02	1.96^{+}	2.03^{+}	1.65	1.44**	1.25***	1.51	1.35**	1.17**
UUC	2.56	2.55^{+}	2.51^{+}	1.88	1.60*	1.41***	1.67	1.47**	1.25***
UUCC	3.03	3.07^{+}	2.89^{+}	2.06	1.74*	1.57**	1.81	1.58*	1.34**
UUCCC	3.40	3.53^{+}	3.25^{+}	2.24	1.87^{+}	1.76^{+}	1.94	1.68*	1.46**
EU	2.55	2.32^{+}	2.51^{+}	1.93	1.53***	1.29***	1.73	1.43***	1.22***
EUC	3.07	2.89^{+}	2.91^{+}	2.18	1.70***	1.46***	1.90	1.57***	1.30***
EUCC	3.55	3.45^{+}	3.29^{+}	2.36	1.84***	1.62**	2.04	1.68**	1.39**
EUCCC	3.91	3.86^{+}	3.57^{+}	2.54	1.97***	1.80**	2.18	1.79**	1.51**
EE	3.12	2.82^{+}	2.91^{+}	2.28	1.65***	1.35***	2.03	1.60***	1.28***
EEC	3.75	3.54^{+}	3.37^{+}	2.58	1.85***	1.55***	2.23	1.75***	1.37***
EECC	4.27	4.19^{+}	3.73^{+}	2.79	2.01***	1.75***	2.39	1.87***	1.48***
EECCC	4.69	4.69^{+}	4.09^{+}	3.02	2.15***	1.94***	2.55	1.97***	1.60***

Note: average equivalence scales and significance levels of Mann–Whitney–U tests.

Notation: each C denotes a child; each E denotes an employed adult; each U denotes an unemployed adult; *** significance at the 1% level; ** significance at the 5% level; * significance at the 10% level; $^{+}$ insignificant.

For $y_r = 1.0$, there is general consensus about equivalence scales across the sample sub–groups in Germany: none of the test statistics is significant. However, there are robust differences for higher reference incomes where respondents with a high adjusted personal income state significantly lower equivalence scales relative to respondents with a low level of y_{adj}. However, there are only few observations for the highest level of adjusted personal income for Germany. For Belgium, the $y_{adj} = 4.0$ sub–sample in general states lower equivalence scales compared to the $y_{adj} = 1.0$ sub–sample, and this gap extends with an increasing level of reference income. As argued in Section 6.8, this finding should not be over–emphasised since the transformation of y_p to y_{adj} at least partly drives this result. Since only a single Belgian respondent is assigned to $y_{adj} = 7.0$ we refrain from testing her/his responses against the other two sub–samples.

Table 7.25. Impacts of Adjusted Personal Income (V_{II}, Belgium)

y_r	1.0		4.0		7.0	
y_{adj}	1.0	4.0	1.0	4.0	1.0	4.0
N	97	51	97	51	97	51
UC	1.53	1.49$^+$	1.26	1.19$^+$	1.19	1.13$^+$
UCC	1.97	1.88$^+$	1.49	1.33*	1.37	1.24$^+$
UCC	2.41	2.26$^+$	1.70	1.48**	1.55	1.36$^+$
E	1.67	1.49**	1.36	1.22**	1.27	1.14***
EC	2.26	2.03**	1.67	1.42***	1.51	1.28***
ECC	2.75	2.47**	1.92	1.58***	1.70	1.41***
ECCC	3.25	2.89**	2.18	1.74***	1.91	1.53***
UU	1.78	1.70**	1.60	1.47***	1.52	1.35***
UUC	2.30	2.21*	1.85	1.63***	1.72	1.47***
UUCC	2.76	2.59$^+$	2.08	1.77***	1.91	1.59***
UUCCC	3.23	2.98*	2.31	1.92***	2.10	1.71**
EU	2.36	2.14**	1.88	1.61***	1.77	1.46***
EUC	2.88	2.61**	2.16	1.78***	1.97	1.58***
EUCC	3.34	3.02**	2.40	1.92***	2.15	1.70***
EUCCC	3.80	3.39**	2.66	2.07***	2.35	1.83***
EE	3.09	2.54***	2.26	1.77***	2.09	1.58***
EEC	3.75	3.11***	2.60	1.97***	2.33	1.72***
EECC	4.28	3.56***	2.87	2.12***	2.54	1.85***
EECCC	4.80	3.97***	3.15	2.28***	2.76	1.99***

Note: average equivalence scales and significance levels of Mann–Whitney–U tests.
Notation: each C denotes a child; each E denotes an employed adult; each U denotes an unemployed adult; *** significance at the 1% level; ** significance at the 5% level; * significance at the 10% level; $^+$ insignificant.

7.10 Reliability

Are respondents able to assess "correctly" the needs of households that differ from their own by their living standard or by their demographic composition? We interpret equivalence scales as the "correct" ones if they are stated by respondents for whom either living standard or demographic composition is the same as for the hypothetical household. Reliability of our method requires that our respondents' are not too rationally bounded to make general judgements about the needs of households even if these households are significantly different from their own. As outlined in Section 6.9, we analyse such effects by restricting the German and Belgium sample in two different ways: the first restriction takes into account the equivalence scales stated for all household types where the reference income is closest to the respondent's *adjusted* personal income (y_{adj}). This conversion rests upon the assumption that the living standard is about the same in each household of the resulting sub–sample. The second restriction considers only those equivalence scales a respondent stated for a hypothetical household type that coincides with or is closest to her/his own. For each restriction, a regression is run, and by evaluating the extent to which regression coefficients of the sub–sample statistically differ from the regression coefficients of the overall sample, we can obtain a better impression of the problematic, on whether the use of hypothetical households is error–generating or not.

As to the first restriction, we run a regression for each reference income separately which takes the form

$$\sigma_{i,j} = c_0 + a_1 * Stim'_j + a_2 * Dy_{adji} + a_3 * Dy_{adji} * Stim'_j + a_4 * Pers(I)_i + \epsilon_{i,j}. \quad (7.3)$$

$\sigma_{i,j}$ is the equivalence scale stated by respondent i corresponding to a vector of stimulus variables *Stim'* taking the values j. *Stim'* comprises a dummy for the second adult (DA_2) and a dummy for each child (DC_1, DC_2, DC_3) but, for obvious reasons, not the stimulus *reference income*. Dy_{adj} is the sample–restricting dummy which is 1.0 if the respondent is assigned to the respective level of adjusted personal income, while it is zero in all other cases. $Dy_{adj} * Stim'$ denotes the products of the sample–restricting dummy and the vector *Stim'*, thus the interactions $Dy_{adj} * DA_2$, $Dy_{adj} * DC_1$, $Dy_{adj} * DC_2$, and $Dy_{adj} * DC_3$. If the respective coefficients were positive, they will indicate differences in the assessments of equivalence scales between the overall sample and the sub–samples obtained from the Dy_{adj}–restriction. *Pers(I)* consists of the personal variables *gender*, *siblings*, and *education*. We refrain from including the vector *Pers(II)* since its explanatory power is negligible. Of course, we did not consider personal income (y_p) either.

Table 7.26 states regression coefficients regarding those variables (Dy_{adj} and $Dy_{adj} * Stim'$) that measure differences between the restricted and the unrestricted sample. Insignificant coefficients for D_{adj} for both countries indicate that the assessments of household needs between the Dy_{adj}–restricted sample and the unrestricted sample are about the same. There is, however, some disagreement regarding the impact of employment on household needs, yet this difference is quantitatively small for both countries. Thus, we can conclude that there is no serious indication that our respondents' rationality is too restricted for making general judgements about the needs of households whose living standard is different from their own. On the contrary, even if interviewees are characterised by rather different living standards, this difference does not affect their evaluations of household needs.

Table 7.26. Regressions with Sample Restricted by Adjusted Personal Income (V_{II})

	Germany			Belgium	
y_{adj}	1.0	4.0	7.0	1.0	4.0
Dy_{adj}	0.000	-0.026	0.005	-0.006	0.005
	(0.007)$^{+}$	(-0.518)$^{+}$	(0.146)$^{+}$	(-0.181)$^{+}$	(0.139)$^{+}$
Dy_{adj}	0.010	-0.050	-0.082	0.030	-0.073
$*DA_2$	(0.286)$^{+}$	(-1.593)$^{+}$	(-3.013)***	(1.053)$^{+}$	(-2.932)***
Dy_{adj}	-0.010	-0.065	-0.012	0.047	-0.034
$*C_1$	(-0.359)$^{+}$	(-2.506)**	(-0.436)$^{+}$	(2.216)**	(-1.040)$^{+}$
Dy_{adj}	-0.020	-0.028	-0.013	0.042	-0.087
$*C_2$	(-0.646)$^{+}$	(-0.795)$^{+}$	(-0.541)$^{+}$	(1.246)$^{+}$	(-4.115)***
Dy_{adj}	-0.023	-0.022	-0.009	0.034	-0.033
$*C_3$	(-0.696)$^{+}$	(-0.871)$^{+}$	(-0.424)$^{+}$	(1.246)$^{+}$	(-1.276)$^{+}$
Dy_{adj}	0.066	-0.128	-0.066	0.157	-0.142
$*n_E$	(2.563)***	(-4.867)***	(-2.411)***	(6.452)***	(-5.749)***
R^2	0.460	0.280	0.307	0.444	0.328
F statistic	272.847	83.685	85.801	283.627	139.395

Note: estimated variable: equivalence scale. Number of observations: Germany: 1,919; Belgium: 2,831.

Notation: t statistics in parentheses; *** significant at the 1% level; ** significant at the 5% level; * significant at the 10% level; $^{+}$ insignificant.

Are interviewees able to assess the needs of households whose demography is different from their own? Unfortunately, we could not conduct the same analysis as for V_I since the size of both samples is too small for distinguishing 20 sub–samples, one for each hypothetical household type. Instead, we will supply suggestions to four questions that seem of particular interest.

Firstly, do interviewees with children state other weights for children than their childless counterparts? To answer this question, we proceed as follows: the samples are subdivided by a dummy variable DC which is zero for childless interviewees and 1.0 else. Then, we run a pooled regression with the cumulated children weights as dependent variable and the independent variables of regression (3) in Section 7.6 plus aforementioned dummy DC. The results are reported in Table A3 in the Appendix. For both countries, DC is significant but with inverse signs: childless Belgian interviewees state higher children needs compared with Belgian interviewees with one child or more, while the opposite is true for Germany. However, the coefficient is quantitatively small in both cases. For Germany (Belgium), the standardised coefficient is 0.077 (−0.049).

Secondly, do interviewees without a partner state different equivalence scales for two–adult households compared to interviewees having a partner? Such a potential structural break can be identified by a dummy variable (DP)

which is 1.0 for interviewees with a partner while else it is zero. A pooled regression is run with two–adult household equivalence scales as the dependent variable and the independent variables of regression (3) in Section 7.6 plus the dummy DP excluding DA_2. Results are reported in Table A4 in the Appendix. For Belgium, interviewees without a partner slightly overestimate the needs of two–adult households while there is no significant pattern for Germany.

Thirdly, in a similar manner we explore whether interviewees having a partner state other equivalence scales for one–adult households than interviewees that do no have a partner. Thus, the dependent variable are equivalence scales for single–adult households. A dummy variable DP distinguishes the interviewees with a partner ($DP = 1.0$) from singles ($DP = 0$). The regression results can be taken from Table A5 in the Appendix. That DP is significantly negative in Belgium means that Belgian interviewees having a partner slightly underestimate the needs of single–adult households compared with interviewees having no partner. For Germany, the difference is insignificant.

Fourthly, do employed interviewees state other weights for employees than their unemployed counterparts? We address this question by splitting the sample into the groups of unemployed and employed respondents. For this, a dummy DW is defined that is zero for interviewees who are unemployed or who work irregularly, and which is 1.0 else. The pooled regression explains the (cumulated) weights for employees by the set of variables according to regression (3), except for the children dummies, and including DW. The regression results can be taken form Table A6 in the Appendix. For both countries, the regression reveals that unemployed or irregularly employed interviewees overestimate the (cumulated) weights for employees. However, this difference again is quantitatively minor.

Altogether, we can sum up in the same way as for V_I: the data suggest some haziness of knowledge in the sense that there are minor differences in the assessment of household needs dependent upon whether the interviewee's welfare level or household type coincides with the respective characteristics of the household of interest or not. However, these quantitative differences are small without exception which is an important indication that the interviewees are capable to deal with the tasks provided in questionnaire V_{II}.

8

Conclusion

The work at hand presented the methodological properties of a new approach to assigning equivalence scales by using our suggested new survey method. We applied it in order to determine the impacts of reference income and employment on equivalence scales.

We have implemented the new method in four studies employing two different sets of stimulus variables. The first two studies have been conducted in Germany and Cyprus, two countries with significantly different socio–economic conditions. These studies' main target has been a test of the IB/ESE assumption by directly asking subjects to state equivalent incomes for different hypothetical households compared with a reference household, a single adult with a pre–specified reference income. Our respondents repeated this task for five different levels of reference income. Despite the differences in the socio–economic conditions of both countries, the equivalence scales obtained are rather similar, and slightly higher equivalence scales for Cyprus can be explained by the adjustment procedure regarding the stimulus *reference income* according to the lower Cypriot GDP. The main result of both surveys is that equivalence scales negatively depend on the level of reference income. This finding strongly questions the results of previous empirical studies on inequality and poverty where equivalence scales have always been assumed to be constant. Obviously, this constancy assumption either means an overestimation of the needs of "rich" or the underestimation of the needs of "poor" multi–person households or the mis–specification of the needs of both.

The other two surveys have been conducted in Germany and Belgium using an extended set of stimulus variables by distinguishing unemployed and employed household members. In both studies the employment status turns out to be an important criterion for the evaluation of household needs. According to our respondents of both countries, equivalence scales are an increasing function of the number of employed household members. The data reveal that the employment status does not only affect the needs of adults but also the needs of children, and a plausible interpretation of this finding is that employment reduces the ability of adults to provide work within the household, hence the ability to care for their children. As we have stressed before, it is therefore necessary to broaden economic models for deriving equivalence scales with respect to household production activities which again are determined by the time restrictions of the household members. Again, all equivalence scales derived are characterised by a negative dependence on the level of reference income, an observation which can be seen as a further confirmation of the conclusion drawn from the two former surveys.

In contrast to other survey methodologies as the one pioneered by the *Leyden School*, we have used income as the dimension for both, stimulus and response, as opposed to two different dimensions, income and a verbal characterisation of household welfare. This also means that there is no necessity to define a functional or parametric utility system for the determination of equivalence scales. The choice of an equal dimension for the stimulus and response variables is mainly motivated by the observation that previous survey methods' results have been biased substantially by respondents' personal characteristics and potential subjective biases. *Preference drift* probably is the most prominent example. Our hope was to avoid such undesirable distortions by evading the problem that verbal characterisations of household welfare evoke different images across the sample of respondents which then are translated into different cash amounts and equivalence scales. Thus, we paid a lot of attention establishing the impacts of our respondents' personal characteristics on equivalence scales. We wish to emphasise that the personal characteristics and circumstances of our respondents have very little if any effect on equivalence scales derived from our specific survey method.

Since we have asked our interviewees to assess the needs of our supplied and given hypothetical households, another important question has risen, and been the subject of our investigation, mainly to establish whether the use of hypothetical households is error–generating or not. We have suggested a consumer model to motivate a number of sample restrictions that allowed for quantifying such errors and we have given evidence that the use of hypothetical households in the questionnaires is reliable: that our respondents have not been too rationally bounded in the assessments of the needs of hypothetical household types that differed from their own as to their income or welfare level, or as to their demographic characteristics.

An interesting topic for future research could be an analysis of the sensitivity of inequality comparisons across heterogeneous populations to the choice of the reference household if one uses income dependent equivalence scales. In this treatise we always used the least needy household r as the reference, normalised its equivalence scale to 1.0, and determined equivalence scales (larger than 1.0) for more needy household types k which decreased with increasing income of the reference household. Of course, correspondingly one could choose any other household type as the reference, for instance the most needy household. Refraining from endowment effects, equivalence scales for less needy household types in this case would be less then 1.0 and *increasing* with rising income of the most needy household. To make this connection clear, imagine the following numerical example with two welfare–equalising income pairs for r and k, namely (1.000, 2.000) and (2.000, 3.000). Taking r as the reference, we obtain equivalence scales for k which are decreasing in the income of r, namely $\frac{2.000}{1.000} = 2.0$ and $\frac{3.000}{2.000} = 1.5$. The alternative choice of k as the reference leads to an equivalence scale of r which is increasing in k's income, namely $\frac{1.000}{2.000} = \frac{1}{2}$ and $\frac{2.000}{3.000} = \frac{2}{3}$. *Ebert* (1999) and *Pyatt* (1990) show that if equivalence scales are *constant*, the adjustment of incomes by equivalence scales and the weighting of resulting equivalent incomes by the same factor is the only way for making consistent comparisons of relative inequality across heterogeneous populations under a set of assumptions. These assumptions especially comprise that the results of the comparisons should not be affected by the chosen type of the reference household and that an income transfer which leads to a reduction of inequality of living standards between two households should not be inequality increasing (*Ebert* 1999, p. 4). However, income dependencies of equivalence scales "might give rise to inconsistencies in normative assessment" (*Ebert* and *Moyes* 2000, p. 27). It seems to be an interesting field for future empirical research to see whether such inconsistencies are of practical relevance when income dependent equivalence scales are applied.

Appendix

Diese Befragung befasst sich mit der Problematik, dass unterschiedliche Haushaltstypen unterschiedliche Einkommensbedürfnisse aufweisen. Diese Einkommensbedürfnisse hängen von der im Haushalt lebenden Zahl der Erwachsenen und Kinder ab. So braucht ein zusammenlebendes Paar aufgrund der gemeinsamen Haushaltsführung in der Regel nicht das doppelte Einkommen eines Einpersonenhaushaltes, um den gleichen Lebensstandard zu erreichen. Auch die Haushaltszusammensetzung spielt eine Rolle, da Kinder möglicherweise andere Bedürfnisse als Erwachsene aufweisen.

Daher ergibt sich folgende Frage: Wie hoch müsste das Einkommen eines Mehrpersonenhaushalts im Vergleich zu einem Einpersonenhaushalt mit gegebenem Einkommen sein, damit beide den gleichen Lebensstandard erreichen?

Da es auf diese Frage keine objektiv richtige Antwort gibt, möchten wir Ihre subjektive Einstellung zu dieser Frage kennenlernen. Gehen Sie bei der Beantwortung der Frage davon aus, dass die Erwachsenen zwischen 35 und 55, die Kinder zwischen 7 und 11 Jahre alt sind.

In den auf der nächsten Seite folgenden Tabellen sollen Sie fünf unterschiedliche Situationen bewerten, die jeweils in einer Tabelle abgebildet sind.

Ein Erwachsener ohne Kind	**Referenz–einkommen**	Zwei Erwachsene ohne Kind	
Ein Erwachsener mit einem Kind		Zwei Erwachsene mit einem Kind	
Ein Erwachsener mit zwei Kindern		Zwei Erwachsene mit zwei Kindern	
Ein Erwachsener mit drei Kindern		Zwei Erwachsene mit drei Kindern	

In der Tabelle variieren wir die Anzahl der Kinder und der Erwachsenen. Die Zahl der Kinder variiert von 0 bis 3, die der Erwachsenen zwischen 1 (erste Spalte) und 2 (dritte Spalte). Nur für den Einpersonenhaushalt ohne Kind ist ein Nettoeinkommen vorgegeben, das Referenzeinkommen, während die Felder neben den anderen Haushaltstypen leer sind.

Wie hoch müsste dann das gesamte familiäre Nettoeinkommen (die Summe der Nettoeinkünfte aller Familienmitglieder) sein, damit alle Haushaltstypen in der Tabelle gleich gut gestellt sind? Bitte geben Sie genau dieses familiäre Nettoeinkommen in den einzelnen Feldern der Tabelle an.

Figure A1. Introduction (V_I, Germany)

1. Bitte geben Sie Ihr Geschlecht an:	[ ] männlich
	[ ] weiblich
2. Leben Sie mit einem Partner zusammen?	[ ] ja
	[ ] nein
3. Wie viele Kinder leben in Ihrem Haushalt?	[ ] 0
	[ ] 1
	[ ] 2
	[ ] 3 oder mehr
4. Wie hoch ist Ihr gesamtes Haushaltsnettoeinkommen?	[ ] weniger als 1.750 DM
	[ ] 1.750–3.249 DM
	[ ] 3.250–4.749 DM
	[ ] 4.750–6.249 DM
	[ ] mehr als 6,249 DM
5. Sind Sie	[ ] Sozialhilfeempfänger,
	[ ] Arbeitsloser,
	[ ] Arbeiter,
	[ ] Angestellter,
	[ ] Beamter,
	[ ] Schüler, Student oder Auszubildender,
	[ ] Selbständiger,
	[ ] Renter oder Pensionär,
	[ ] Hausmann oder Hausfrau?
6. Welchen Schulabschluss besitzen Sie?	[ ] kein Abschluss
	[ ] Hauptschule
	[ ] Realschule
	[ ] Gymnasium
	[ ] Universität oder Fachhochschule
7. Mit wie vielen Geschwistern lebten Sie während Ihrer Jugend zusammen?	[ ] 0
	[ ] 1
	[ ] 2
	[ ] 3 oder mehr

Figure A2. Personal Questionnaire (V_I, Germany)

Hier sehen Sie die oben angesprochenen Tabellen, die sich aufgrund des Nettoeinkommens des Einpersonenhaushalts unterscheiden. Tragen Sie bitte in jeder Tabelle die Haushaltsnettoeinkommen für die übrigen sieben Haushaltstypen ein, so dass alle Haushalte den gleichen Lebensstandard erreichen wie der Einpersonenhaushalt.

Ein Erwachsener ohne Kind	1000 DM	Zwei Erwachsene ohne Kind	
Ein Erwachsener mit einem Kind		Zwei Erwachsene mit einem Kind	
Ein Erwachsener mit zwei Kindern		Zwei Erwachsene mit zwei Kindern	
Ein Erwachsener mit drei Kindern		Zwei Erwachsene mit drei Kindern	

Ein Erwachsener ohne Kind	2500 DM	Zwei Erwachsene ohne Kind	
Ein Erwachsener mit einem Kind		Zwei Erwachsene mit einem Kind	
Ein Erwachsener mit zwei Kindern		Zwei Erwachsene mit zwei Kindern	
Ein Erwachsener mit drei Kindern		Zwei Erwachsene mit drei Kindern	

Ein Erwachsener ohne Kind	4000 DM	Zwei Erwachsene ohne Kind	
Ein Erwachsener mit einem Kind		Zwei Erwachsene mit einem Kind	
Ein Erwachsener mit zwei Kindern		Zwei Erwachsene mit zwei Kindern	
Ein Erwachsener mit drei Kindern		Zwei Erwachsene mit drei Kindern	

Ein Erwachsener ohne Kind	5500 DM	Zwei Erwachsene ohne Kind	
Ein Erwachsener mit einem Kind		Zwei Erwachsene mit einem Kind	
Ein Erwachsener mit zwei Kindern		Zwei Erwachsene mit zwei Kindern	
Ein Erwachsener mit drei Kindern		Zwei Erwachsene mit drei Kindern	

Ein Erwachsener ohne Kind	7000 DM	Zwei Erwachsene ohne Kind	
Ein Erwachsener mit einem Kind		Zwei Erwachsene mit einem Kind	
Ein Erwachsener mit zwei Kindern		Zwei Erwachsene mit zwei Kindern	
Ein Erwachsener mit drei Kindern		Zwei Erwachsene mit drei Kindern	

Figure A3. General Questionnaire (V_I, Germany)

Προσοχή: Αφού απαντήσετε σε όλες τις ερωτήσεις κας των δύν επ΄μενων σελίδων, τελευταία σελίδα του ερωτηματολογίου αυτού Θα σφραγιστεί σε ένα συνηΘισμένο, ασημάδευτο φάκελο. Με αυτή την τακτική διασφαλιξέται η ανωνυμία σας. Σας παρακαλούε να απαντήσετε σε όλες τις ερωτήσεις ανεξαιρέτως.

1. *Πληροφορίες: Κατά το σχεδιασμό ενός συστήματος κοινωνιών παροχών ή < δίκαιων > φορολογικών κλιμάκων, παρουσιάξεται το εξής κρίσιμο πρόβλημα: νοικ– οκυριά διαφορετικού μεγέΘους ή σύνΘεσης έχουν διαφορετικές. Για παράδειμα, ένα ξευγάρι χωρίς παιδιά που ξει στο ίδιο σπιτι και μοιράξετι το κόστος διαβίωσης (νοίκι κλπ.), δε χρειάξεται δύο φορές το εισόδημα ενός εργεύη για να επιτύχει το ίδιο βιοτικό επίπεδο.* Από *την άλλη πλευρά, οικογένειες με παιδιά έχουν διαφορετικές ανάγκες, διότι απλά οι ανάγκες των παιδιών διαφέρουν από αυτές των ενηλικών. Δεδομενόυ ότι δεν υπάρχουν αντικειμενικά αποδεκτές απαντησέις όσον αφορά το ξήτημα των αναγκών νοικοκυριών διαφορετικής δημογραφικής σύνθεσης, ενδιαφερόμαστε να μάθουμε ποιές είναι οι δικές σας προσωπικές απόψεις επάνω σ' αυτό το κρίσιμο θέμα.*

2. *Οδηγίες: Στην επόμενη σελίδα υπάρχουν πέντε κουτιά* (1–5) *τα οποιά αντιστοιχούν σε πέντε διαφορετικές περιπιώσεις. Παρακαλούμε να εξετάσετε το κάθε κουτί ξεχωριστά. Σας παρεχουμε έναν αριθμό, ο οποίος αντιστοιχεί στο μηνιαίο καθαρό εισόδημα (δηλ. οι φόροι έξω), ενός νοικοκυριού με ένα μόνο ενήλικα χωρίς παιδιά. Σας δίνουμε επίσης οικογένειες διαφορετικού μεγέθους και σύνθεσης με κενά δίπλα τους. Σας παρακαλο– ύμε να συμπληρώσετε τα κενά με το ερωτηματικό* <?> *βάξοντας το οικογενειακό ειόδημα που πιστεύετε ότι φέρνει την αντίστοιχη οικογένεια στο ίδιο βιοτικό επίπεδο με αυτό του εργένη. Για παράδειγμα, πολλοί πιστεύουν ότι ένα νοικοκυριό με ενά μόνο γονεά και δύο παιδιά χρειάξεται μηνιαίο οικογενειακό εισόδημα* 410 *λιρών για να επιτύχει το ίδιο βιοτικό επίπεδο με έναν εργένη που λαμβάνει* 200 *λίρες το μήνα. Στα υπόλοιπα κουτιά σας ξητάμε να επαναλάβετε την ίδια διαδικασία, με τη μόνη διαφορά ότι σε κάθε κουτί θα πρέπει τώρα να βάλετε τέτοια οικογενειακά εισοδήματα ούτως ώστε όλες οι οικογενέιες να επιτύχουν το νέο υψηλότερο βιοτικό επίπεδο που αντιστοιχεί στο νέο υψηλότερο εισόδημα του εργένη που σας δίνουμε. Για παράδειγμα, πολλοί πιστεύουν ότι ένα νοικοκυριό με ένα μόνο γονέα και δύο παιδιά χρειάξεται μηνιαίο οικογενειακό εισόδημα* 1400*ων λιρών για να επιτύχει το ίδιο βιοτικό επίπεδο με έναν εργένη που λαμβάνει* 800 *λίρες το μήνα. Σας υπενθυμίξουμε ότι καλείστε να συμπληρώσετε ό, τι εσείς θεωρείτε πιο λογικό με βάση τις δικές σας αντιλήψεις. Προσέξτε ότι σε κάθε στήλη ενός κουτιού* (1–5), *τα εισοδήματα που βάξετε δε θα πρέπει να μειώνονται διαβάξοντας τη στήλη από πάνω προς τα κάτω μέσα στο ίδιο κουτί. Σας παρακαλούμε επίσης να συμπληρώσετε όλα τα κενά.*

Figure A4. Introduction (V_I, Cyprus)

1.*Φύλο* :	[ ] ἴΑνδρας [ ] *Γυναίκα*
2.*Ζείτε μαξί με σύξυγο ή αρραβωνιαστικό/ιά;*	[ ] *Ναι* [ ] ἴΟχι
3.*Αν στην προηγούμενη ερώτ– ηση απαντήσατε «ἴΟχι» τότε ξείτε με τους γονείς σας;*	[ ] *Ναι* [ ] ἴΟχι
4.*Πόσα παιδιά (ηλικίας κάτω των* 16) *ζουν στο σπίτι σας;*	[ ] *Κανένα* [ ] ἴΕνα [ ] *Δύο* [ ] *Τρια ή παραπάνω*
5. *Ποιό είναι το καθαρό μηνι– αίο (οι φόροι έξω) οικογενε– ιακό σας εισόδημα;*	[ ] *Κάτω από* 300 *λίρες* [ ] 300–579 *λίρες* [ ] 580–839 *λίρες* [ ] 840–1099 *λίρες* [ ] 1100 *ή περισσότερο*
6. *Είστε*:	[ ] *Λήπτης κοινωνικής πρόνοιας;* [ ] ἴΑνεργος/η; [ ] *Εργάτης/ρια σε βιομηχανία ή βιοτεχνία ή αγρότης/ισσα;* [ ] *Ιδιωτικός υπάλληλος;* [ ] *Δημόσιος υπάλληλος;* [ ] *Επιχειρηματίας/ιδιώτης;* [ ] *Μαθητής/ρια ή φοιτητής/ρια ή μαθητευόμενος/η σε επιχείρηση;* [ ] *Συνταξιούχος;* [ ] *Νοικοκυρά;*
7. *Ποιό είναι το επίπεδο της σχολικής εκπαίδευσής σας;*	[ ] *Κάτω από Γυμνάσιο* [ ] *Απόφοιτος Γυμνασίου* [ ] *Απόφοιτος Λυκείου* [ ] *Απόφοιτος Τεχνικής Σχολής* [ ] *Απόφοιτος Πανεπιστημίου ή παραπάνω*
8. *Πόσα ακόμη αδέλφια (εκτός από εσάς) ζούσαν στο σπίτι σας κατά την παιδική σας ηλικία;*	[ ] Κανένα [ ] ἴΕνα [ ] *Δύο* [ ] Τρία *ή παραπάνω*

Figure A5. General Questionnaire (V_I, Cyprus)

Σας παρακαλούμε να βάλετε ένα σταυρό σε κάθε σωστή απάντηση. Αν είστε φοιτητής/τρια και ζείτε μόνος/η (ή και με άλλους συγκάτοικους φοιτητές) εκτός του τόπου κατοικίας των γονέων σας αλλά συντηρείστε από αυτούς, παρακαλούμε να συμπληρώσετε ως «οικογενειακό» εισόδημά σας το μηνιαίο χαρτζηλίκι σας. Θα τηρηθεί απόλυτη εχεμύθεια όσον αφορά τις πληροφορίες που μας παρέχετε. Σας υπενθυμίζουμε ότι αυτή η σελίδα θα σφραγιστεί σε ένα συνηθισμένο φάκελο αφού την απαντήσετε.

Νοικοκυριό ενός ενήλικα χωρίς παιδιά	200 λίρες το μήνα	Νοικοκυριό δύο ενηλίκων χωρίς παιδιά	
Νοικοκυριό ενός γονέα με 1 παιδί		Νοικοκυριό δύο γονέων με 1 παιδί	
Νοικοκυριό ενός γονέα με 1 παιδιά		Νοικοκυριό δύο γονέων με 1 παιδιά	
Νοικοκυριό ενός γονέα με 3 παιδιά		Νοικοκυριό δύο γονέων με 3 παιδιά	

Νοικοκυριό ενός ενήλικα χωρίς παιδιά	500 λίρες το μήνα	Νοικοκυριό δύο ενηλίκων χωρίς παιδιά	
Νοικοκυριό ενός γονέα με 1 παιδί		Νοικοκυριό δύο γονέων με 1 παιδί	
Νοικοκυριό ενός γονέα με 1 παιδιά		Νοικοκυριό δύο γονέων με 1 παιδιά	
Νοικοκυριό ενός γονέα με 3 παιδιά		Νοικοκυριό δύο γονέων με 3 παιδιά	

Νοικοκυριό ενός ενήλικα χωρίς παιδιά	800 λίρες το μήνα	Νοικοκυριό δύο ενηλίκων χωρίς παιδιά	
Νοικοκυριό ενός γονέα με 1 παιδί		Νοικοκυριό δύο γονέων με 1 παιδί	
Νοικοκυριό ενός γονέα με 1 παιδιά		Νοικοκυριό δύο γονέων με 1 παιδιά	
Νοικοκυριό ενός γονέα με 3 παιδιά		Νοικοκυριό δύο γονέων με 3 παιδιά	

Νοικοκυριό ενός ενήλικα χωρίς παιδιά	1100 λίρες το μήνα	Νοικοκυριό δύο ενηλίκων χωρίς παιδιά	
Νοικοκυριό ενός γονέα με 1 παιδί		Νοικοκυριό δύο γονέων με 1 παιδί	
Νοικοκυριό ενός γονέα με 1 παιδιά		Νοικοκυριό δύο γονέων με 1 παιδιά	
Νοικοκυριό ενός γονέα με 3 παιδιά		Νοικοκυριό δύο γονέων με 3 παιδιά	

Νοικοκυριό ενός ενήλικα χωρίς παιδιά	1400 λίρες το μήνα	Νοικοκυριό δύο ενηλίκων χωρίς παιδιά	
Νοικοκυριό ενός γονέα με 1 παιδί		Νοικοκυριό δύο γονέων με 1 παιδί	
Νοικοκυριό ενός γονέα με 1 παιδιά		Νοικοκυριό δύο γονέων με 1 παιδιά	
Νοικοκυριό ενός γονέα με 3 παιδιά		Νοικοκυριό δύο γονέων με 3 παιδιά	

Figure A6. General Questionnaire (V_I, Cyprus)

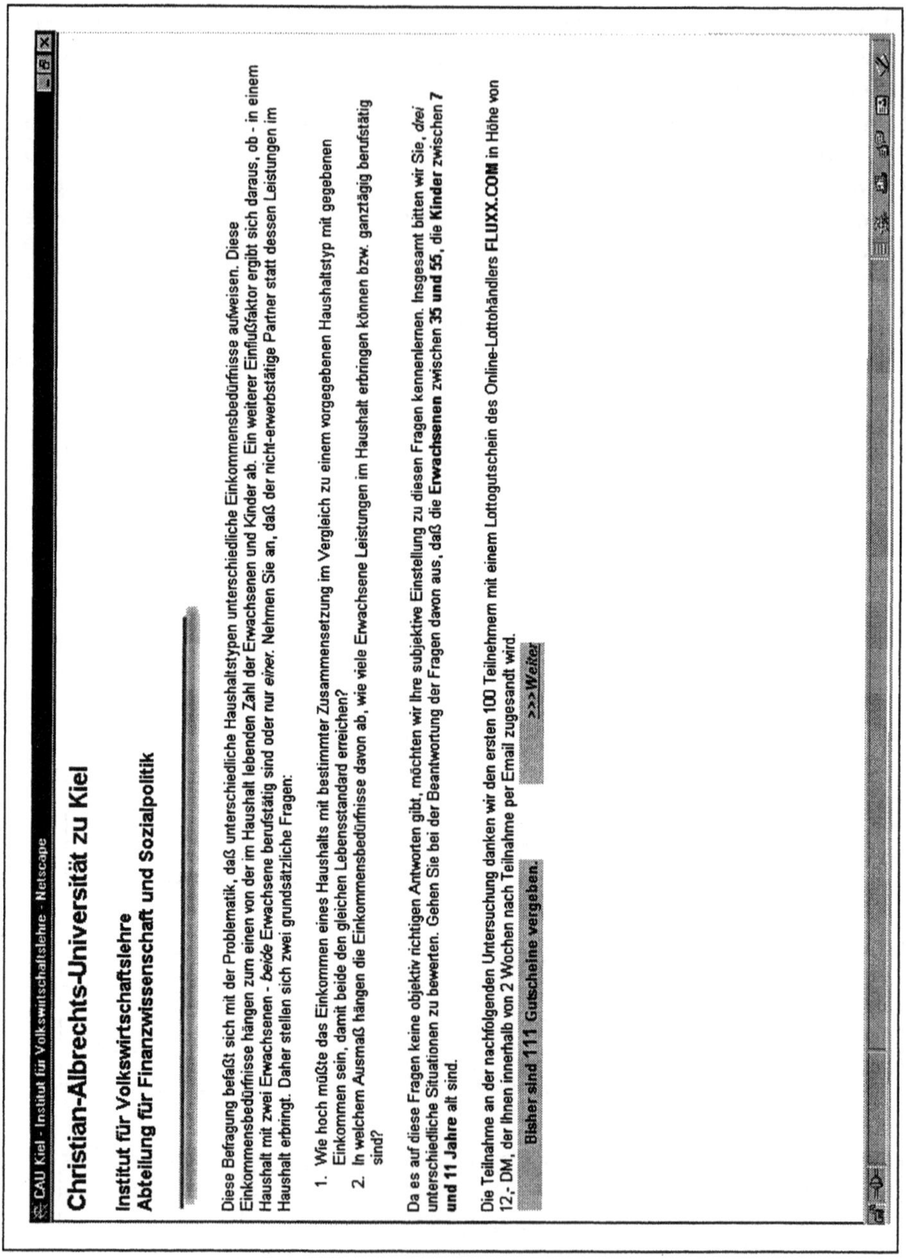

CAU Kiel - Institut für Volkswirtschaftslehre - Netscape

Christian-Albrechts-Universität zu Kiel

Institut für Volkswirtschaftslehre
Abteilung für Finanzwissenschaft und Sozialpolitik

Diese Befragung befaßt sich mit der Problematik, daß unterschiedliche Haushaltstypen unterschiedliche Einkommensbedürfnisse aufweisen. Diese Einkommensbedürfnisse hängen zum einen von der im Haushalt lebenden Zahl der Erwachsenen und Kinder ab. Ein weiterer Einflußfaktor ergibt sich daraus, ob - in einem Haushalt mit zwei Erwachsenen - *beide* Erwachsene berufstätig sind oder nur *einer*. Nehmen Sie an, daß der nicht-erwerbstätige Partner statt dessen Leistungen im Haushalt erbringt. Daher stellen sich zwei grundsätzliche Fragen:

1. Wie hoch müßte das Einkommen eines Haushalts mit bestimmter Zusammensetzung im Vergleich zu einem vorgegebenen Haushaltstyp mit gegebenen Einkommen sein, damit beide den gleichen Lebensstandard erreichen?
2. In welchem Ausmaß hängen die Einkommensbedürfnisse davon ab, wie viele Erwachsene Leistungen im Haushalt erbringen können bzw. ganztägig berufstätig sind?

Da es auf diese Fragen keine objektiv richtigen Antworten gibt, möchten wir Ihre subjektive Einstellung zu diesen Fragen kennenlernen. Insgesamt bitten wir Sie, *drei* unterschiedliche Situationen zu bewerten. Gehen Sie bei der Beantwortung der Fragen davon aus, daß die **Erwachsenen** zwischen **35 und 55**, die **Kinder** zwischen **7 und 11 Jahre** alt sind.

Die Teilnahme an der nachfolgenden Untersuchung danken wir den ersten 100 Teilnehmern mit einem Lottogutschein des Online-Lottohändlers **FLUXX.COM** in Höhe von 12,- DM, der Ihnen innerhalb von 2 Wochen nach Teilnahme per Email zugesandt wird.

Bisher sind 111 Gutscheine vergeben. >>>Weiter

Figure A7. Introduction, Part 1 (V_{II})

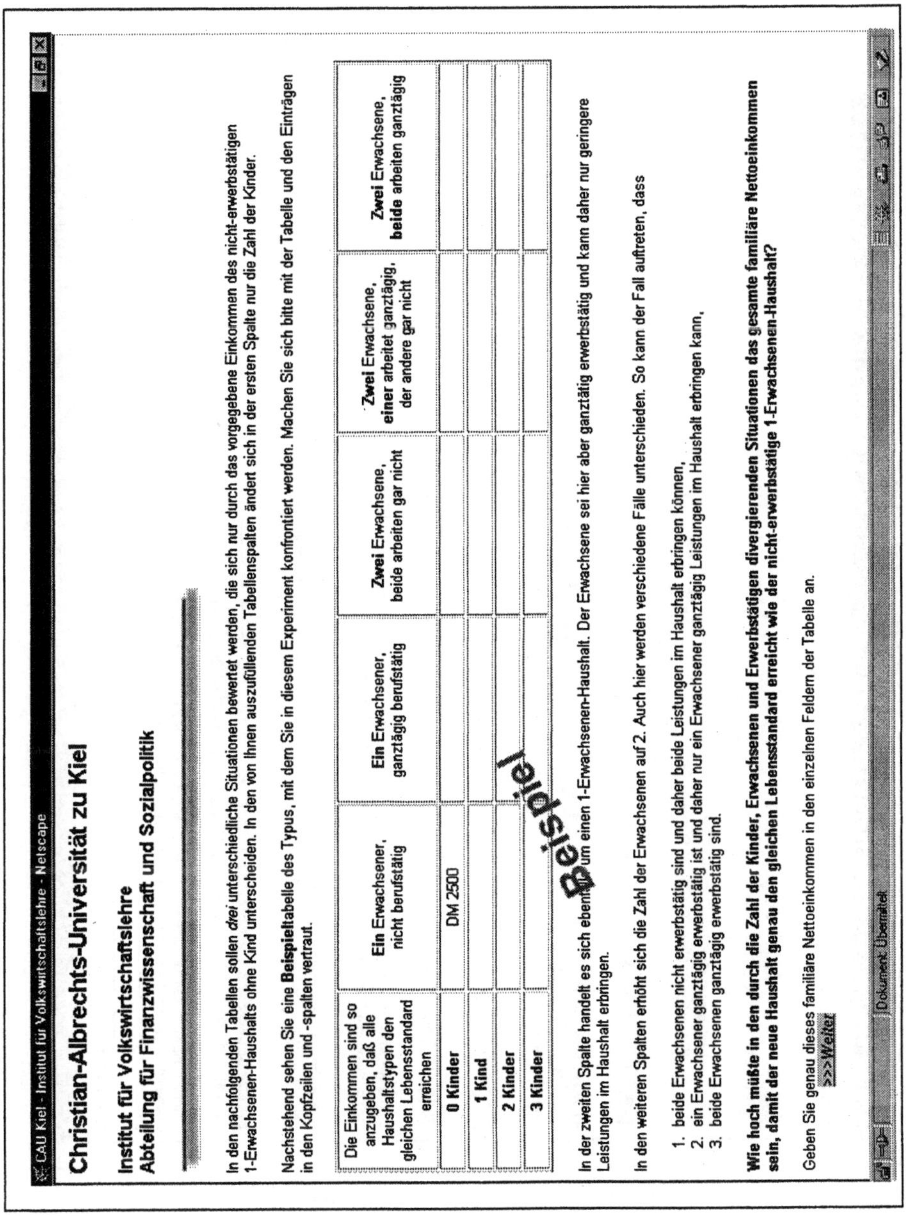

CAU Kiel - Institut für Volkswirtschaftslehre - Netscape

Christian-Albrechts-Universität zu Kiel

Institut für Volkswirtschaftslehre
Abteilung für Finanzwissenschaft und Sozialpolitik

In den nachfolgenden Tabellen sollen *drei* unterschiedliche Situationen bewertet werden, die sich nur durch das vorgegebene Einkommen des nicht-erwerbstätigen 1-Erwachsenen-Haushalts ohne Kind unterscheiden. In den von Ihnen auszufüllenden Tabellenspalten ändert sich in der ersten Spalte nur die Zahl der Kinder.

Nachstehend sehen Sie eine **Beispiel**tabelle des Typus, mit dem Sie in diesem Experiment konfrontiert werden. Machen Sie sich bitte mit der Tabelle und den Einträgen in den Kopfzeilen und -spalten vertraut.

Die Einkommen sind so anzugeben, daß alle Haushaltstypen den gleichen Lebensstandard erreichen	**Ein** Erwachsener, nicht berufstätig	**Ein** Erwachsener, ganztägig berufstätig	**Zwei** Erwachsene, beide arbeiten gar nicht	**Zwei** Erwachsene, **einer** arbeitet ganztägig, der andere gar nicht	**Zwei** Erwachsene, **beide** arbeiten ganztägig
0 Kinder	DM 2500				
1 Kind					
2 Kinder					
3 Kinder					

Beispiel

In der zweiten Spalte handelt es sich ebenfalls um einen 1-Erwachsenen-Haushalt. Der Erwachsene sei hier aber ganztätig erwerbstätig und kann daher nur geringere Leistungen im Haushalt erbringen.

In den weiteren Spalten erhöht sich die Zahl der Erwachsenen auf 2. Auch hier werden verschiedene Fälle unterschieden. So kann der Fall auftreten, dass

1. beide Erwachsenen nicht erwerbstätig sind und daher beide Leistungen im Haushalt erbringen können,
2. ein Erwachsener ganztägig erwerbstätig ist und daher nur ein Erwachsener ganztägig Leistungen im Haushalt erbringen kann,
3. beide Erwachsenen ganztägig erwerbstätig sind.

Wie hoch müßte in den durch die Zahl der Kinder, Erwachsenen und Erwerbstätigen divergierenden Situationen das gesamte familiäre Nettoeinkommen sein, damit der neue Haushalt genau den gleichen Lebensstandard erreicht wie der nicht-erwerbstätige 1-Erwachsenen-Haushalt?

Geben Sie genau dieses familiäre Nettoeinkommen in den einzelnen Feldern der Tabelle an.

>>>Weiter

Dokument: Übermittelt

Figure A8. Introduction, Part 2 (V_{II})

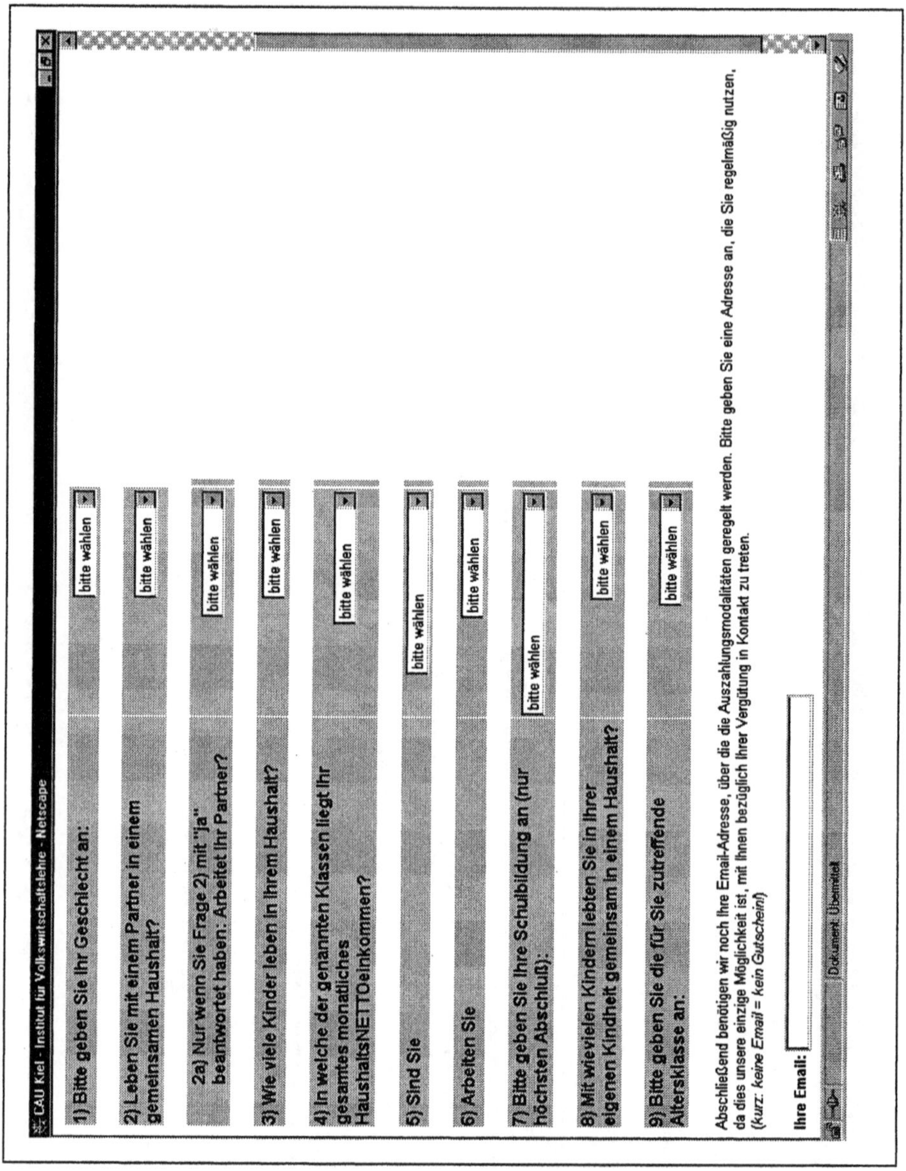

Figure A9. Personal Questionnaire (V_{II})

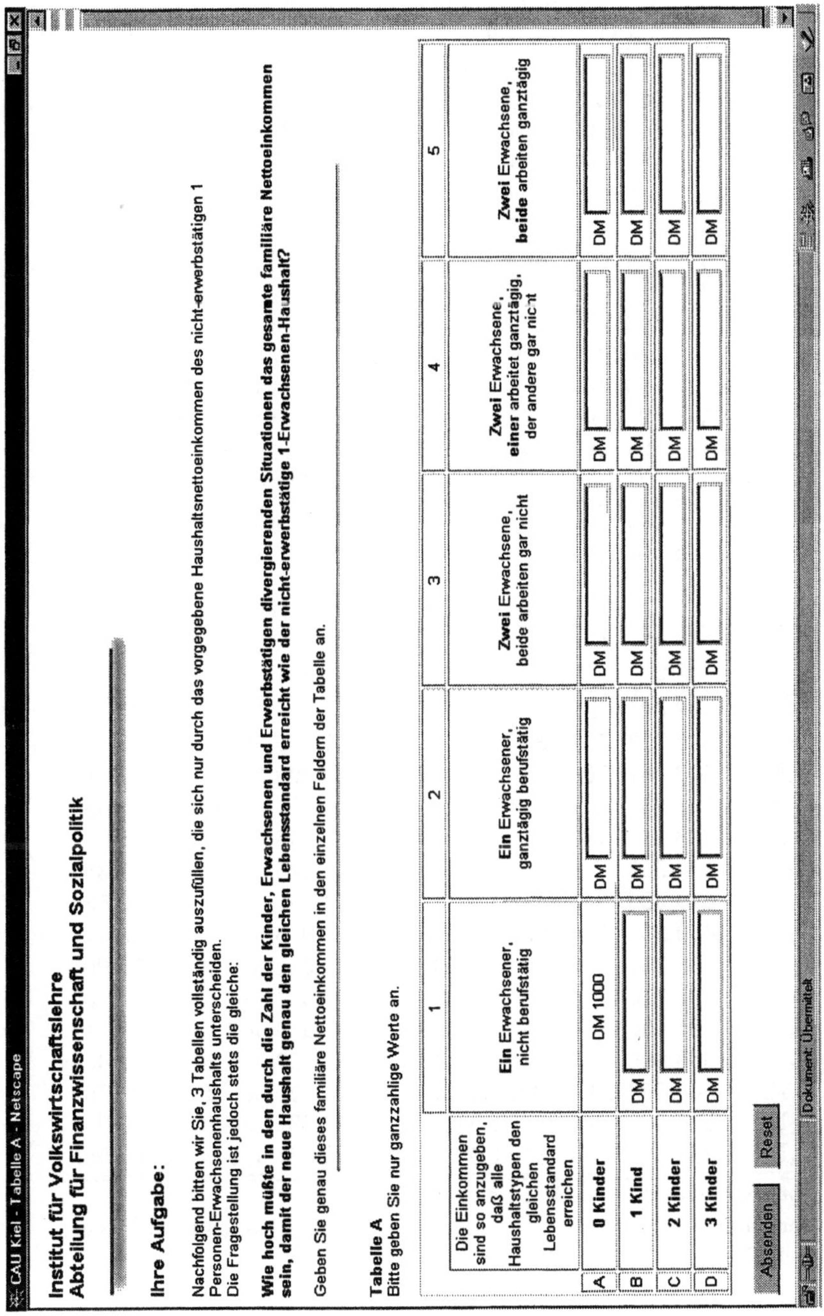

Figure A10. General Questionnaire (V_{II})

Table A1. Children Costs (V_I)

y_r	1.0	2.5	4.0	5.5	7.0
			Germany		
C_1A	569.521	603.293	696.287	702.156	782.994
C_2A	450.838	487.126	564.311	579.641	655.150
C_3A	452.994	481.587	544.431	581.287	624.132
C_1AA	516.228	557.485	610.060	666.257	726.407
C_2AA	455.808	503.743	571.018	587.874	655.988
C_3AA	448.922	489.671	529.581	613.892	635.868
			Cyprus		
C_1A	146.477	165.131	211.823	253.092	278.354
C_2A	120.962	140.692	178.308	217.115	230.008
C_3A	126.800	138.108	175.069	201.608	225.262
C_1AA	126.685	145.692	183.077	221.615	251.600
C_2AA	124.692	144.185	175.531	211.338	227.400
C_3AA	122.146	135.577	168.385	198.077	219.908

Note: data for Germany in DM; data for Cyprus in CP.
Notation: each A denotes an adult; C_i denotes the ith child.

Table A2. Children Costs (V_{II})

	Germany			Belgium		
y_r	1.0	4.0	7.0	1.0	4.0	7.0
C_1U	598.002	1,018.813	1,013.368	258.369	465.651	598.564
C_2U	528.713	731.680	918.812	211.752	395.946	543.510
C_3U	463.861	706.438	868.321	209.409	386.758	546.282
C_1E	591.584	1,010.402	1,225.736	286.523	537.094	709.698
C_2E	488.116	783.662	981.193	237.849	444.134	596.215
C_3E	434.653	741.575	950.502	233.275	446.020	621.362
C_1UU	549.505	859.412	1,045.046	254.691	445.067	589.584
C_2UU	480.204	670.786	875.251	216.933	394.752	579.577
C_3UU	385.151	698.019	908.423	219.919	399.107	576.966
C_1EU	527.716	924.258	1,130.201	252.597	475.839	589.154
C_2EU	485.150	674.255	890.592	221.544	407.430	568.711
C_3EU	368.806	708.912	932.182	212.067	441.208	602.483
C_1EE	644.063	1,112.384	1,315.349	315.128	566.242	708.752
C_2EE	532.666	773.271	1,022.770	249.785	456.765	650.000
C_3EE	433.665	852.484	1,030.201	240.691	479.946	669.550

Note: German data in DM; Belgian data in Euro.
Notation: C_i denotes the ith child; each E denotes an employed adult; each U denotes an unemployed adult.

Table A3. Differences in the Assessment of Children (V_{II})

	Germany	Belgium
c_0	0.698	0.082
	(13.791)***	(9.729)***
y_r	-0.504	-0.392
	(-43.666)***	(-37.873)***
DA_2	-0.031	0.045
	(-2.542)***	(4.094)***
DC_2	0.209	0.163
	(15.701)***	(13.630)***
DC_3	0.188	0.210
	(14.128)***	(17.517)***
n_E	0.049	0.119
	(3.994)***	(10.846)***
y_p	-0.113	-0.009
	(-8.579)***	(-0.729)+
Gender	0.083	0.025
	(6.881)***	(2.395)**
Siblings	0.038	-0.022
	(3.178)***	(-2.111)**
Education	0.049	0.015
	(4.088)***	(1.446)**
DC	0.077	-0.049
	(5.705)***	(-4.720)***
R^2	0.394	0.281
F statistic	296.042	327.976

Note: dependent variable: cumulated children weights; pooled estimations; standardized coefficients; number of observations: Germany: 4,546; Belgium: 6,705.

Notation: t statistics in parentheses; *** significant at the 1% level; ** significant at the 5% level; + insignificant.

Table A4. Differences in the Assessment of Two–adult Households (V_{II})

	Germany	Belgium
c_0	2.456	1.266
	(35.922)***	(6.241)***
y_r	-0.489	-0.403
	(-37.896)***	(-36.322)***
DC_1	0.121	0.124
	(7.680)***	(9.094)***
DC_2	0.115	0.123
	(6.329)***	(7.828)***
DC_3	0.089	0.107
	(5.642)***	(7.871)***
n_E	0.260	0.284
	(20.154)***	(25.591)***
y_p	-0.077	0.053
	(-5.891)***	(3.421)**
Gender	0.063	0.024
	(4.875)***	(2.100)**
Siblings	0.081	0.025
	(6.226)***	(2.216)**
Education	0.015	0.066
	(1.111)+	(5.772)***
DP	-0.012	-0.113
	(-0.695)+	(-7.263)***
R^2	0.395	0.341
F statistic	297.641	276.521

Note: dependent variable: equivalence scale of AA–households; pooled estim.; standardised coefficients; number of observations: Germany: 3,636; Belgium: 5,364.

Notation: t statistics in parentheses; *** significant at the 1% Level; ** significant at the 5% level; + insignificant.

Table A5. Differences in the Assessment of Single–adult Households (V_{II})

	Germany	Belgium
c_0	1.565	1.446
	(25.629)***	(29.847)***
y_r	-0.519	-0.433
	(-32.626)***	(-31.227)***
DC_1	0.160	0.176
	(8.365)***	(10.602)***
DC_2	0.187	0.187
	(8.899)***	(10.315)***
DC_3	0.156	0.170
	(8.115)***	(10.256)***
n_E	0.269	0.310
	(15.679)***	(20.869)***
y_p	-0.060	0.057
	(-3.748)***	(2.946)***
Gender	0.061	0.002
	(3.812)***	(0.167)+
Siblings	0.061	0.005
	(3.798)***	(0.344)+
Education	-0.004	0.021
	(-0.266)+	(1.510)+
DP	-0.011	-0.106
	(-0.544)+	(-5.518)***
R^2	0.455	0.397
F statistic	222.342	295.803

Note: dependent variable: equivalence scale of A–households; pooled estimations; standardized coefficients; number of observations: Germany: 2,121; Belgium: 3,129.
Notation: t statistics in parentheses; *** significant at the 1% level; + insignificant.

Table A6. Differences in the Assessment of Employees (V_{II})

	Germany	Belgium
c_0	0.237	0.234
	(2.165)**	(0.178)+
y_r	-0.313	-0.272
	(-9.304)***	(-10.638)***
DA_2	-0.074	-0.043
	(-1.912)*	(-1.460)+
n_E	0.259	0.245
	(7.692)***	(9.577)***
y_p	0.035	0.036
	(0.959)+	(0.960)+
Gender	0.003	-0.060
	(0.095)+	(-2.344)**
Siblings	0.114	0.059
	(3.362)***	(2.303)**
Education	0.022	0.038
	(0.624)+	(1.467)+
DW	-0.117	-0.074
	(-3.440)***	(-2.893)***
R^2	0.184	0.143
F statistic	41.603	44.929

Note: dependent variable: cumulated weights for employees; pooled estimations; number of observations: Germany: 720; Belgium: 1,314; standardised coefficients.
Notation: t-statistics in parentheses; *** significant at the 1% level; ** significant at the 5% level; * significant at the 10% level; + insig.

List of Symbols

$a_0, a_1, ...$	regression coefficients.
c_0	regression intercept.
$c(.)$	cost function.
df	degrees of freedom.
$f_i(n_A, n_C)$	congestion function of good i.
G	vector of congestion functions.
i	index.
j	index.
ins	logarithm of insufficient income.
j	stimulus variables have values of j.
$k = 1, ..., K$	household type.
l_i	translating parameter of good i.
log	logarithm.
m_i	equivalence scale of good i.
n_A	number of adults.
n_C	number of children.
n_E	number of employees.
p	price/price vector.
p_i	price of good i.
r	reference–household type.
s	household demography.
t	t statistic.
$u(.)$	utility function.
$\bar{u}$	given level of utility.
$v(.)$	indirect utility function.
x_A	quantity of adult good.
x_B^a	quantity of non–adult good that is also consumed by adults.
x_B^c	quantity of non–adult good that is exclusively consumed by children.
x_i	quantity of good i.
x_i^h	Hicksian demand function of good i.
x_i^m	Marshallian demand function of good i.
y	income.
y_{adj}	adjusted personal income.
y_{dis}	disposable income.
y_{ins}	insufficient income.

y_{min}	minimal income.
y_p	personal income.
y_r	reference income.
y_{suf}	sufficient income.
A	adult.
C	child.
C_2	second child in the household.
CD	country dummy.
CP	Cypriot Pounds.
DC_3	dummy third child.
DA_2	dummy second adult.
Dy_{adj}	dummy $y_a dj$ correspondence.
DM	Deutschmarks.
DHC	dummy household size correspondence.
EUR	Euro.
DP	dummy partner.
DW	dummy working.
E	employed adult.
F	F statistic.
$F(.)$	function.
F_k	equivalence factor of household type k.
FS	family size/number of household members.
$H \equiv (h_i)$	function which maps income to a non–negative real number.
HSE	household size elasticity.
$Pers(I)$	vector (I) of personal characteristics.
$Pers(II)$	vector (II) of personal characteristics.
S	level of household satisfaction.
$Stim$	vector of stimulus variables.
$StimInt$	vector of interactions of stimulus variables.
N	number of observations.
P	poverty line.
R^2	coefficient of determination.
$\bar{R}^2$	adjusted coefficient of determination.
U	unemployed adult.
V	parameter.
V_I, V_{II}	surveys.
W	individual weight.
Z	vector of household characteristics or Z value of test statistic.
ESE	equivalence scale exactness.
HSE	household–size elasticity.
IB	independence of base.
IEQ	income evaluation question.
MIQ	minimal income question.
α_{FS}	coefficient of the logarithm of family size.
α_{iA}	congestion parameter adults, good i.

α_{iC} congestion parameter children, good i.
α_{FS} coefficient of the logarithm of household income.
β_i income elasticity of good i.
γ subsistence quantity.
ϵ disturbance term.
η elasticity.
$\mu(y)$ average income.
σ equivalence scale.
φ publicness of optimal consumption budget.

List of Figures and Tables

References

AABERGE, R., AND I. MELBY (1998), "The Sensitivity of Income Inequality to Choice of Equivalence Scales," *The Review of Income and Wealth*, 44,4, 565–569.

AGUILAR, R., AND B.GUSTAFSSON (1988), "Public Opinion About Social Assistance in Sweden," *European Journal of Political Research*, 16, 251–276.

ANDREWS, F., AND S. WITHEY (1976), Social Indicators of Well–being: Americans Perception of Life Quality, New York: Plenum Press.

APPS, P.F., KILLINGSWORTH, M., AND R. REES (1996), "On the Specification of Labour Supply and Household Production Models," Working Paper No. 300, Australian National University, Canberra.

APPS, P.F., AND R. REES (1988), "Taxation and the Household," *Journal of Public Economics*, 35, 155–169.

APPS, P.F., AND R. REES (1995), "Household Production, the Costs of Children and Equivalence Scales," Working Papers in Economics and Econometrics, Research School of Social Sciences, Australian National University, Canberra.

APPS, P.F., AND R. REES (1996), "Labour Supply, Home Production and Intra-family Welfare Distribution," *Journal of Public Economics*, 60, 199–219.

APPS, P.F., AND R. REES (1997), "Collective Labour Supply and Household Production," *Journal of Political Economy*, 105, 178–190.

APPS, A., AND E. SAVAGE (1989), "Labour Supply, Welfare Rankings and the Measurement of Inequality," *Journal of Public Economics*, 39, 335–364.

ATKINSON, A.B. (1983), *The Economics of Inequality*, 2nd Edition, Oxford: Clarendon Press.

BARTEN, A.B. (1964), "Family Composition, Prices and Expenditure Patterns," in: Hart, P.E., Mills, G., and J.K. Whitaker (Eds.), Econometric Analysis for National Economic Planning, London: Butterworth, 277–297.

BARTEN, A.B. (1968), "Estimating Demand Functions," *Econometrica*, 36, 231–251.

BARTEN, A.B. (1969), "Maximum Likelihood Estimator of a Complete System of Demand Equations," *European Economic Review*, 1, 7–73.

BARTEN, A.B. (1977), "The Systems of Consumer Demand Functions Approach: A Review," *Econometrica*, 45, 23–51.

BECKER, G. (1965), "A Theory of the Allocation of Time," *Economic Journal*, 75, 493–517.

BECKER, G. (1981), A Treatise on the Family, Cambridge (MA): Harvard University Press.

BETTI, G. (1999), "A Non-Parametric Approach to Equivalence Scales," *Statistics in Transition : Journal of the Polish Statistical Association*, 4,2, 181-194.

BLACKORBY, C., AND D. DONALDSON (1988), "Adult-Equivalence Scales and the Economic Implementation of Interpersonal Comparisons of Well-Being," University of British Columbia Discussion Paper, 88-27.

BLACKORBY, C., AND D. DONALDSON (1991), "Adult Equivalence-Scales and the Interpersonal Comparisons of Well-Being, and Applied Welfare Economics," in: Elster, J. Roemer, J., (Eds.), Interpersonal Comparisons and Distributive Justice, Cambridge: Cambridge University Press.

BLACKORBY, C., AND D. DONALDSON (1993), "Adult Equivalence Scales and its Implementation of Interpersonal Comparisons of Well–being," *Social Choice and Welfare*, 10, 335–361.

BLUNDELL, R., AND A. LEWBEL (1990), "The Information Content of Equivalence Scales," Institut for Fiscal Studies London Working Paper W90/4.

BLUNDELL, R., AND A. LEWBEL (1991), "The Information Content of Equivalence Scales," *Journal of Econometrics*, 50, 49–68.

BRADBURY, B. (1989), "Family Size Equivalence Scales and Survey Evaluations of Income and Well-Being," *Journal of Social Policy*, 18,3, 383–408.

BRADSHAW, J. (1991), "How Much is Enough?," Basic Income Research Group Bulletin 12, 13–14.

BRADSHAW, J., MITCHELL, D., AND J. MORGAN (1987), "Evaluating Adequacy: The Potential of Budget Standards," *Journal of Social Policy*, 16, 165–181.

BRADSHAW, J., DITCH, J., HOLMES, H., AND P. WHITEFORD (1993), "A Comparative Study of Child Support in Fifteen Countries," *Journal of European Social Policy*, 3,4, 255–271.

BREITER, A., AND B. BATINIC (1997), "Das Internet als Basis für elektronische Befragungen," *Jahrbuch der Absatz– und Verbrauchsforschung*, 2, 214–229.

BROWN, M., AND D. HEIEN (1972), "The S–Branch Utility Tree: A Generalization of the Linear Expenditure System," *Econometrica*, 40, 737–747.

BROWNING, M. (1992), "Children and Household Economic Behavior," *Journal of Economic Literature*, 30, 1434–1475.

BUCHEGGER, R. (1986), "Konsumnachfrage und Haushaltsstruktur," München: Florentz.

CALLAN, T. (1989), Poverty, Income and Welfare in Ireland, Economic and Social Research Institute, Paper 146, Dublin.

CAPLOVITZ, D. (1967) The Poor Pay More: Consumer Practices of Low–Income Families. New York: The Free Press.

CHADEAU, A., AND A. FOUQET (1981), "Peut-on Mesurer le Travail Domestique?," *Economie et Statistique*, 136, 29–42.

COLASANTO, D., KAPTEYN, A., AND J. VAN DER GAAG (1984), "Two Subjective Definitions of Poverty: Results from the Wisconsin Basic Needs Study," *The Journal of Human Resources*, 19,1, 127–138.

CONNIFFE, D. (1992), "The Non-Constancy of Equivalence Scales," *Review of Income and Wealth*, 4, 429–443.

CONSTANTINIDES, G.M. (1990), "Habit Formation: A Resolution of the Equity Premium Puzzle," *The Journal of Political Economy*, 98,3, 519–543.

COULTER, F.A.E., COWELL, F.A., AND S.P. JENKINS (1992), "Differences in Needs and Assessment of Income Distributions," *Bulletin of Economic Research*, 44, 77–124.

DANZIGER, S., VAN DER GAAR, J., TAUSSIG, M., AND E. SMOLENSKY (1984), "The Direct Measurement of Welfare Levels: How Much Does it Cost to Make Ends Meet?, *Review of Economics and Statistics*, 66, 500–504.

DEATON, A.S. (1997), The Analysis of Household Surveys; a Microeconomic Approach to Development Policy, The John Hopkins University Press, Baltimore, London.

DEATON, A.S., AND A. CASE (1988), "Analysis of Household Expenditures, Living Standards Measurement Study," Working Paper No.11, World Bank, Washington (D.C.).

DEATON, A.S., AND J. MUELLBAUER (1980), Economics and Consumer Behaviour, Cambridge: Cambridge University Press.

DEATON, A.S., AND J. MUELLBAUER (1986), "On Measuring Child Costs: With Applications to Poor Countries," *Journal of Political Economy*, 94, 720–744.

DEATON, A.S., RUIZ-CASTILLO, J., AND D. THOMAS (1989), "The Influence of Household Composition on Household Expenditure Patterns," *Journal of Political Economy*, 97, 179–200.

DE COSTER, A., HOUTHUYS, D., NICAISE, I., PACOLET, J., AND R. WOUTERS (1984), Sociale Zekerheid en Personenbelasting, Katholieke Universiteit Leuven.

DEISS, J., GUILLAUME, M.-L., AND A.P. LÜTHI (1988), *Kinderkosten in der Schweiz. Untersuchung über die Aequivalenzskalen der Einkommen*, Freiburg (Switzerland): Univ.–Verlag.

DELEECK, H. (1989), "The Adequacy of the Social Security System in Belgium, 1976–1985," *Journal of Social Policy*, 18,1, 91–117.

DE VOS, K., HAGENAARS, A., AND B.M.S. VAN PRAAG (1987), "Armoede, Arbeid en Sociale Zekerheid," Den Haag: Ministerie can Sociale Zaken en Werkgelgenheid.

DE VOS, K., AND T.I. GARNER (1991), "An Evaluation of Subjective Poverty Definitions: Comparing Results from the US and the Netherlands", *The Review of Income and Wealth*, 37,3, 267–285.

DICKENS, R., FRY, V., AND P. PASHARDES (1993), "Nonlinearities, Aggregation and Equivalence Scales," *Economic Journal*, 103, 359–368.

DONALDSON, D., AND K. PENDAKUR (2003), "Equivalent–Income Functions and Income–Dependent Equivalence Scales," forthcoming in the *Journal of Public Economics.*

DOUTHITT, R., MACDONALD, M., AND R. MULLIS (1992), "The Relationship between Measures of Subjective and Economic Well-being", *Social Indicators Research*, 26, 407–422.

DUBNOFF, S. (1985), "How much Income is Enough? Measuring Public Judgements," *Public Opinion Quarterly*, 49, 285–299.

DUBNOFF, S., VAUGHAN, D., AND C. LANCASTER (1981), Income Satisfaction Measures in Equivalence Scale Applications, Proceedings of the Social Statistics Section, American Statistical Association, 348–352.

EBERT, U. (1999), "Using Equivalent Income of Equivalent Adults to Rank Income Distributions when Household Types are Different," *Social Choice and Welfare*, 16, 233–258.

EBERT, U., AND P. MOYES (2000), "Adjusting Incomes for Needs: Can one Avoid Equivalence Scales?," Working Paper V–204–00, Volkswirtschaftliche Reihe, Universität Oldenburg.

EINHORN, H.J., AND R.M. HOGARTH (1981), "Behavioral Decision Theory: Processes of Judgement and Choice," *Journal of Accounting Research*, 19, 1–41.

ELSTER, J. (1990), "When Rationality Fails," in: Cook, K.S. and M. Levi (eds.), The Limits of Rationality, University of Chicago Press, Chicago, 19–59.

ENGEL, E. (1857), "Die Productions– und Consumptionsverhältnisse des Königreichs Sachsen," *Zeitschrift des Statistischen Büreaus des Königlich Sächsischen Ministeriums des Inneren*, No. 8 and 9, Reprint: Engel, E. (1895), "Die Lebenshaltungskosten belgischer Arbeiter–Familien früher und jetzt," Appendix I, 1-54, Dresden: C. Heinrich.

ENGEL, E. (1895), "Die Lebenshaltungskosten belgischer Arbeitnehmerfamilien früher und jetzt," International Statistical Institute Bulletin 44, 1–74.

FAIK, J. (1995), Äquivalenzskalen. Theoretische Erörterungen, empirische Ermittlung und verteilungsbezogene Anwendung für die Bundesrepublik Deutschland, Berlin: Duncker&Humblot.

FIEGEHEN, G.C., LANSLEY, P.S., AND A.D. SMITH (1977), Poverty and Progress in Britain 1953–1973, Cambridge.

FISCHHOFF, B., SLOVIC, P., AND S. LICHTENSTEIN (1980), "Knowing what You Want: Measuring Labile Values," in: Wallstein, T.S. (ed.), Cognitive Processes in Choice and Decision Behavior, Erlbaum, Hillsdale, 117–141.

FISHER, F. (1987), "Household Equivalence Scales and Interpersonal Comparisons," *Review of Economic Studies*, 54, 519–524.

FITZGERALD, J., SWENSON, M., AND J. WICKS (1996), "Valuation of Household Production and Market Prices and Estimation of Production Functions," *Review of Income and Wealth*, 42,2, 165–180.

FLIK, R.J., AND B.M.S. VAN PRAAG (1991), "Subjective Poverty Line Definitions", *De Economist*, 139,3, 311–330.

FLIK, R.J., AND B.M.S. VAN PRAAG (1992), " Poverty Lines and Equivalence Scales", in: Polskie Towarzystwo Statystyczne, Poverty Measurement for Economies in Transition in Eastern European Countries: International Scientific Conference, Warsaw, 7–9 October 1991, 65–97.

FRIEDMAN, R.D. (1965), Poverty, Definition and Perspective, Washington (D.C.): American Enterprise Institute.

GARFINKEL, I., AND R. HAVEMAN (1977), Earnings Capacity, Poverty, and Inequality, New York: Academic Press.

GEARY, R.C. (1950), "A Note on 'A Constant Utility Index of the Cost of Living,' " *The Review of Economic Studies*, 18, 65-66.

GFK MEDIENFORSCHUNG (2001), *GfK Online–Monitor*, 7th Wave, www.gfk.de/produkte/eigene-pdf/jupiterMMXIEU250401.pdf.

GOEDHART, T., HALBERSTADT, V., KAPTEYN, A., AND B.M.S. VAN PRAAG (1977), "The Poverty Line. Concept and Measurement," *Journal of Human Resources*, 12, 503–520.

GORMAN, W.M. (1976), "Tricks with Utility Functions," in: Artis, M., and R. Nobay (ed.), Essays in Economic Analysis, Cambridge: Cambridge University Press, 211–243.

GOZALO, P. (1997), "Nonparametric Bootstrap Analysis with Applications to Demographic Effects in Demand Functions," *Journal of Public Econometrics*, 81, 357–393.

GRÄF, L., AND M. HEIDINGSFELDER (1999), "Bessere Datenqualität bei WWW–Umfragen. Erfahrungen aus einem Methodenexperiment mit dem Internet–Rogator," in: Batinic, B., Werner, A., Gräf, L. and W. Bandilla (ed.), Online Research. Methoden, Anwendungen und Ergebnisse, Göttingen: Hogrefe.

GRAHAM, J., AND C. GREEN (1984), "Estimating Parameters of a Household Production Function with Joint Products," *Review of Economics and Statistics*, 66, 277–282.

GRONAU, R. (1988), "Consumption Technology and the Intrafamily Distribution of Resources: Adult Equivalence Scales Reexamined," *Journal of Political Economy*, 96, 1183–1205.

GRONAU, R. (1997), "The Theory of Home Production: The Past Ten Years," *Journal of Labor Economics*, 15,2, 197–205.

GUJARATI, D.N. (1988), Basic Econometrics, New York: McGraw–Hill Book Company.

HAGENAARS, A. (1985), "The Perception of Poverty," Academic Thesis, University of Leyden. Published 1986, Amsterdam: North–Holland.

HAGENAARS, A., HOMAN, M., AND B.M.S. VAN PRAAG (1984), "Draag- krachtverschillen Tussen Huishoudens Met Één, Resp. Twee Kostwinners," *Economisch Statistische Berichten*, 69, 552–559.

HAGENAARS, A., AND B.M.S. VAN PRAAG (1985), "A Synthesis of Poverty Line Definitions," *The Review of Income and Wealth*, 31,2, 139–154.

HALLEROED, B. (1991), "The Truly Poor. Direct and Indirect Consensual Measurement of Poverty in Sweden", *Journal of European Social Policy*, 5,2, 111–129.

HALLEROED, B. (1995), " Making Ends Meet: Perceptions of Poverty in Sweden," *Scandinavian Journal of Social Welfare*, 4, 174–189.

HANSEN, G. (1993), Quantitative Wirtschaftsforschung, München: Vahlen.

HARTOG, J. (1988), "Book Review, Poverty and the Measurement of Individual Welfare: A Review of A.J.M. Hagenaars' The Perception of Poverty," *Journal of Human Resources*, 23, 243–266.

HAUPTMANNS, P. (1999), "Grenzen und Chancen von quantitativen Befragungen mit Hilfe des Internet," in: Batnic, B., Werner, A., Gräf, L. and W. Bandilla (ed.), Online Research. Methoden, Anwendungen und Ergebnisse, Göttingen: Hogrefe.

HAVEMAN, R., AND L. BURON (1993), "Escaping Poverty through Work: The Problem of Low Earnings capacity in the United States," *The Review of Income and Wealth*, 39,2, 141–157.

HEADEY, B., HAMPEL, J., AND W. MEYER (1990), "The Relationship Between Objective and Subjective Indicators: A Reciprocal Causation Model Linking Changes in Income, Income Satisfaction and Life Satisfaction," Working Paper 332, J.W. Goethe–Universität Frankfurt and Universität Mannheim.

HENDERSON, A.M. (1949), "The Cost of Children," *Population Studies*, 3, 30–150 and 267–298.

HOMAN, E., HAGENAARS, A., AND B.M.S. VAN PRAAG (1986), Interhuishoudelijke vergelijkingen van consumptie, welvaart en tijdsallocatie. Eindverslag van het onderzoek Kostwinnersproblematiek, Leiden en Rotterdam: Centrum voor Onderzoek van de Economie van de Publieke Sector, Erasmus Universiteit Rotterdam.

HOMAN, E., HAGENAARS, A., AND B. VAN PRAAG (1991), "Income Inequality between One-earner and Two-earner Households: Is it Real or Artificial, *De Economist*, 139,4, 530–549.

JANSSENS, P., AND L. SCHULPEN (1985), "Het Sociaal Levensminimum, een Vergelijking van Twee Methodes," *Tijdschrift voor Sociologie*, 6, 107–131.

JORGENSON, D.W. (1990), "Aggregate Consumer Behaviour and the Measurement of Social Welfare, *Econometrica*, 58, 1007–1040.

JORGENSON, D.W., AND D.T.S. SLESNICK (1987), "Aggregate Consumer Behaviour and Household Equivalence Scales," *Journal of Business and Economic Statistics*, 5, 219–232.

JOVANOVIC, B. (1995), "A CES Indirect Production Function," NBER Technical Working Paper No. T0188.

KAPTEYN, A., AND B.M.S. VAN PRAAG (1976), "A New Approach to the Construction of Family Equivalence Scales," *European Economic Review*, 7, 313–335.

KAPTEYN, A., VAN DE GEER, S., AND H. VAN DE STADT (1984), "The Impact of Changes in Income and Family Composition on Subjective Measures of Well-Being," Netherlands Central Bureau of Statistics, Department for Statistics of Income and Consumption, Voorburg.

KAPTEYN, A., AND T. WANSBEEK (1985), "The Individual Welfare Function, A Review," *Journal of Economic Psychology*, 6, 333–363.

KAPTEYN, A., KOOREMAN, P., AND R. WILLEMSE (1988), "Some Methodological Issues in the Implementation of Subjective Poverty Definitions", *Journal of Human Resources*, 23,2, 222-242.

KILPATRICK, R. (1973), "The Income Elasticity of the Poverty Line," *The Review of Economics and Statistics*, 55, 327–332.

KING, M.A. (1983), "Welfare Analysis of Tax Reforms Using Household Data," *Journal of Public Economics*, 21, 183–214.

KLEIN, T. (1986), "Äquivalenzskalen - Ein Literatursurvey," SfB 3, Arbeitspapier 195, Frankfurt am Main und Mannheim.

KLEIN, T. (1994), "Einkommen und Bedarf im Haushaltszusammenhang - Äquivalenzskalen als Instrument der Wohlfahrtsmessung," in: Hauser, R., Ott, N., and G. Wagner (eds.), Mikroanalytische Grundlagen der Gesellschaftspolitik, Volume 2, Berlin: Akademie–Verlag, 278–294.

KLEIN, L.R., AND H. RUBIN (1948), "A Constant Utility Index of the Cost of Living," *The Review of Economic Studies*, 15, 84-87.

KOULOVATIANOS, C., SCHRÖDER, C., AND U. SCHMIDT (2003), "On the Income Dependence of Equivalence Scales," Working Paper, Kiel.

LANCASTER, C., AND R. RAY (1998), "Comparison of Alternative Models of Household Equivalence Scales: The Australian Evidence on Unit Data," *The Economic Record*, 74,224, 1–14.

LEWBEL, A. (1985), "A Unified Approach to Incorporating Demographic or Other Effects into Demand Systems," *Review of Economic Studies*, 52, 1–18.

LEWBEL, A. (1989), "Household Equivalence Scales and Welfare Comparisons," *Journal of Public Economics*, 39, 377–391.

MAS-COLELL, A., WHINSTON, M.D., AND J.R. GREEN (1995), Microeconomic Theory, Oxford: Oxford University Press.

MATHESON, G., AND P. SAUNDERS (1992), Perceptions of Poverty, Income Adequacy and Living Standards in Australia, Kensington, New South Wales.

McCLEMENTS, L.D. (1977), "Equivalence Scales for Children," *Journal of Public Economics*, 8, 91–210.

McCLEMENTS, L.D. (1978), "The Economics of Social Security," London: Heinemann.

MELENBERG, B., AND A. VAN SOEST (1995), "Semiparametric Estimation of Equivalence Scales Using Subjective Information," Discussion Paper, Tilburg University.

MISSONG, M. (2002), Demographisch gegliederte Nachfragesysteme und Äquivalenzskalen für Deutschland. Eine empirische Überprüfung neoklassischer Ansätze anhand der Daten der Einkommens- und Verbrauchsstichproben, Habilitation, Kiel University.

MORIANI, C. (1990), "Italian Experience of Harmonized Poverty Measures: a Summary", in: Teekens, R. and B.M.S. Van Praag, Analysing Poverty in the European Community, Eurostat News Special Edition, Luxemburg: Office for Official Publications of the European Communities, 139–152.

MUELLBAUER, J. (1977), "Testing the Barten Model of Household Composition Effects and the Cost of Children," *Economic Journal*, 87, 460–487.

MUELLBAUER, J. (1978), "Equivalence Scales," Selected Evidence Submitted to the Royal Commission for Report No. 6: Lower Incomes, HMSO, London.

MUELLBAUER, J. (1980), "The Estimation of the Prais-Houthakker Model of Equivalence Scales," *Econometrica*, 48, 153–176.

MUELLBAUER, J. (1990), "Professor Sen and the Standard of Living," in: Hawthorn, G. (Ed.), The Standard of Living, Cambridge: Cambridge University Press, 39–58.

MUFFELS, R., KAPTEYN, A., DE VRIES, A., ET AL. (1990), "Poverty in the Netherlands: Report on the Durch Contribution to an International Comparative Study on Poverty and the Financial Efficacy of the Social Security System," VUGA, The Hague.

MURTHI, M. (1992), "Engel Equivalence Scales in Sri Lanka: Exactness, Specification, Measurement, Error," Working Paper, School of Social Sciences, University of Sussex, Brighton.

MUTH, R.F. (1966), "Household Production and Consumer Demand Functions," *Econometrica*, 34,3, 699–708.

NELSON, J.A. (1993), "Household Equivalence Scales: Theory versus Policy?," *Journal of Labor Economics*, 11, 471–493.

NICHOLLS, W.L., AND D.E. DE LEEUW (1996), "Factors in Acceptance of Computer–Assisted Interviewing Methods. A Conceptual and Historical Review," in: American Statistic Association, Proceedings of the Section on Survey Research Methods, Volume II, 758–763.

NICHOLSON, J.L. (1949), "Variations in Working Class Family Expenditure," *Journal of the Royal Statistical Society*, Series A, 112, 359–413.

O'CONNELL, D., ROSEN, R.J., AND R.L. CLAYTON (1996), "Long–Term Results of Touchtone Data Entry in the Current Employment Statistics Survey Program," in: American Statistic Association, Proceedings of the Section on Survey Research Methods, Volume II, 764–767.

O'HIGGINS, M. (1980), "Poverty in Europe – The Subjective Assessment of Poverty Lines: An Evaluation," Unpublished Manuscript in Two Parts, University of Bath.

ORGANISATION FOR ECONOMIC CO-OPERATION AND DEVELOPMENT (1995), "Household Production in OECD Countries. Data Sources and Measurement Methods," OECD, Paris.

ORSHANSKY, M. (1965), "Counting the Poor: Another Look at the Poverty Profile," *Social Security Bulletin*, 28, 3–29.

PASHARDES, P. (1995), "Equivalence Scales in a Rank-3 Demand System," *Journal of Public Economics*, 58, 143–158.

POLLAK, R.A., AND T.J. WALES (1979), "Welfare Comparisons and Equivalence Scales," *American Economic Review*, 69,2, 216–221.

POLLAK, R.A., AND T.J. WALES (1981), "Demographic Variables in Demand Analysis," *Econometrica*, 49, 1533–1551.

POLLAK, R.A., AND T.J. WALES (1992), "Demand System Specification and Estimation," New York et al.: Oxford University Press.

POULIN, S. (1988), An Application of Analytic Techniques to Canadian Income Satisfaction Data, Ottawa: Statistics Canada, Labour and Household Surveys Analysis Division, Staff Reports.

PRAIS, S.J., AND H.S. HOUTHAKKER (1955), "The Analysis of Family Budgets. With an Application to Two British Surveys Conducted in 1937-9 and Their Related Results," Cambridge: Cambridge University Press.

PYATT, G. (1990), "Social Evaluation Criteria," in: Dagum, C., and M. Zenga (eds.), Income and Wealth Distribution, Inequality and Poverty, Berlin: Springer.

QUAH, E. (1987), "Valuing Family Household Production: A Contingent Evaluation Approach," *Applied Economics*, 19, 875–889.

RAINWATER, L. (1974), "What Money Buys: Inequality and the Social Meanings of Income," New York: Basic Books.

RAINWATER, L. (1990), "Poverty and Equivalence as Social Constructions," LIS Working Paper 55, Walferdange: The Luxembourg Income Study.

RAY, R. (1983), "Measuring the Costs of Children: An Alternative Approach," *Journal of Public Economics*, 22, 89–102.

REIN, M. (1974), "Problems in the Definition and Measurement of Poverty," in: Townsend, P. (Ed.), The Concept of Poverty, London: Heinemann, 46–63.

REIPS, U.-D. (1997), "Das psychologische Experimentieren im Internet," in Batinic, B. (ed.), Internet für Psychologen, Göttingen: Hogrefe.

RIFFAULT, H., AND J. RABIER (1977), "La Perception de la Misère en Europe," Brussels: Commission des Communautés Européennes.

RONNING, G. (1991), *Mikroökonometrie*, Berlin: Springer.

ROTHBARTH, E. (1943), "Note on a Method of Determining Equivalent Income for Families of Different Composition," in: Madge, C. (Ed.), Wartime Pattern of Saving and Spending, London: Faber and Faber Limited, 123–130.

ROWNTREE, B.S. (1901), *Poverty: A Study of Town Life*, London: Macmillan.

ROWNTREE, B.S. (1941) *Poverty and Progress: A Second Social Survey of York*, London: Longmans, Green and Co.

RYDER, H.E., AND G.M. HEAL (1973), "Optimal Growth with Intertemporally Dependent Preferences," *The Review of Economic Studies*, 40,1, 1–31.

SAMUELSON, P. (1948), "Some Implications of Linearity," *The Review of Economic Studies*, 15, 88-90.

SAUNDERS, P., AND B. BRADBURY (1991), "Some Australian Evidence on the Consensual Approach to Poverty Measurement," *Economic Analysis and Policy*, 21,1, 47–78.

SAUNDERS, P., AND G. MATHESON (1992), "Perceptions of Poverty, Income, Adequacy and Living Standards in Australia," Social Policy Research Center Reports and Proceedings No. 99, Kensington: The University of New South Wales.

SAUNDERS, P., AND G. MATHESON (1993), "Politics, Income Perception and Living Standards," *Australian Journal of Political Science*, 28, 1–18.

SAUNDERS, P., HALLERÖD, B., AND G. MATHESON (1994), "Making Ends Meet in Australia and Sweden: A Comparative Analysis Using the Subjective Poverty Line Methodology," *Acta Sociologica*, 37,1, 3–22.

SCHNELL, R., Hill, P.B., AND E. ESSER (1995), Methoden der empirischen Sozialforschung, 5th Edition, München: Oldenbourg.

SEEL, B. (1992), "Standardmodell zur Analyse und Planung ökonomi–scher Problemlagen privater Haushalte," Studien zur Haushaltsökonomik, 4, Frankfurt a.M. et al.

SEIDL, C. (1987), "Hagenaars, A.J.M.: The Perception of Poverty," Book Review, *Journal of Economics*, 47, 92–98.

SEIDL, C. (1994), "How Sensible is the Leyden Individual Welfare Function of Income," *European Economic Review*, 38, 1633–1659.

SEN, A.K. (1984), Resources, Values and Development, Oxford: Basil Blackwell.

SEN, A.K. (1985), Commodities and Capabilities, Amsterdam: North Holland.

SEN, A.K. (1993), Capability and Well-being, in: Sen, A. and M. Nussbaum, The Quality of Life, 30–53, Oxford: Clarendon Press.

SENECA, J.J., AND M.K. TAUSSIG (1971), "Family Equivalence Scales and Personal Income Tax Exemptions for Children," *Review of Economics and Statistics*, 53, 253–262.

SIMON, H.A. (1957), Models of Man. Social and Rational. Mathematical Essays on Rational Human Behavior in a Social Setting, New York: Wiley.

STANOVNIK, T. (1992), "Perception of Poverty and Income Satisfaction. An Empirical Analysis of Slovene Households," *Journal of Economic Psychology*, 13, 57–69.

STONE, J.R.N. (1954), "Linear Expenditure Systems and Demand Analysis: An Application to the Pattern of British Demand," *The Economic Journal*, 64, 511–527.

THEOBALD, A. (1998), "Möglichkeiten und Grenzen der Marktforschung im Internet. Eine anwendungsorientierte Betrachtung," URL: http://www.uni-kl.de/FB–SoWi/LS–Bliemel/mitarb/theobald/paper01.htm.

TOWNSEND, P. (1962), "The Meaning of Poverty," *British Journal of Sociology*, 13, 210–227.

TSAKLOGLOU, P. (1991), "Estimation and Comparison of Two Simple Models of Equivalence Scales for the Cost of Children," *Economic Journal*, 101, 343–357.

VAN DEN BOSCH, K. (1999), Identifying the Poor, Using Subjective and Consensual Measures, Doctoral Thesis, University of Antwerpen.

VAN DER GAAG, J., AND E. SMOLENSKY (1982), "True Household Equivalence Scales and Characteristics of the Poor in the United States," *The Review of Income and Wealth*, 28, 17–28.

VAN HERWAARDEN, F., KAPTEYN, A., AND B.M.S. VAN PRAAG (1977) "Twelve Thousand Individual Welfare Functions of Income: A Comparison of Six Samples in Belgium and The Netherlands," *European Economic Review*, 19, 283–300.

VAN HOA, T. (1986), "Measuring Equivalence Scales. A New System–Wide Method," *Economic Letters*, 20, 95–99.

VAN PRAAG, B.M.S. (1968), "Individual Welfare Functions and Consumer Behavior. A Theory of Rational Irrationality," Amsterdam: North–Holland.

VAN PRAAG, B.M.S. (1971a), "The Individual Welfare Function in Belgium: An Empirical Investigation," *European Economic Review*, 2, 227–269.

VAN PRAAG, B.M.S. (1971b), "The Welfare Function of Income in Belgium: An Empirical Investigation," *European Economic Review*, 2, 337–369.

VAN PRAAG, B.M.S., AND R. FLIK (1992), "Poverty Lines and Equivalence Scales: A Theoretical and Empirical Evaluation," Paper Presented at the Multidisciplinary Research Conference on Poverty and Distribution, Oslo, November 16–17, 1992.

VAN PRAAG, B.M.S., HAGENAARS, A., AND J. VAN WEEREN (1980), "Poverty in Europe," Report to the European Community, Center for Research in Public Economics, University of Leyden.

VAN PRAAG, B.M.S., HAGENAARS, A., AND J. VAN WEEREN (1982), "Poverty in Europe," *The Review of Income and Wealth*, 28, 345–359.

VAN PRAAG, B.M.S., AND N.L. VAN DER SAR (1988), "Household Cost Functions and Equivalence Scales," *The Journal of Human Resources*, 23, 193–210.

VAN PRAAG, B.M.S. (1994), "How Sensible is the Leyden individual welfare function of income? A Reply," *European Economic Review*, 38, 1817–1825.

VAUGHAN, D. (1984), "Using Subjective Assessments of Income to Estimate Family Equivalence Scales: A Report on Work in Progress," Proceedings of the Social Statistics Section of the American Statistical Association, 496–501.

VAUGHAN, D. (1993), "Exploring the Use of the Public's Views to Set Income Poverty Thresholds and Adjust Them over Time," *Social Security Bulletin*, 56,2, 22–46.

WEDELL, D.H. (1991), "Distinguishing among Models of Contextually Induced Preference Reversals," *Journal of Experimental Psychology: Learning, Memory, and Cognition*, 17, 767–778.

WIDMER, R., AND A. SOUSA-POZA (1997), "Eine kritische Analyse der Methoden unbezahlter Arbeit," Diskussionspapier 49 des Forschungsinstituts für Arbeit und Arbeitsrecht an der Universität St. Gallen.

WILL, C., AND J. DABURGER (1996), "Interaktive Befragungen: Eine Alternative zu klassischen Marktforschungserhebungen," *Planung und Analyse*, 6, 22–23.

Printing and Binding: Strauss GmbH, Mörlenbach